# BL metamorphosis

story and art by
**Kaori Tsurutani**

# C O N T E N T S

# Chapter 41

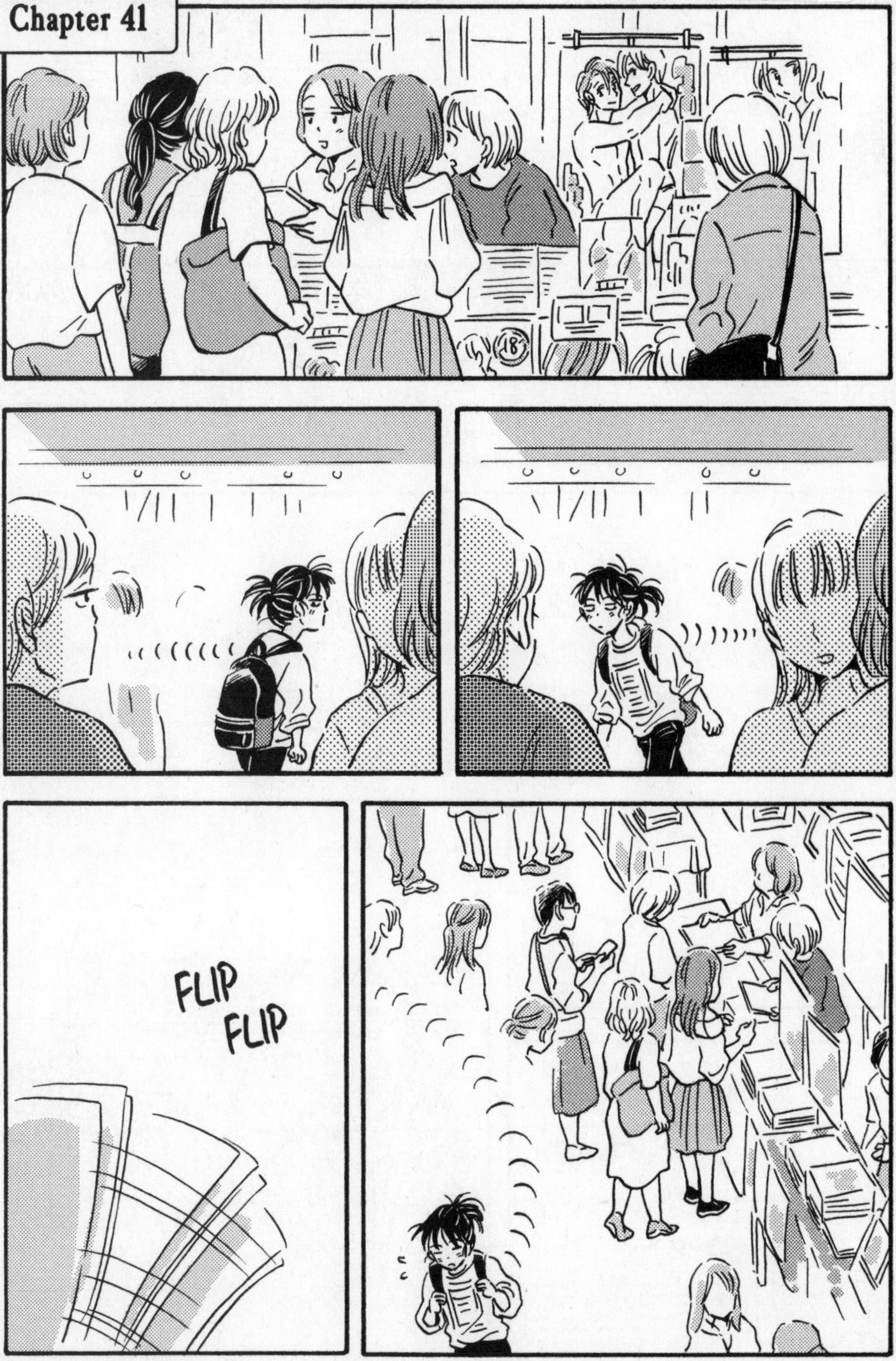
18
FLIP
FLIP

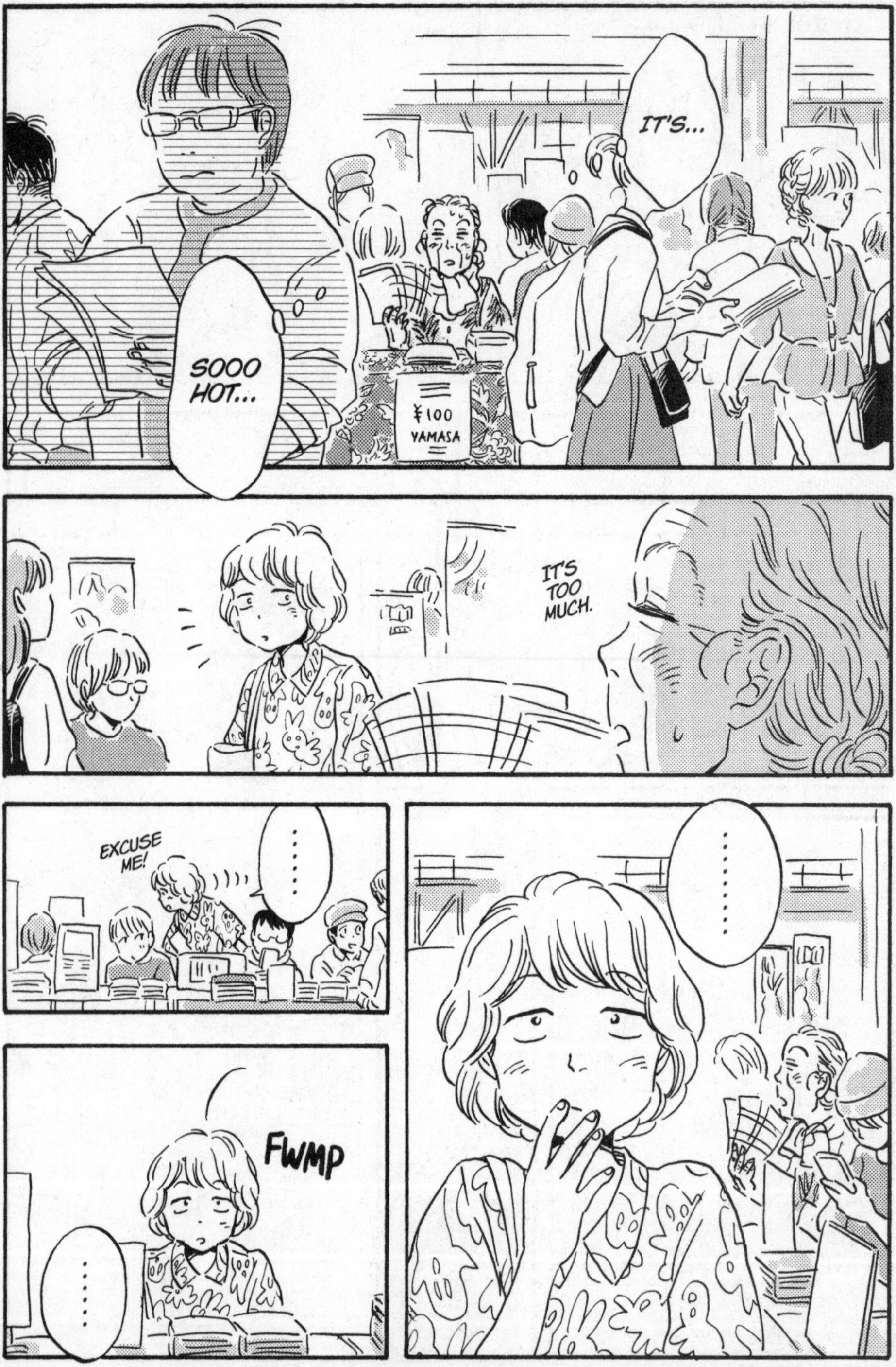

IT'S...
SOOO HOT...
¥100
YAMASA
IT'S TOO MUCH.
......
......
EXCUSE ME!
FWMP
......

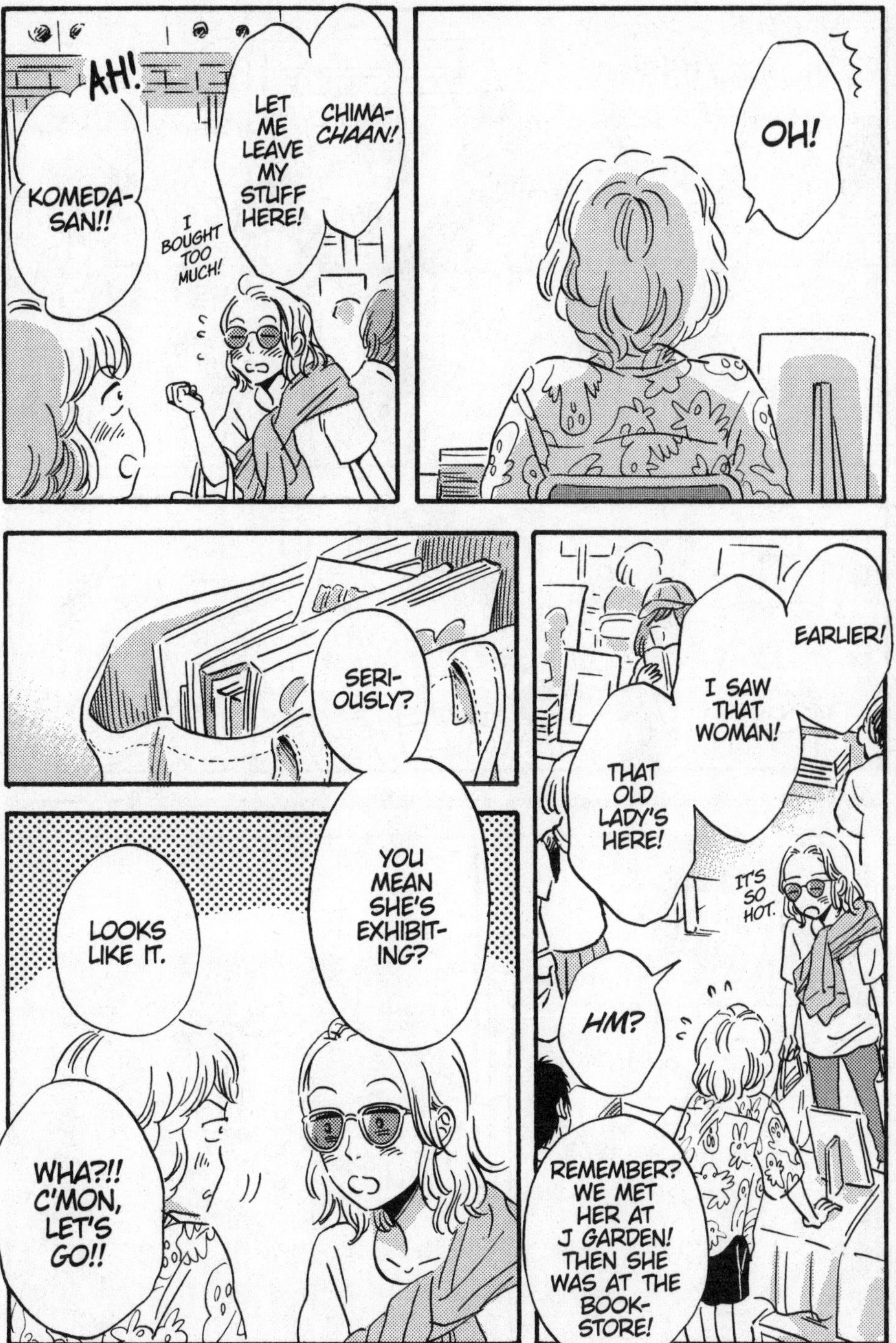
OH!
CHIMA-CHAAN!
LET ME LEAVE MY STUFF HERE!
AH!
KOMEDA-SAN!!
I BOUGHT TOO MUCH!
EARLIER!
I SAW THAT WOMAN!
THAT OLD LADY'S HERE!
IT'S SO HOT.
HM?
REMEMBER? WE MET HER AT J GARDEN! THEN SHE WAS AT THE BOOK-STORE!
SERI-OUSLY?
YOU MEAN SHE'S EXHIBIT-ING?
LOOKS LIKE IT.
WHA?!! C'MON, LET'S GO!!

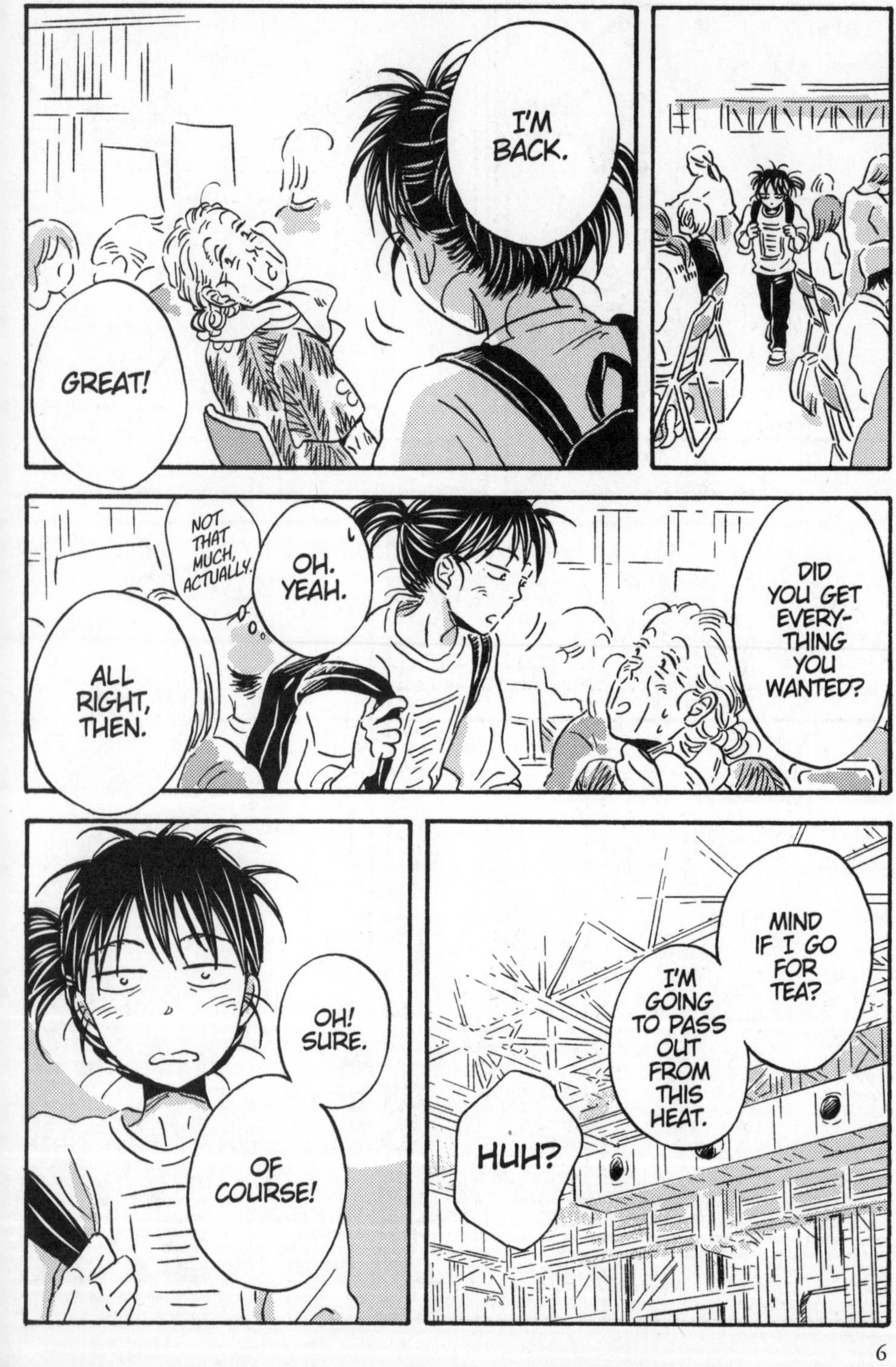
I'M BACK.
GREAT!
DID YOU GET EVERYTHING YOU WANTED?
OH. YEAH.
NOT THAT MUCH, ACTUALLY.
ALL RIGHT, THEN.
MIND IF I GO FOR TEA?
I'M GOING TO PASS OUT FROM THIS HEAT.
HUH?
OH! SURE.
OF COURSE!

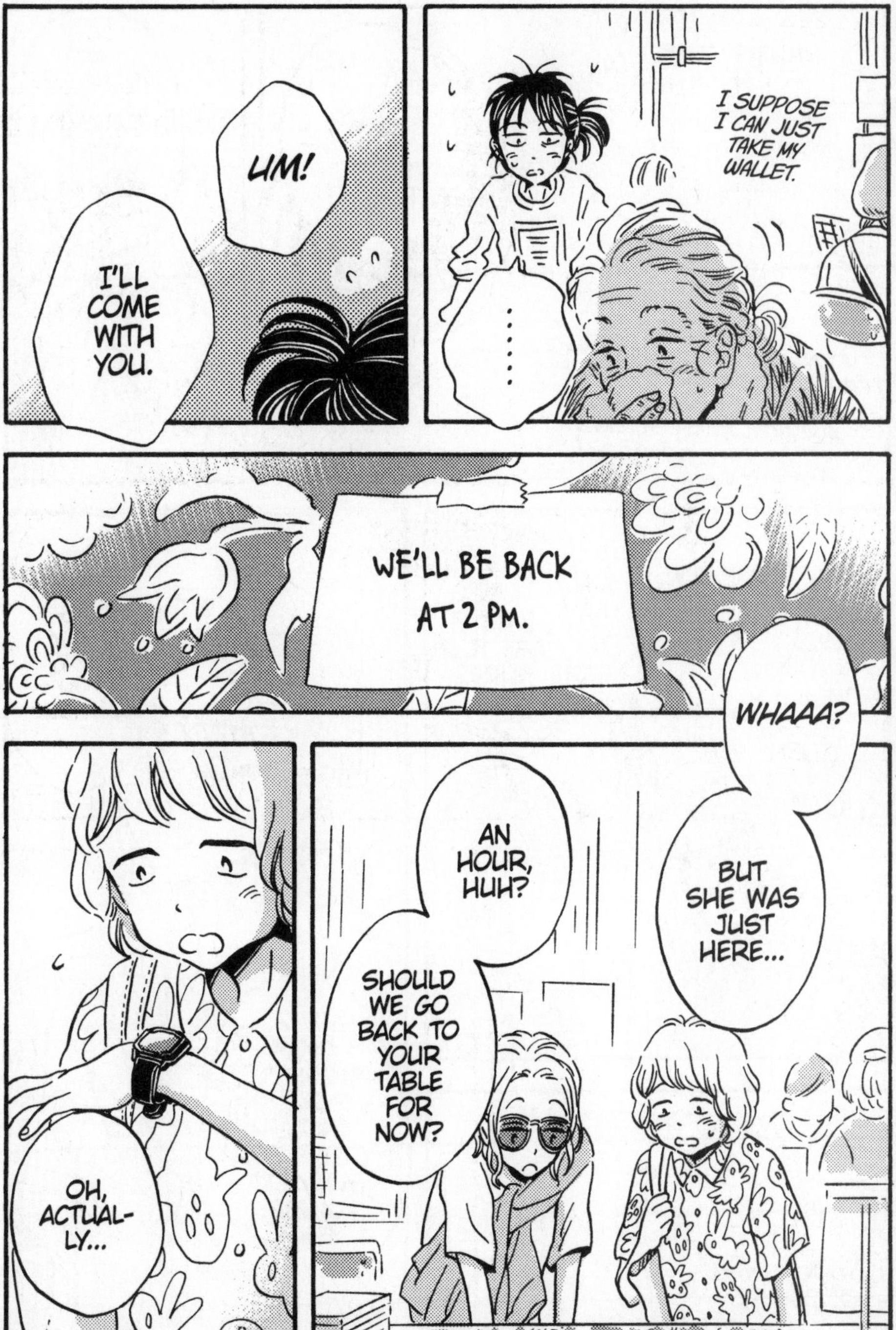
I SUPPOSE I CAN JUST TAKE MY WALLET.
......
UM!
I'LL COME WITH YOU.
WE'LL BE BACK AT 2 PM.
WHAAA?
BUT SHE WAS JUST HERE...
AN HOUR, HUH?
SHOULD WE GO BACK TO YOUR TABLE FOR NOW?
OH, ACTUAL-LY...

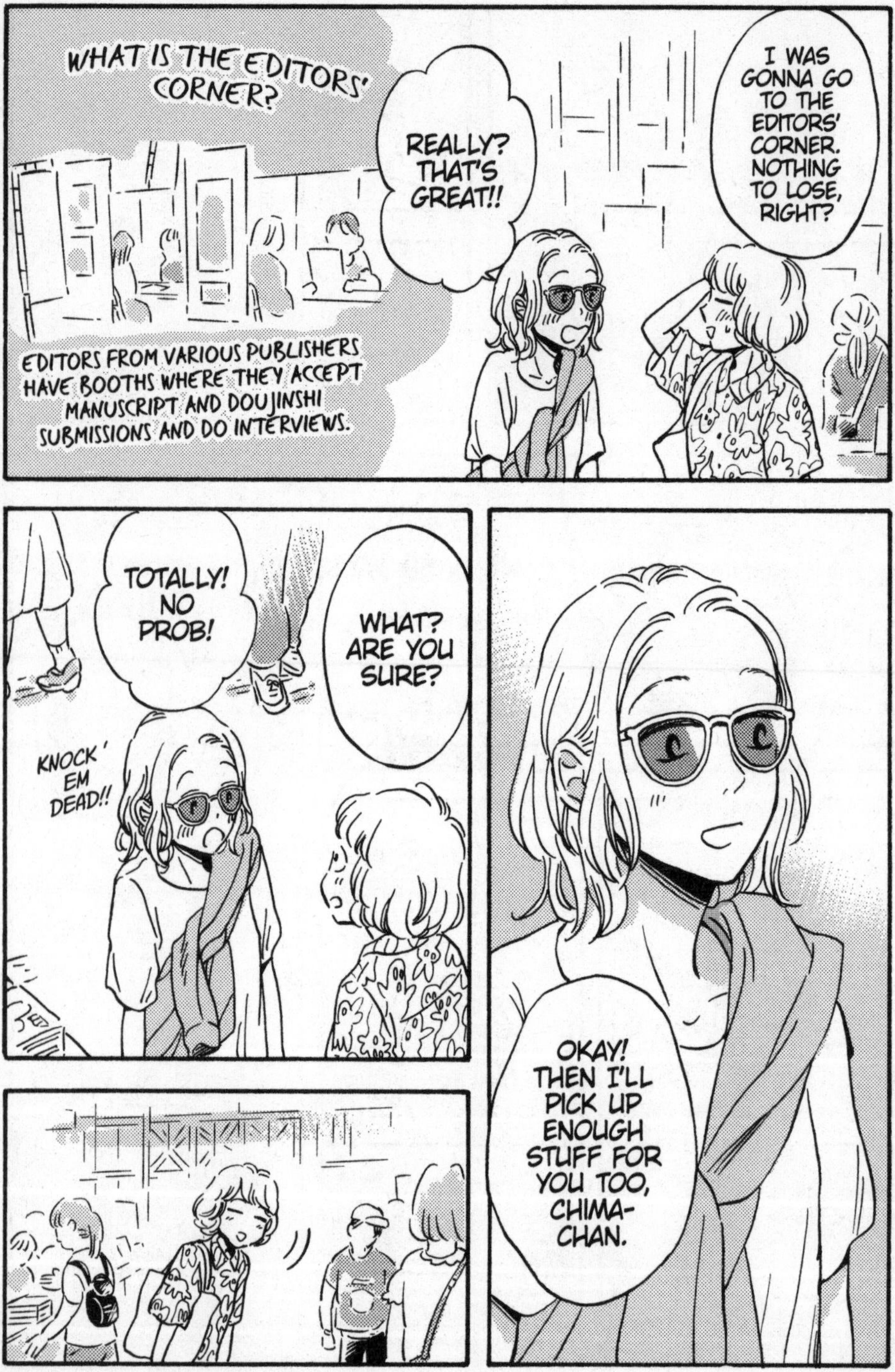
I WAS GONNA GO TO THE EDITORS' CORNER. NOTHING TO LOSE, RIGHT?
REALLY? THAT'S GREAT!!
WHAT IS THE EDITORS' CORNER?
EDITORS FROM VARIOUS PUBLISHERS HAVE BOOTHS WHERE THEY ACCEPT MANUSCRIPT AND DOUJINSHI SUBMISSIONS AND DO INTERVIEWS.
OKAY! THEN I'LL PICK UP ENOUGH STUFF FOR YOU TOO, CHIMA-CHAN.
WHAT? ARE YOU SURE?
TOTALLY! NO PROB!
KNOCK 'EM DEAD!!

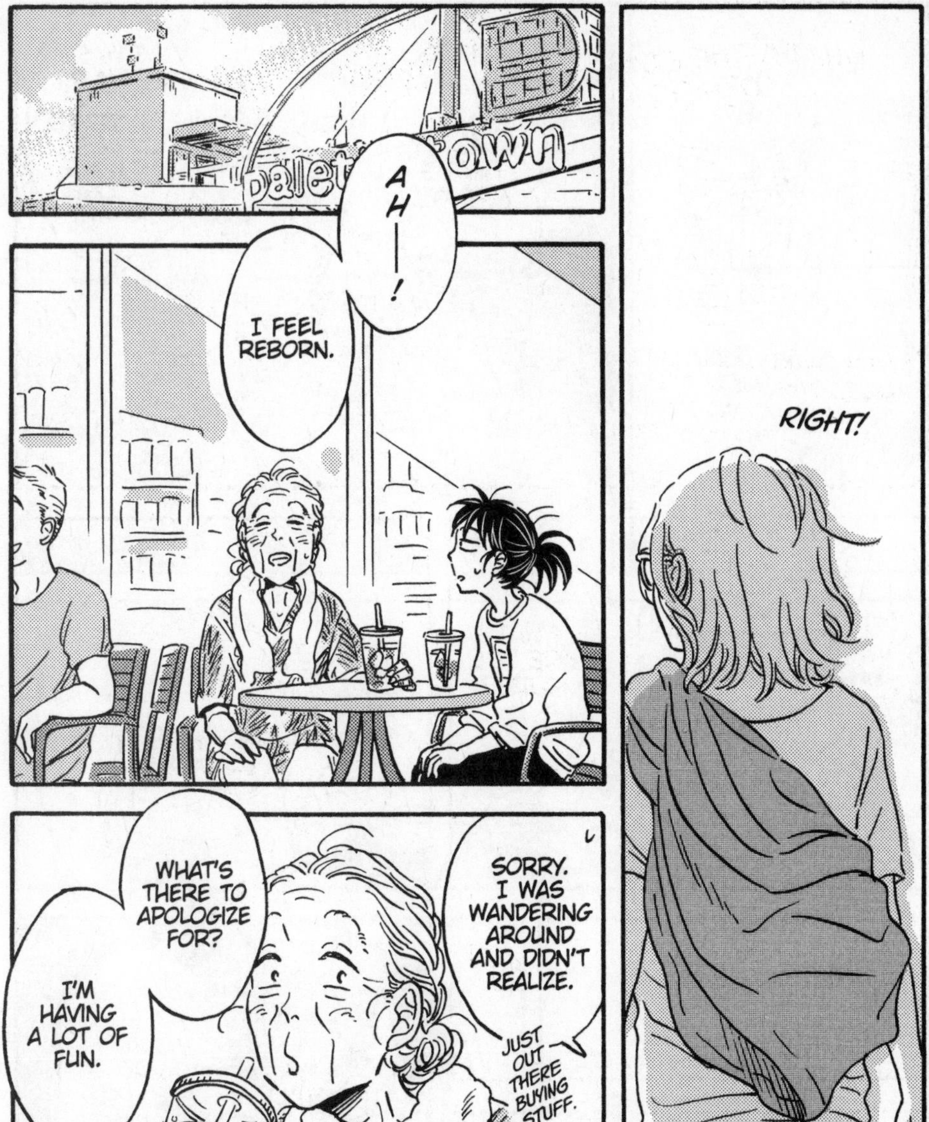
RIGHT!
AH—!
I FEEL REBORN.
SORRY. I WAS WANDERING AROUND AND DIDN'T REALIZE.
JUST OUT THERE BUYING STUFF.
WHAT'S THERE TO APOLOGIZE FOR?
I'M HAVING A LOT OF FUN.
BUT SHE SURE MOVED FAST TO GET HERE.
SHE MUST BE PRETTY TIRED.
IS THERE SOMEPLACE NEARBY WHERE ONE MIGHT HAVE TEA?
URARA-SAN, THIS WAY!!

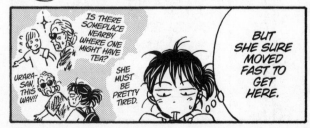

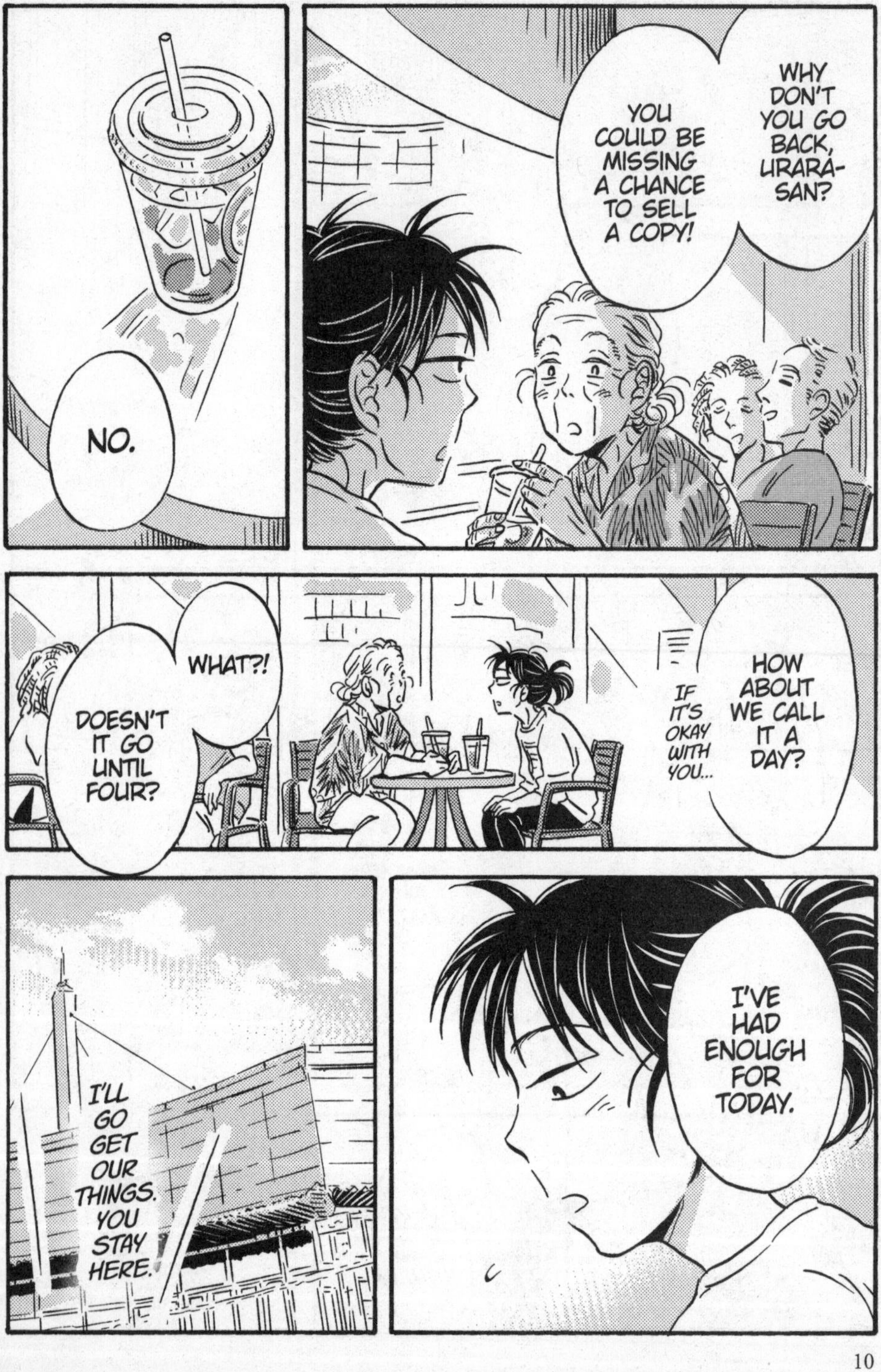
WHY DON'T YOU GO BACK, URARA-SAN?
YOU COULD BE MISSING A CHANCE TO SELL A COPY!
NO.
IF IT'S OKAY WITH YOU... HOW ABOUT WE CALL IT A DAY?
WHAT?!
DOESN'T IT GO UNTIL FOUR?
I'VE HAD ENOUGH FOR TODAY.
I'LL GO GET OUR THINGS. YOU STAY HERE.

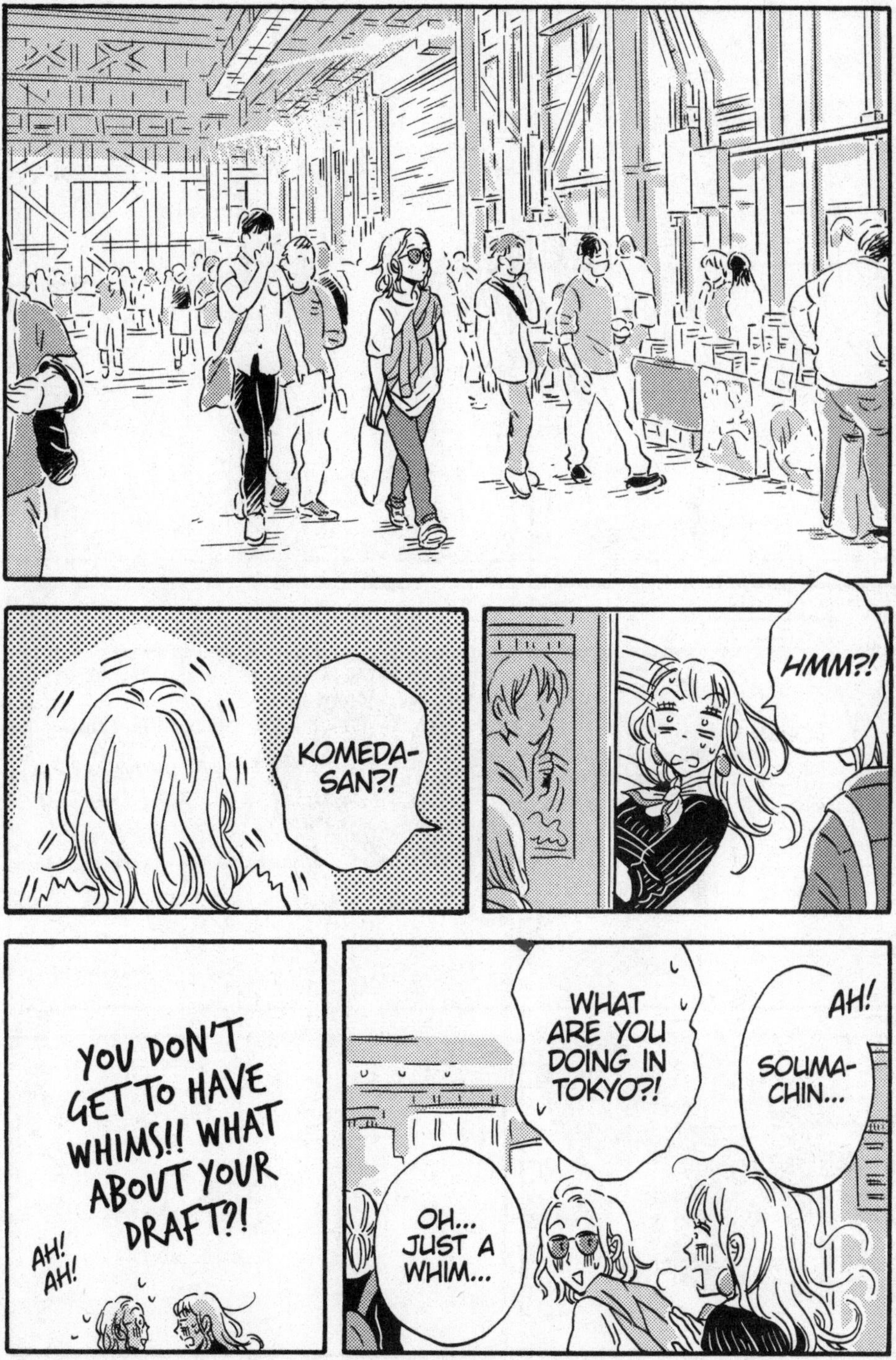
HMM?!
KOMEDA-SAN?!
AH! SOUMA-CHIN...
WHAT ARE YOU DOING IN TOKYO?!
OH... JUST A WHIM...
YOU DON'T GET TO HAVE WHIMS!! WHAT ABOUT YOUR DRAFT?!
AH! AH!

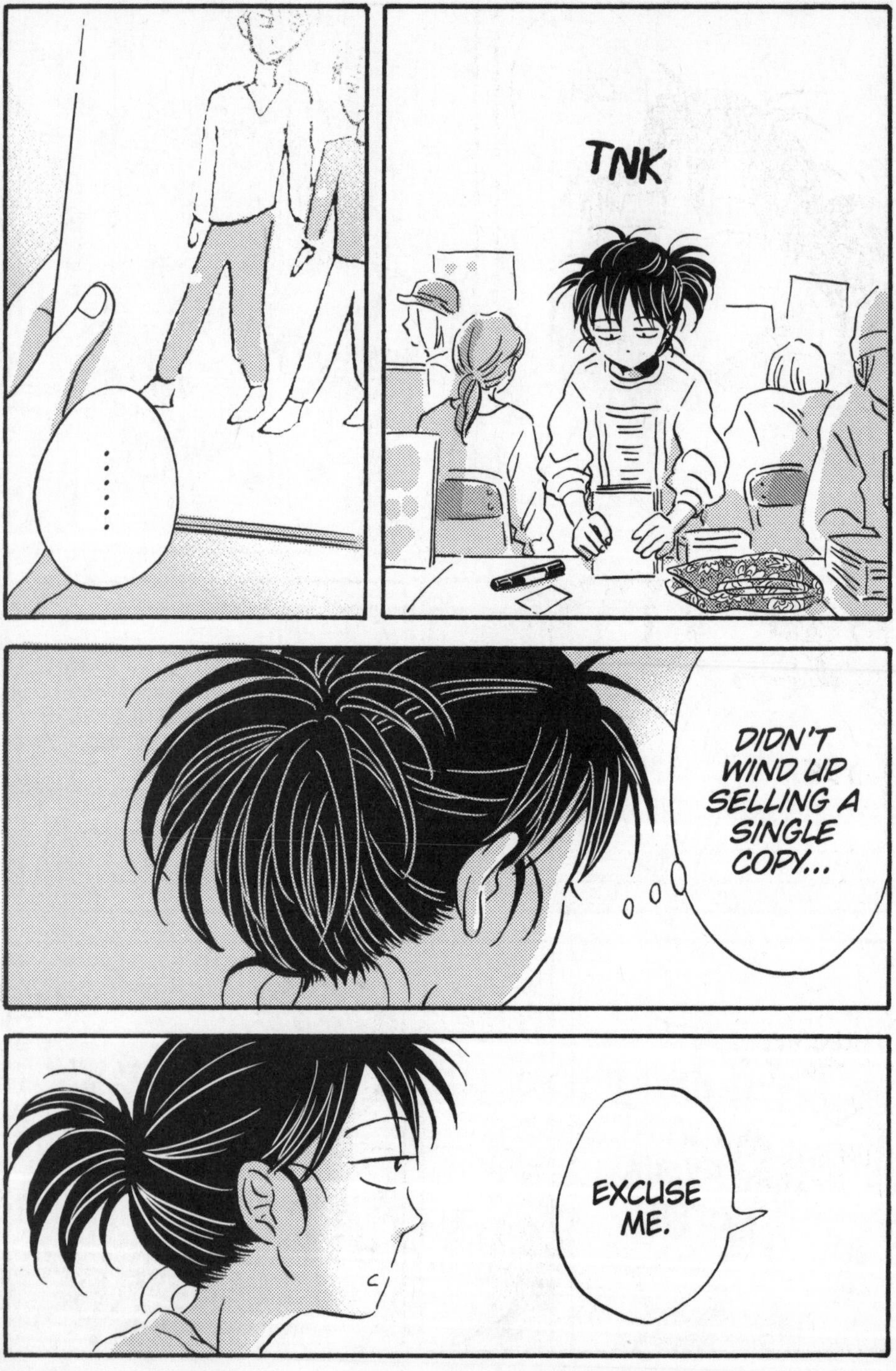
TNK
......
DIDN'T WIND UP SELLING A SINGLE COPY...
EXCUSE ME.

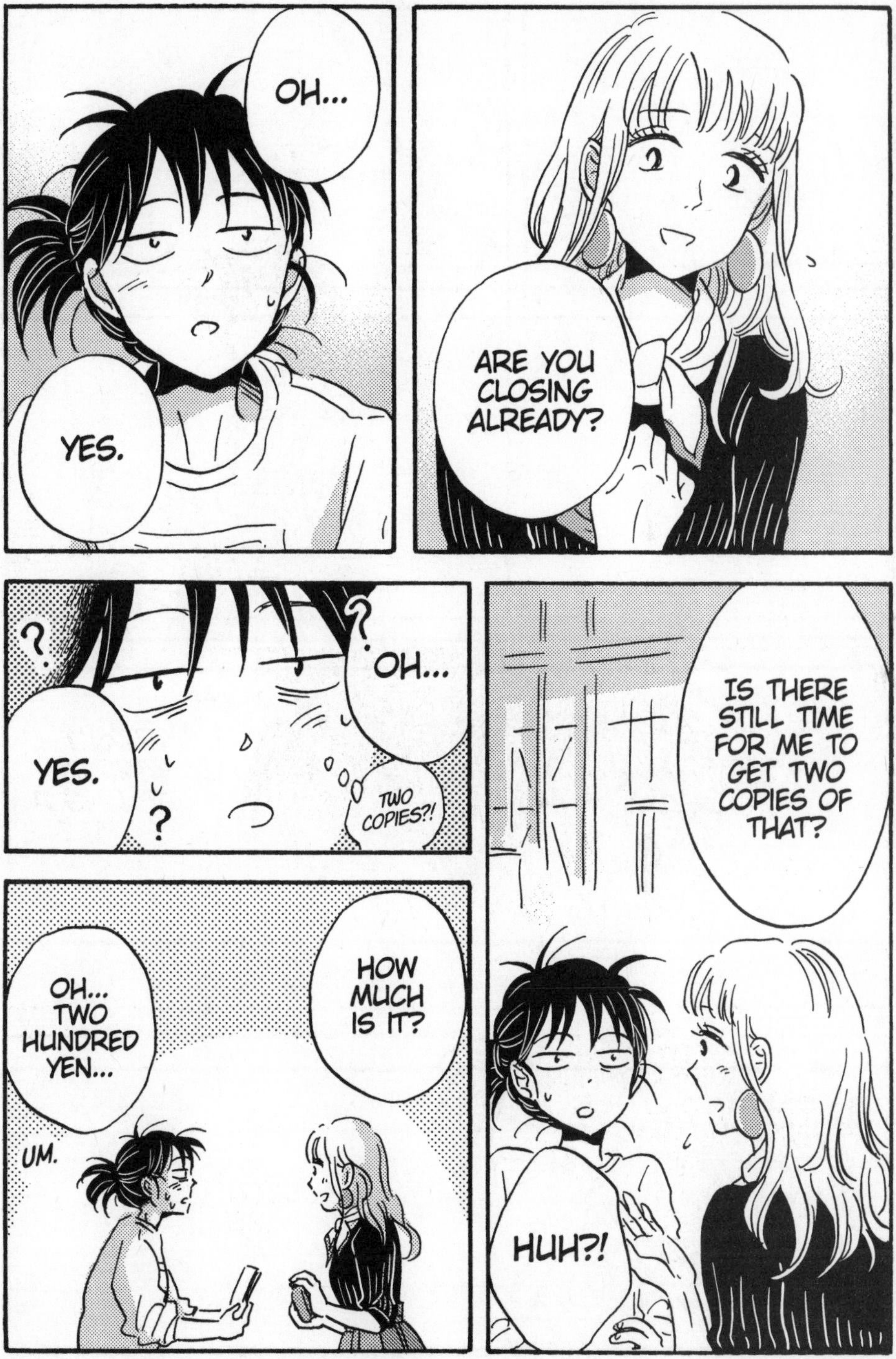
ARE YOU CLOSING ALREADY?
OH...
YES.
IS THERE STILL TIME FOR ME TO GET TWO COPIES OF THAT?
HUH?!
OH...
TWO COPIES?!
YES.
HOW MUCH IS IT?
OH... TWO HUNDRED YEN...
UM.

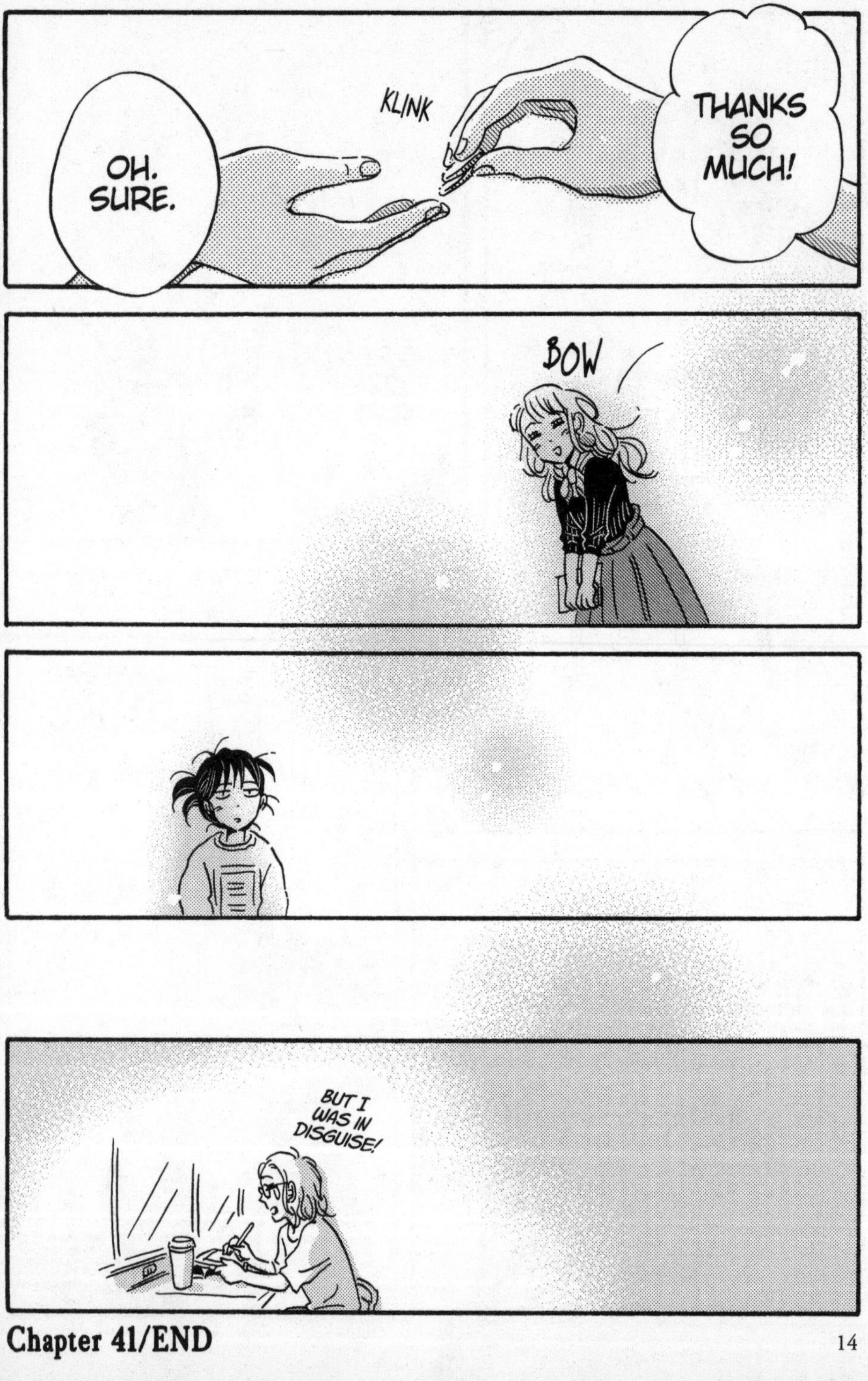
THANKS SO MUCH!
KLINK
OH. SURE.
BOW
BUT I WAS IN DISGUISE!

Chapter 41/END

metamorphosis

# Chapter 42

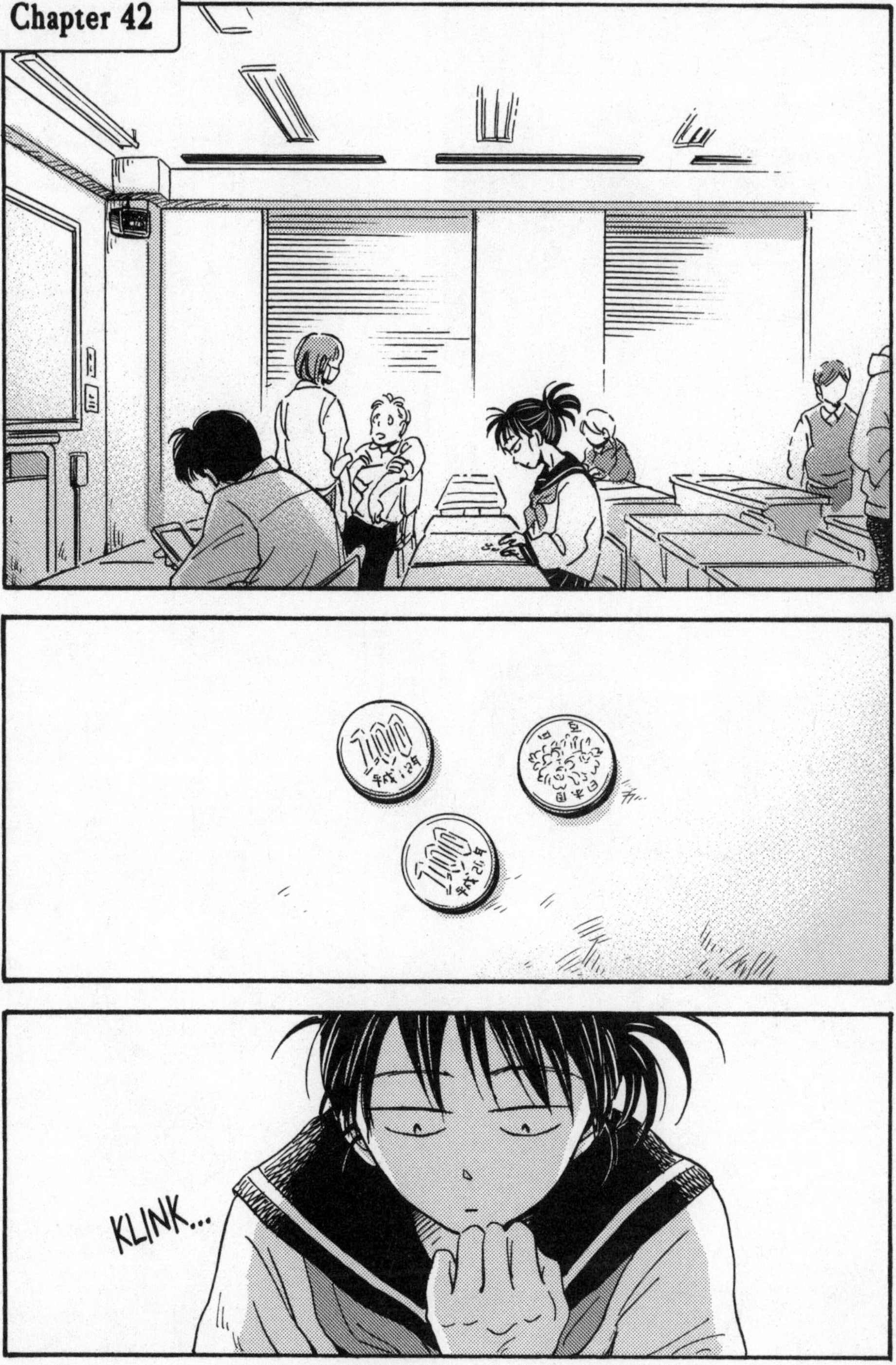
KLINK...

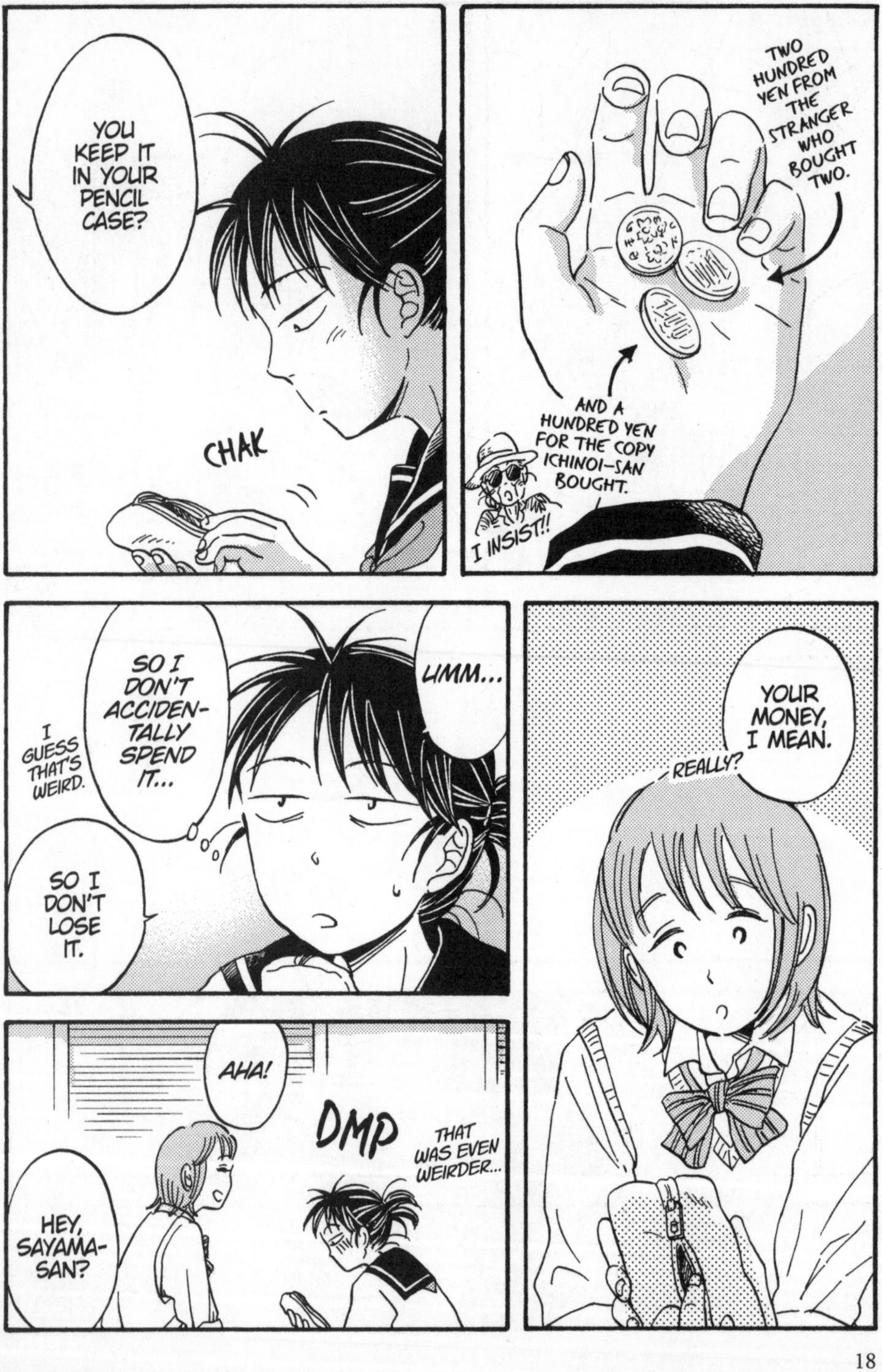
TWO HUNDRED YEN FROM THE STRANGER WHO BOUGHT TWO.
AND A HUNDRED YEN FOR THE COPY ICHINOI-SAN BOUGHT.
I INSIST!!
YOU KEEP IT IN YOUR PENCIL CASE?
CHAK
YOUR MONEY, I MEAN.
REALLY?
UMM...
SO I DON'T ACCIDENTALLY SPEND IT...
I GUESS THAT'S WEIRD.
SO I DON'T LOSE IT.
AHA!
THAT WAS EVEN WEIRDER...
DMP
HEY, SAYAMA-SAN?

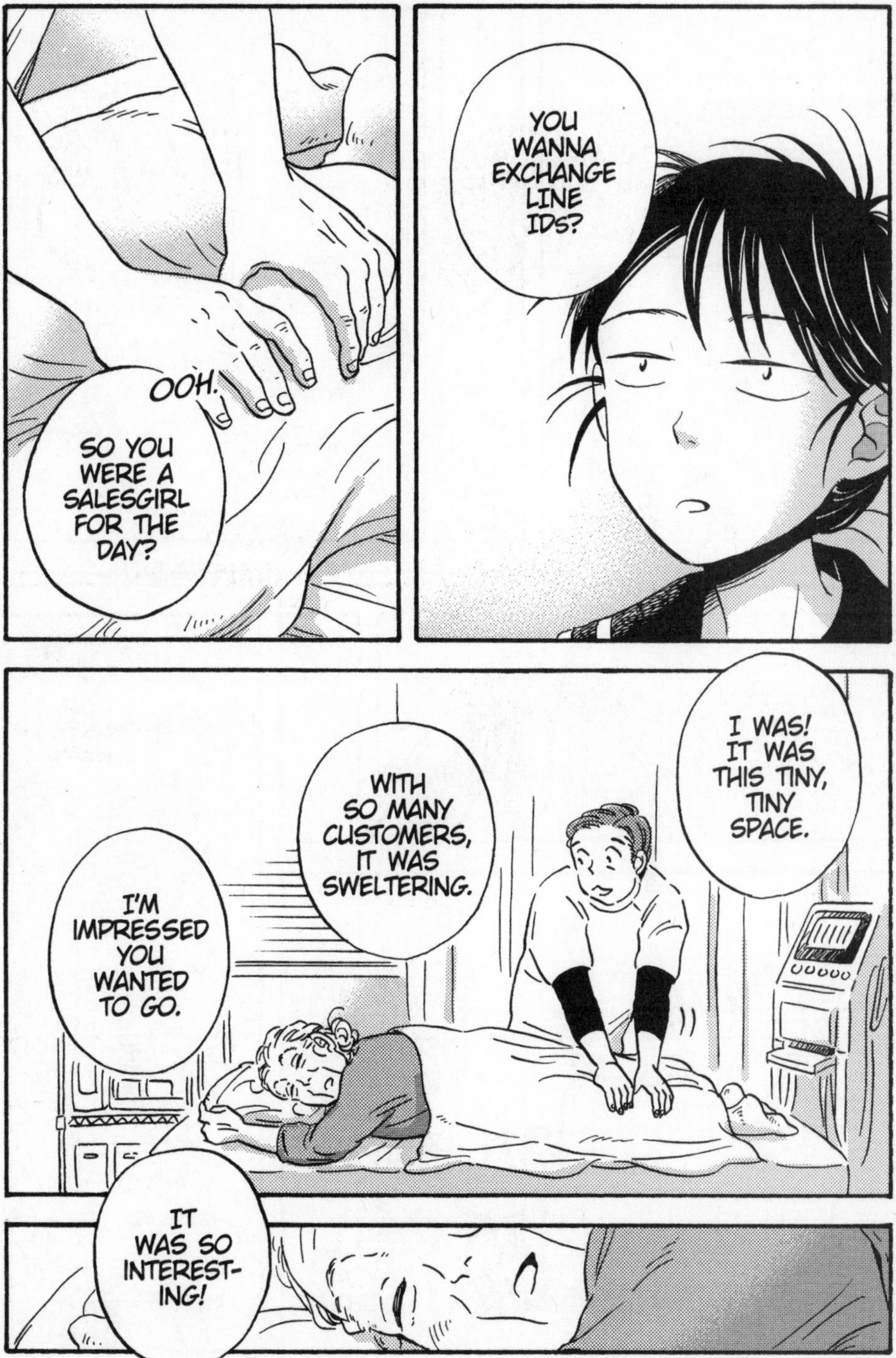
YOU WANNA EXCHANGE LINE IDS?
OOH.
SO YOU WERE A SALESGIRL FOR THE DAY?
I WAS! IT WAS THIS TINY, TINY SPACE.
WITH SO MANY CUSTOMERS, IT WAS SWELTERING.
I'M IMPRESSED YOU WANTED TO GO.
IT WAS SO INTEREST-ING!

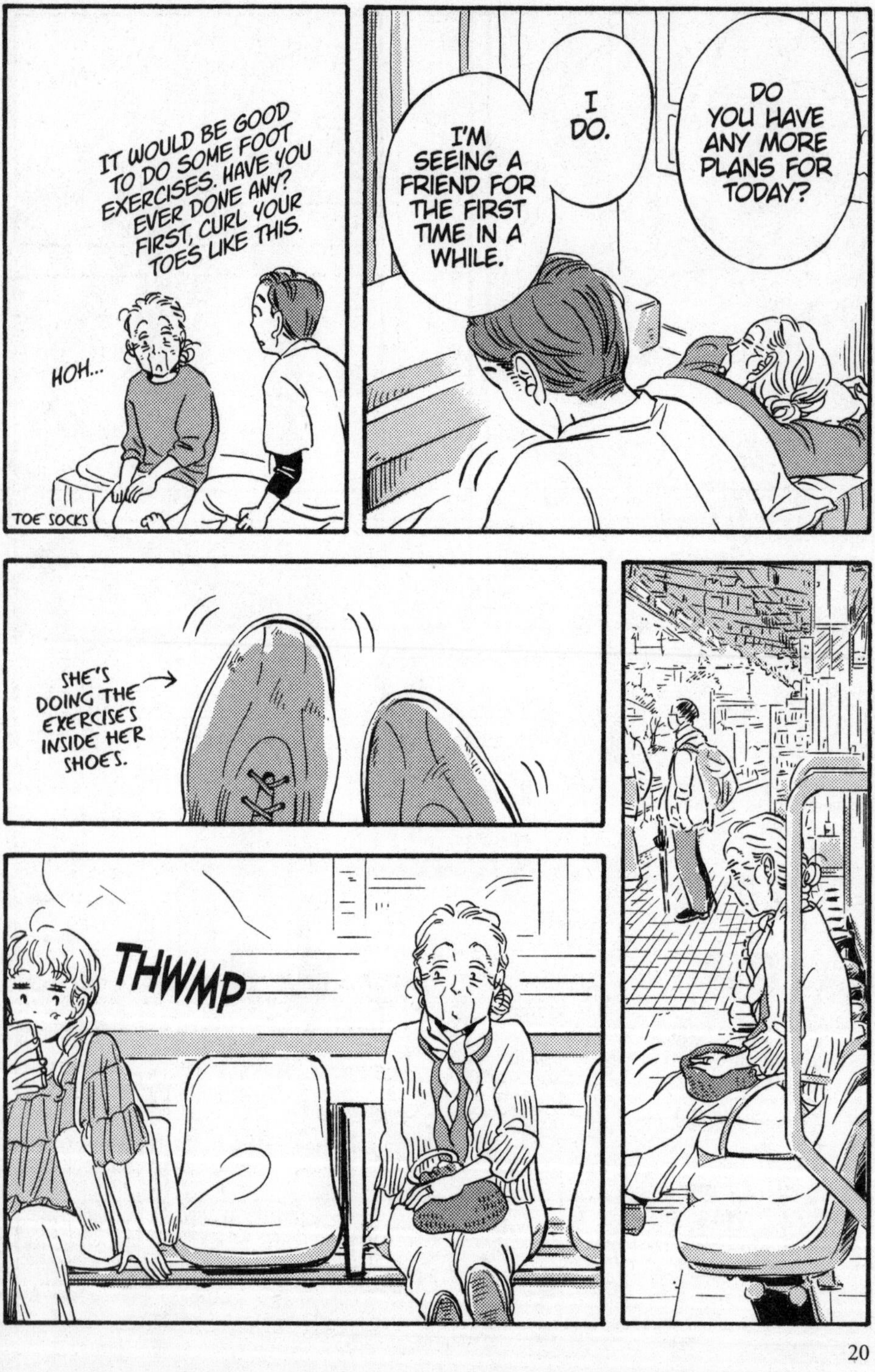
DO YOU HAVE ANY MORE PLANS FOR TODAY?
I DO.
I'M SEEING A FRIEND FOR THE FIRST TIME IN A WHILE.
IT WOULD BE GOOD TO DO SOME FOOT EXERCISES. HAVE YOU EVER DONE ANY? FIRST, CURL YOUR TOES LIKE THIS.
HOH...
TOE SOCKS
SHE'S DOING THE EXERCISES INSIDE HER SHOES.
THWMP

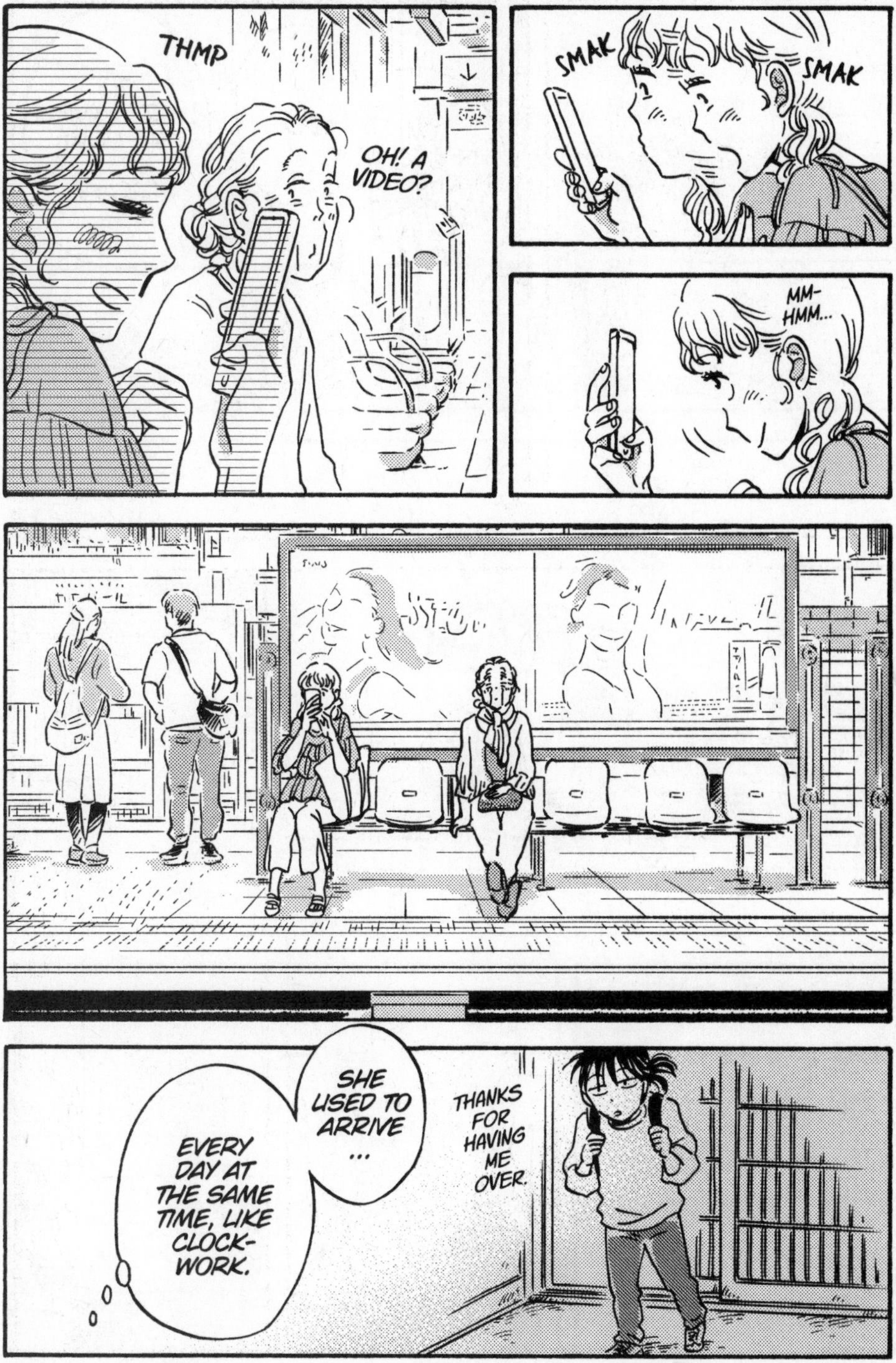
SMAK
SMAK
MM-HMM...
THMP
OH! A VIDEO?
THANKS FOR HAVING ME OVER.
SHE USED TO ARRIVE ...
EVERY DAY AT THE SAME TIME, LIKE CLOCK-WORK.

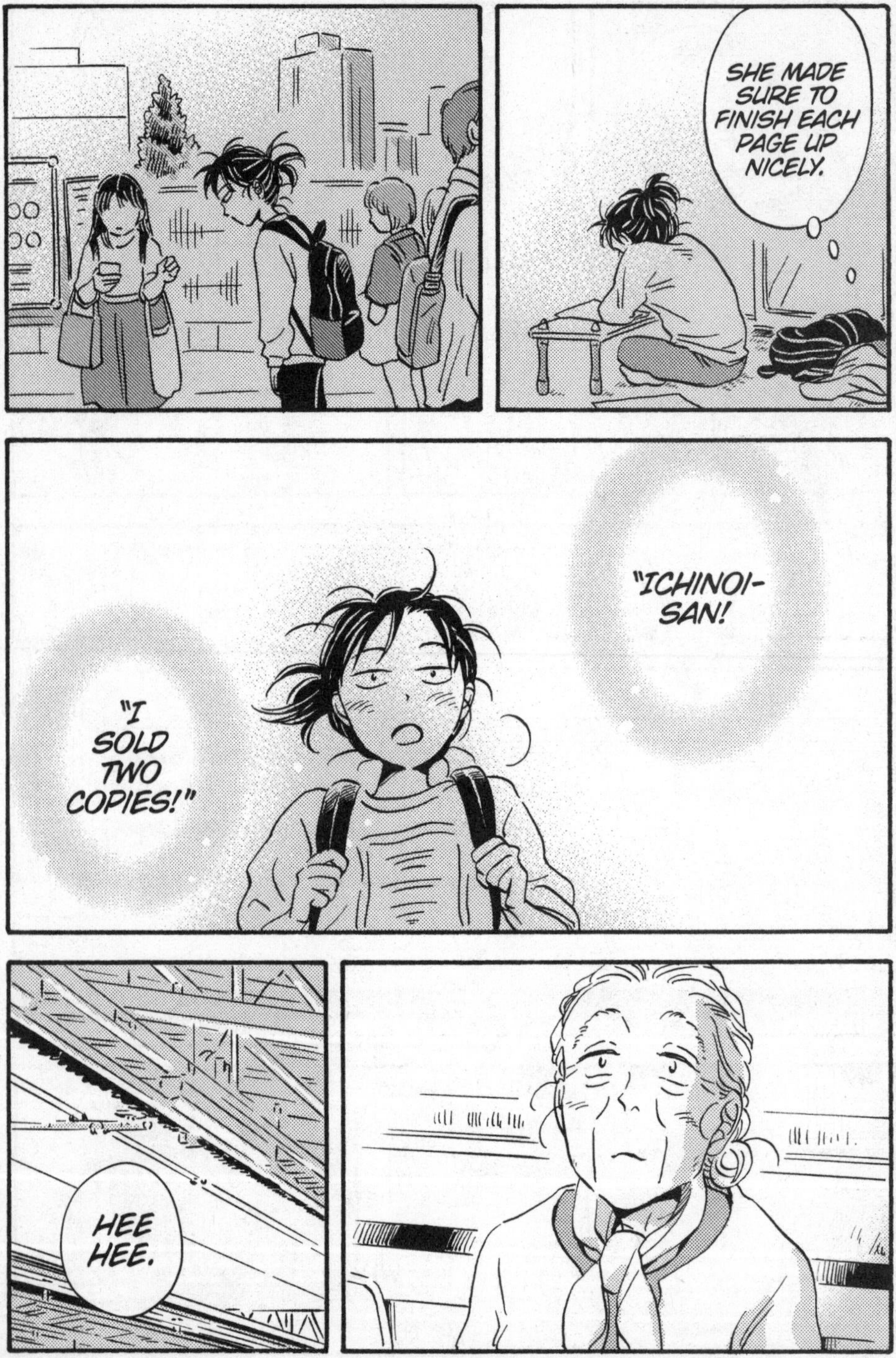
SHE MADE SURE TO FINISH EACH PAGE UP NICELY.
"ICHINOI-SAN!
"I SOLD TWO COPIES!"
HEE HEE.

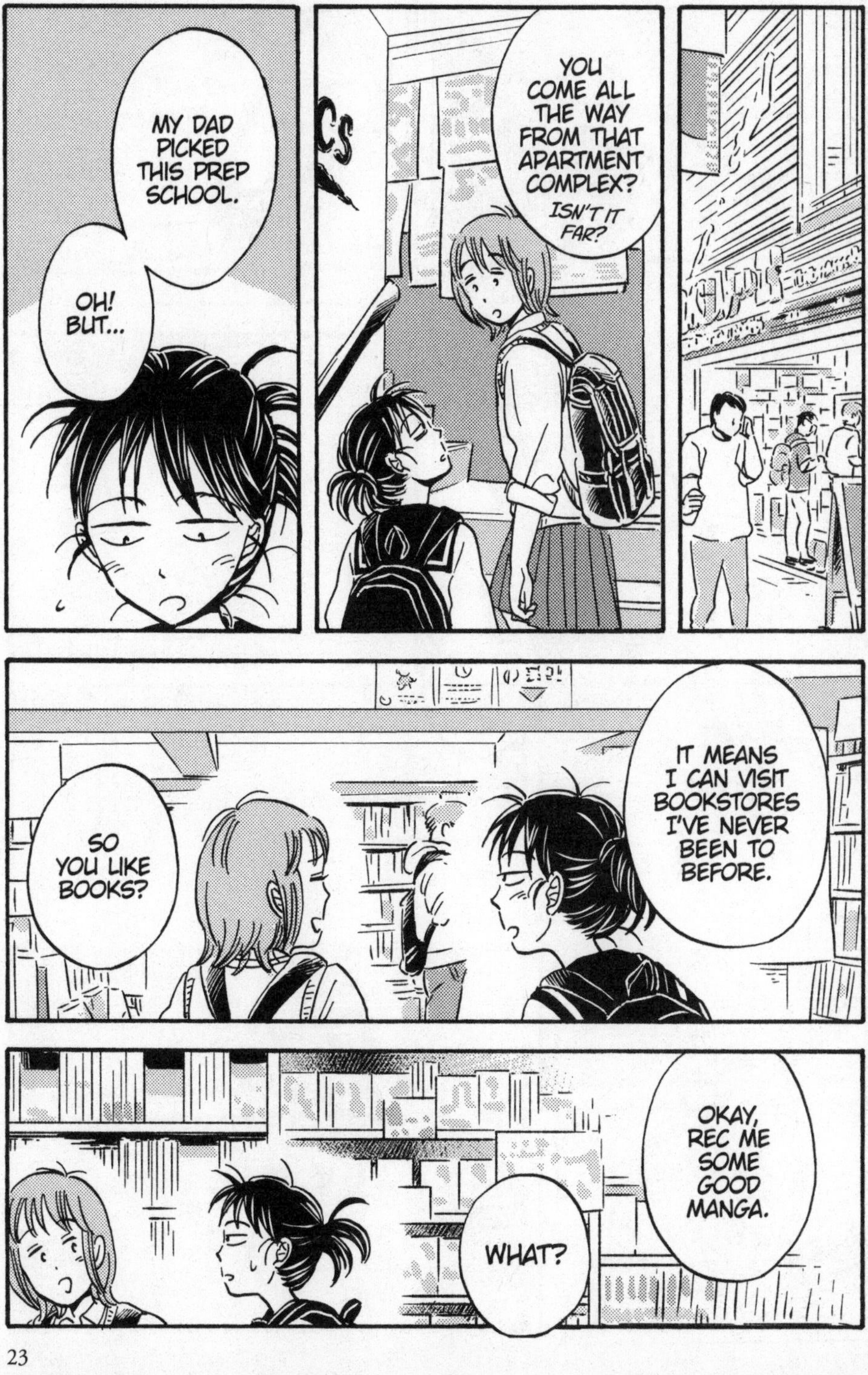
YOU COME ALL THE WAY FROM THAT APARTMENT COMPLEX?
ISN'T IT FAR?
MY DAD PICKED THIS PREP SCHOOL.
OH! BUT...
IT MEANS I CAN VISIT BOOKSTORES I'VE NEVER BEEN TO BEFORE.
SO YOU LIKE BOOKS?
OKAY, REC ME SOME GOOD MANGA.
WHAT?

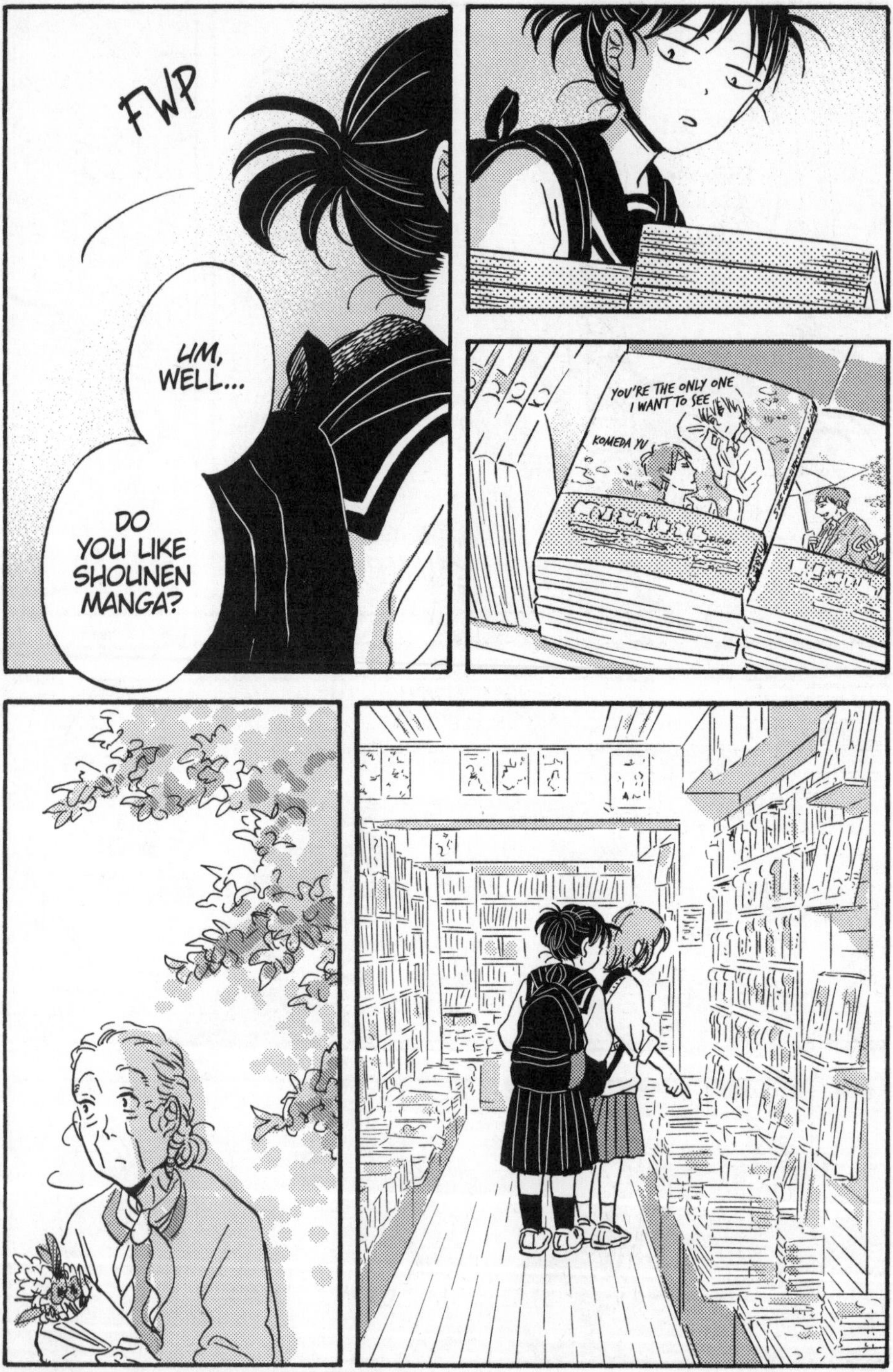
YOU'RE THE ONLY ONE I WANT TO SEE
KOMEDA YU
FWP
UM, WELL...
DO YOU LIKE SHOUNEN MANGA?

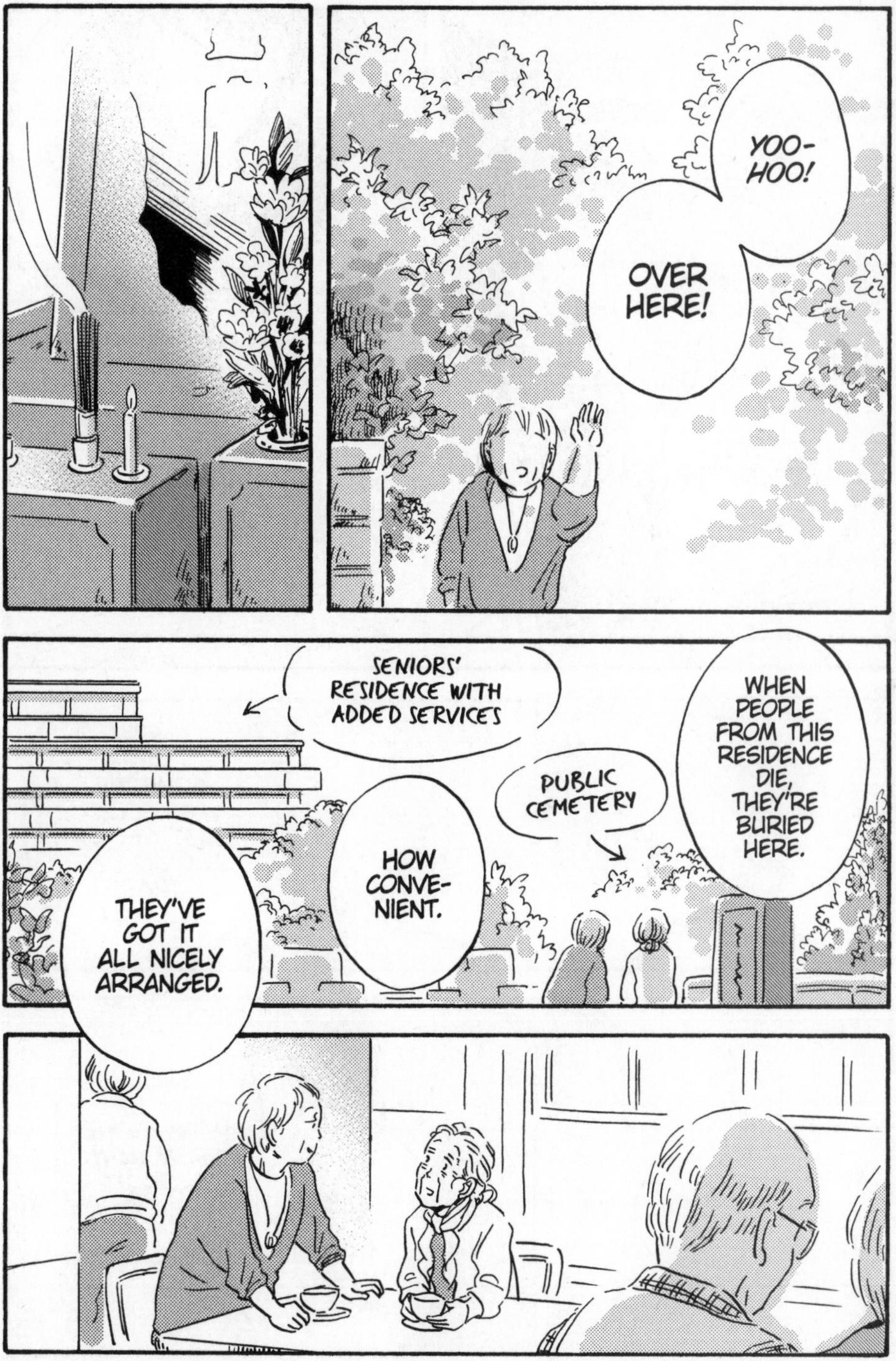
YOO-HOO!
OVER HERE!
WHEN PEOPLE FROM THIS RESIDENCE DIE, THEY'RE BURIED HERE.
SENIORS' RESIDENCE WITH ADDED SERVICES
PUBLIC CEMETERY
HOW CONVENIENT.
THEY'VE GOT IT ALL NICELY ARRANGED.

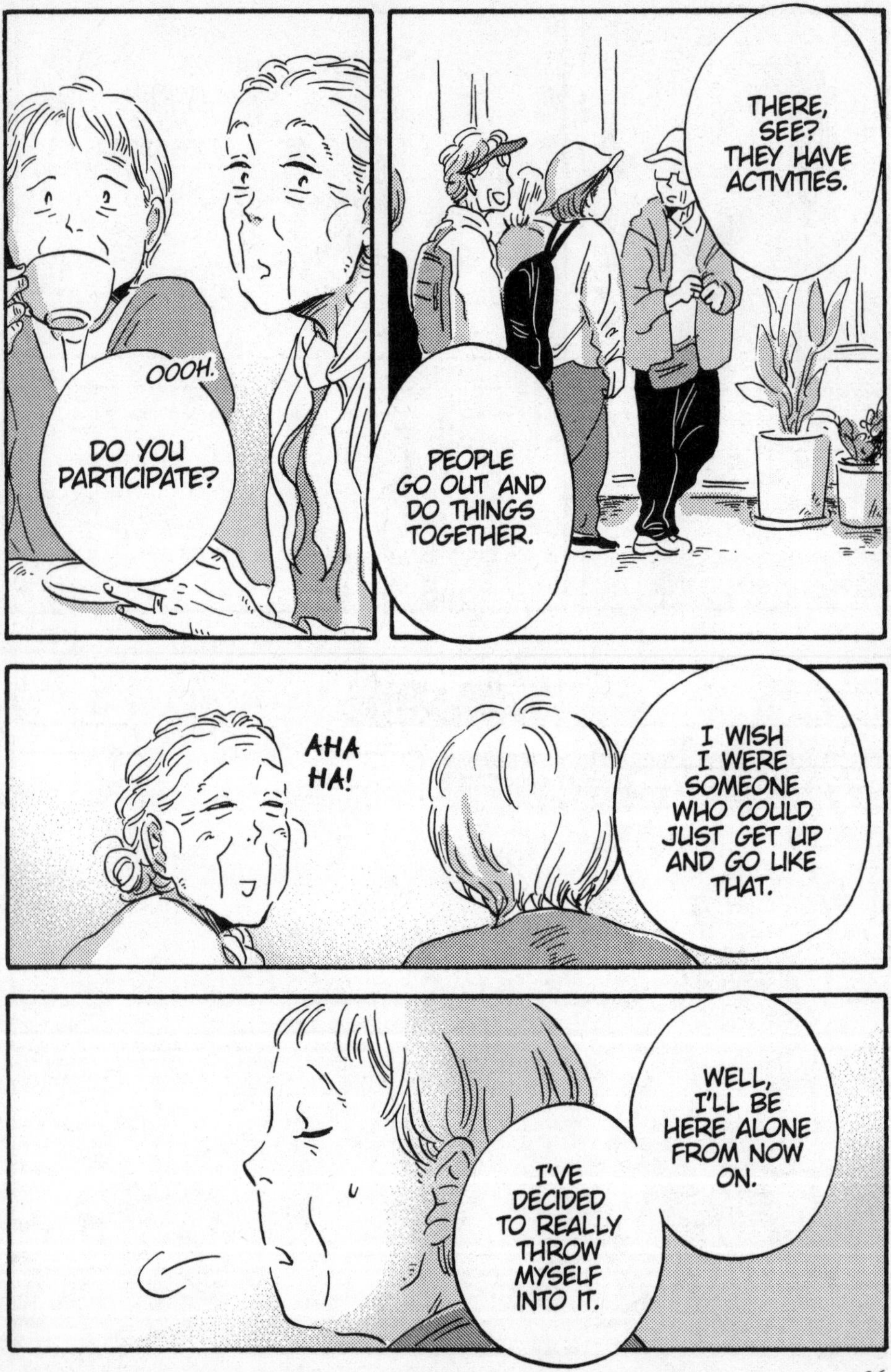
THERE, SEE? THEY HAVE ACTIVITIES.
PEOPLE GO OUT AND DO THINGS TOGETHER.
OOOH.
DO YOU PARTICIPATE?
I WISH I WERE SOMEONE WHO COULD JUST GET UP AND GO LIKE THAT.
AHA HA!
WELL, I'LL BE HERE ALONE FROM NOW ON.
I'VE DECIDED TO REALLY THROW MYSELF INTO IT.

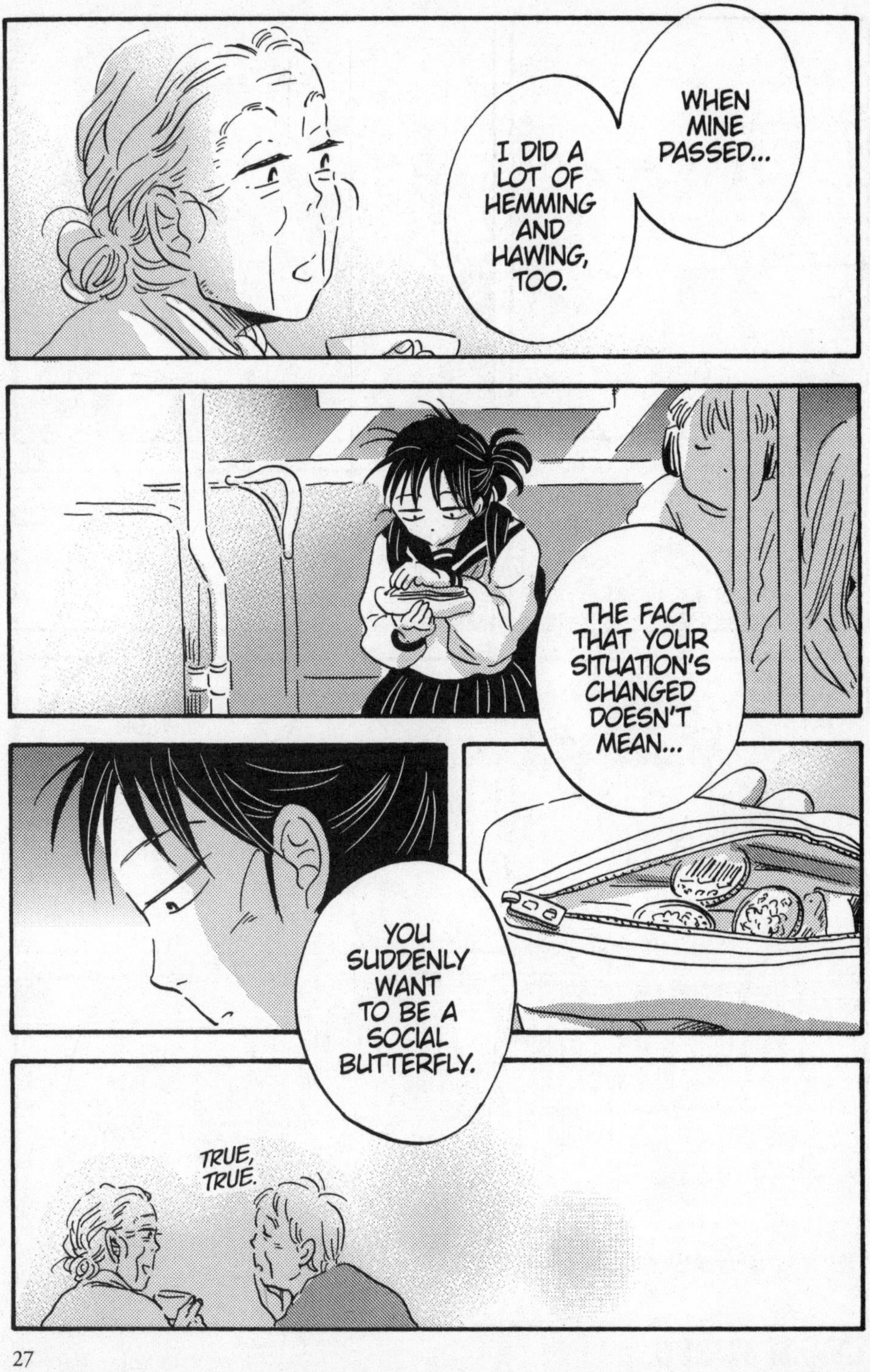
WHEN MINE PASSED...
I DID A LOT OF HEMMING AND HAWING, TOO.
THE FACT THAT YOUR SITUATION'S CHANGED DOESN'T MEAN...
YOU SUDDENLY WANT TO BE A SOCIAL BUTTERFLY.
TRUE, TRUE.

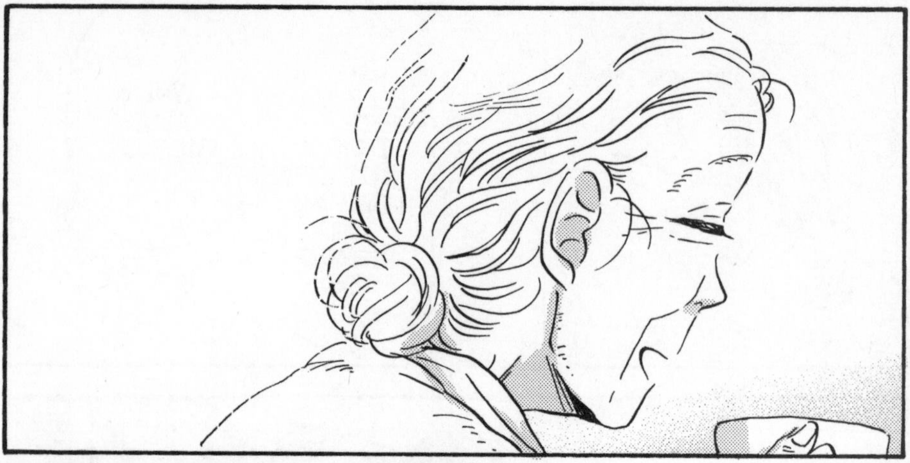

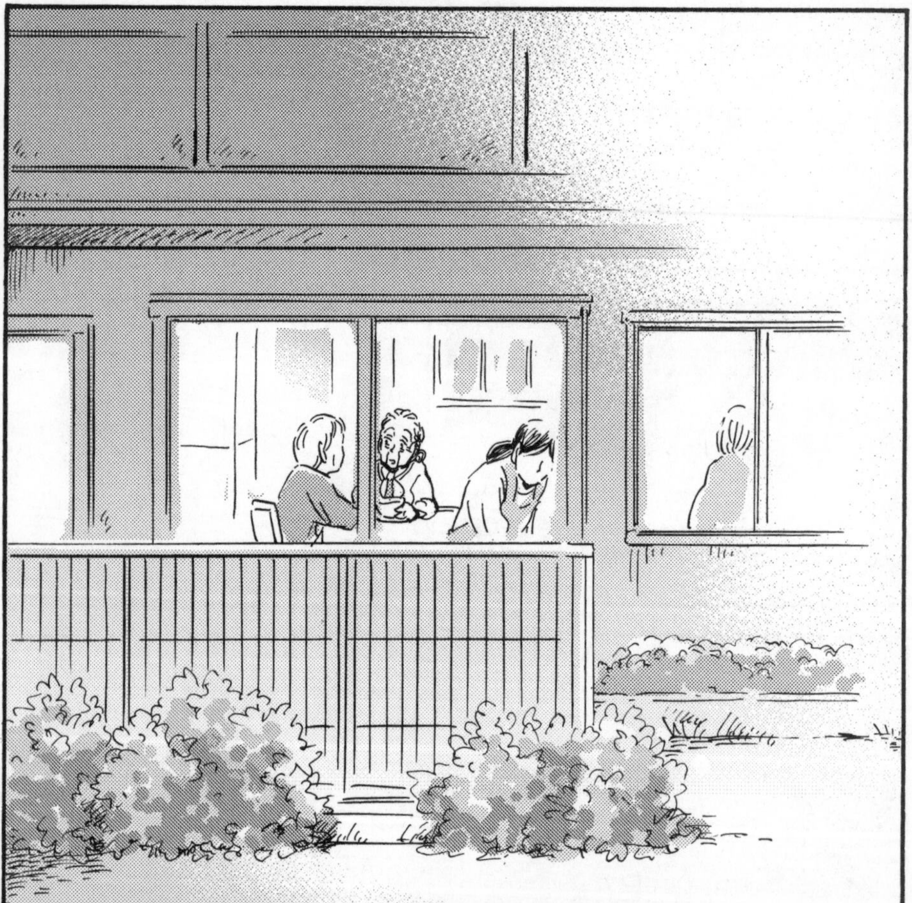

**Chapter 42/END**

metamorphosis

# Chapter 43

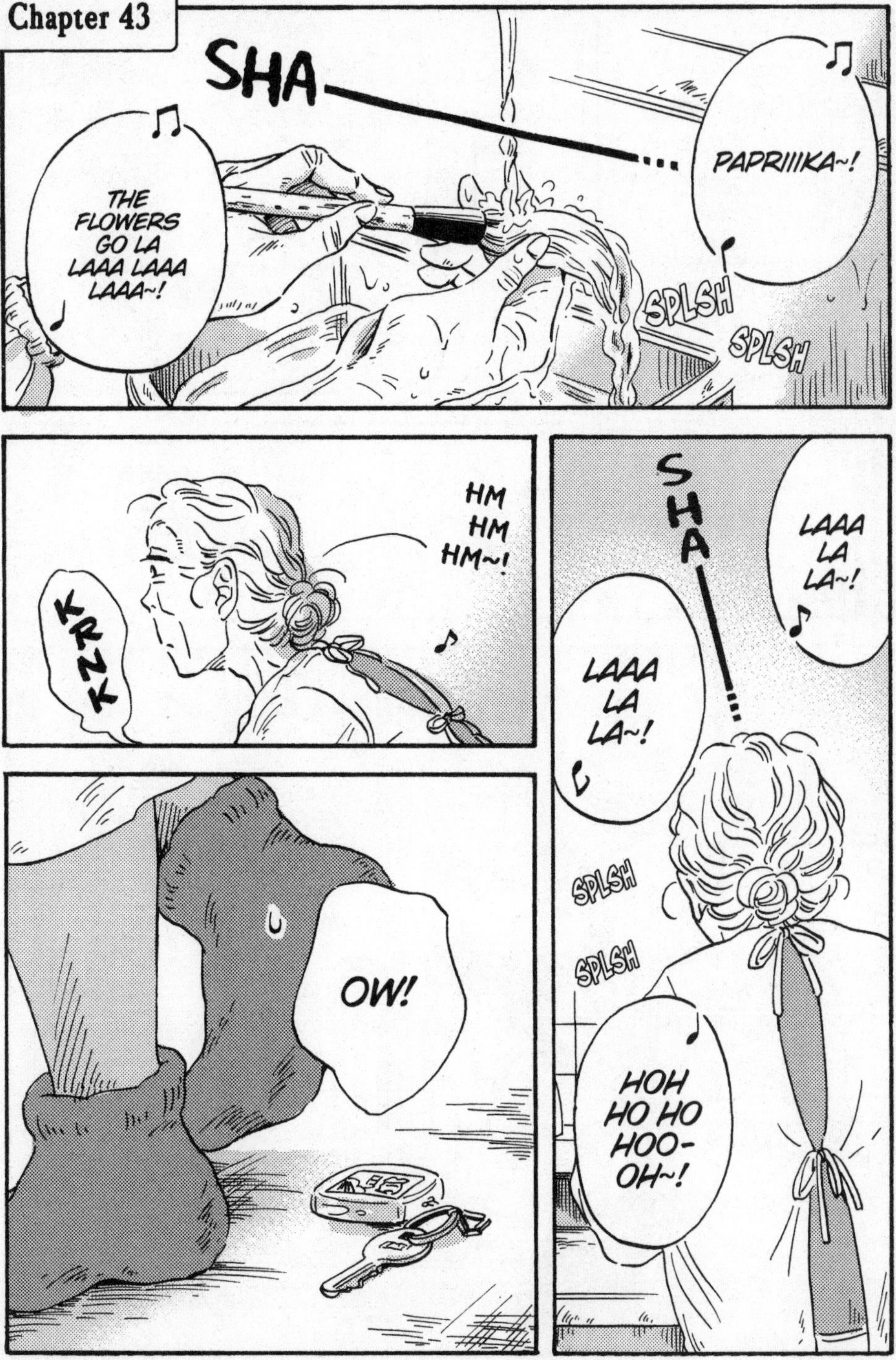
SHA
PAPRIIIKA~!
THE FLOWERS GO LA LAAA LAAA LAAA~!
SPLSH
SPLSH
SHA
LAAA LA LA~!
LAAA LA LA~!
SPLSH
SPLSH
HOH HO HO HOO-OH~!
HM HM HM~!
KRNK
OW!

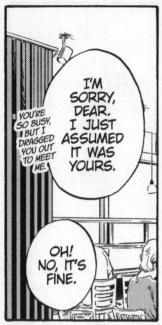

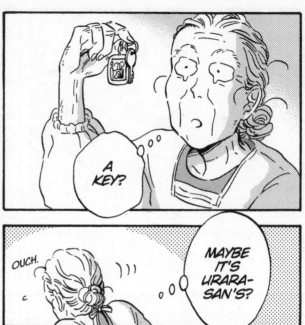

A KEY?
MAYBE IT'S URARA-SAN'S?
OUCH.
I'M SORRY, DEAR. I JUST ASSUMED IT WAS YOURS.
YOU'RE SO BUSY, BUT I DRAGGED YOU OUT TO MEET ME.
OH! NO, IT'S FINE.
I HAVEN'T SEEN YOU SINCE COMITIA.
THINKING ABOUT IT STILL PUTS THE BIGGEST SMILE ON MY FACE.
SAME HERE.
IT SURE WAS CROWDED, HUH?
AND SO HOT...
IT WAS QUITE DIFFERENT SEEING IT FROM THE INSIDE!
SUCH A TINY BOOTH!

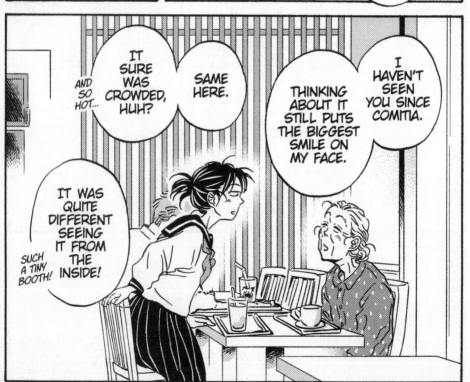

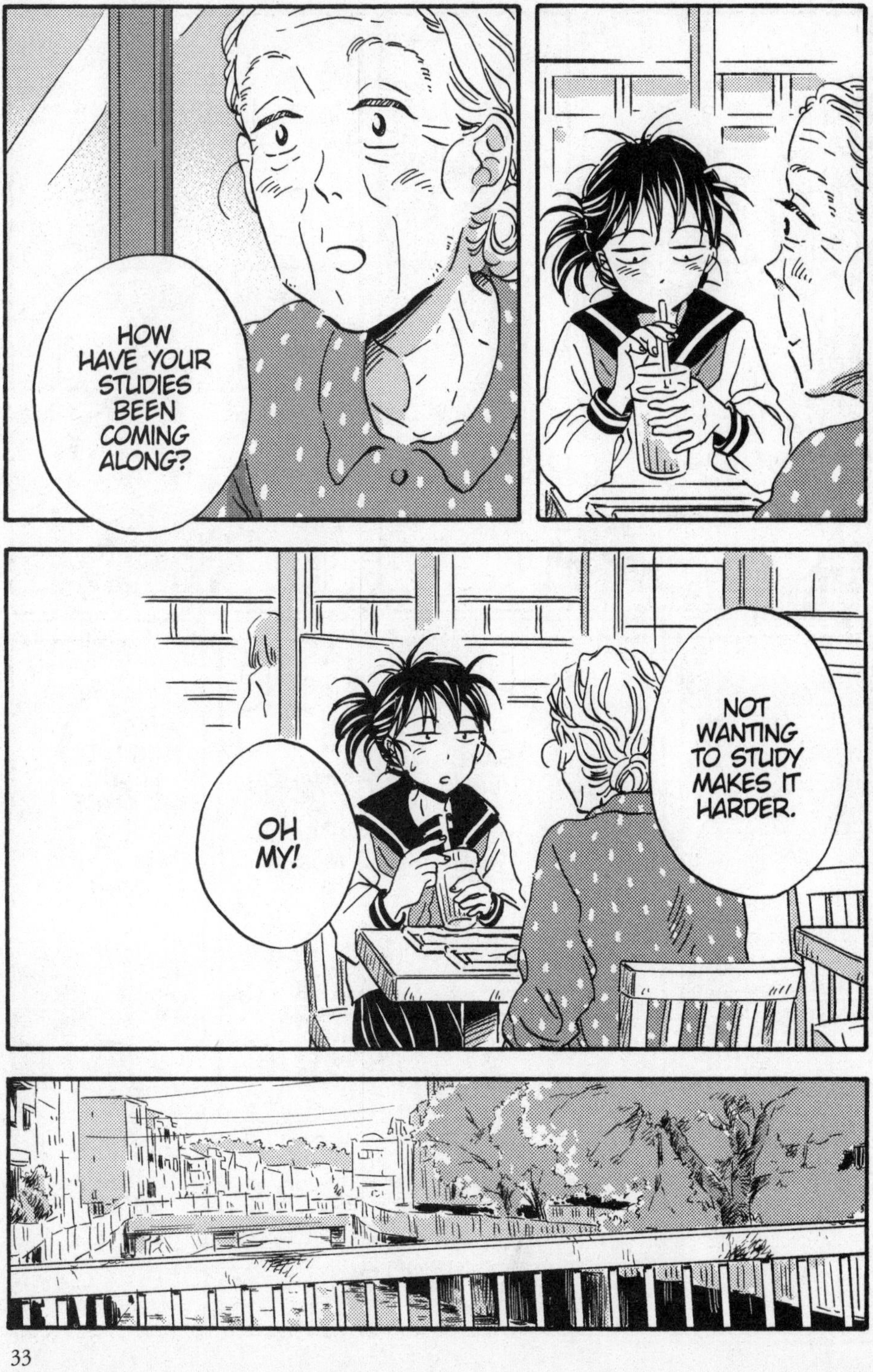
HOW HAVE YOUR STUDIES BEEN COMING ALONG?
NOT WANTING TO STUDY MAKES IT HARDER.
OH MY!

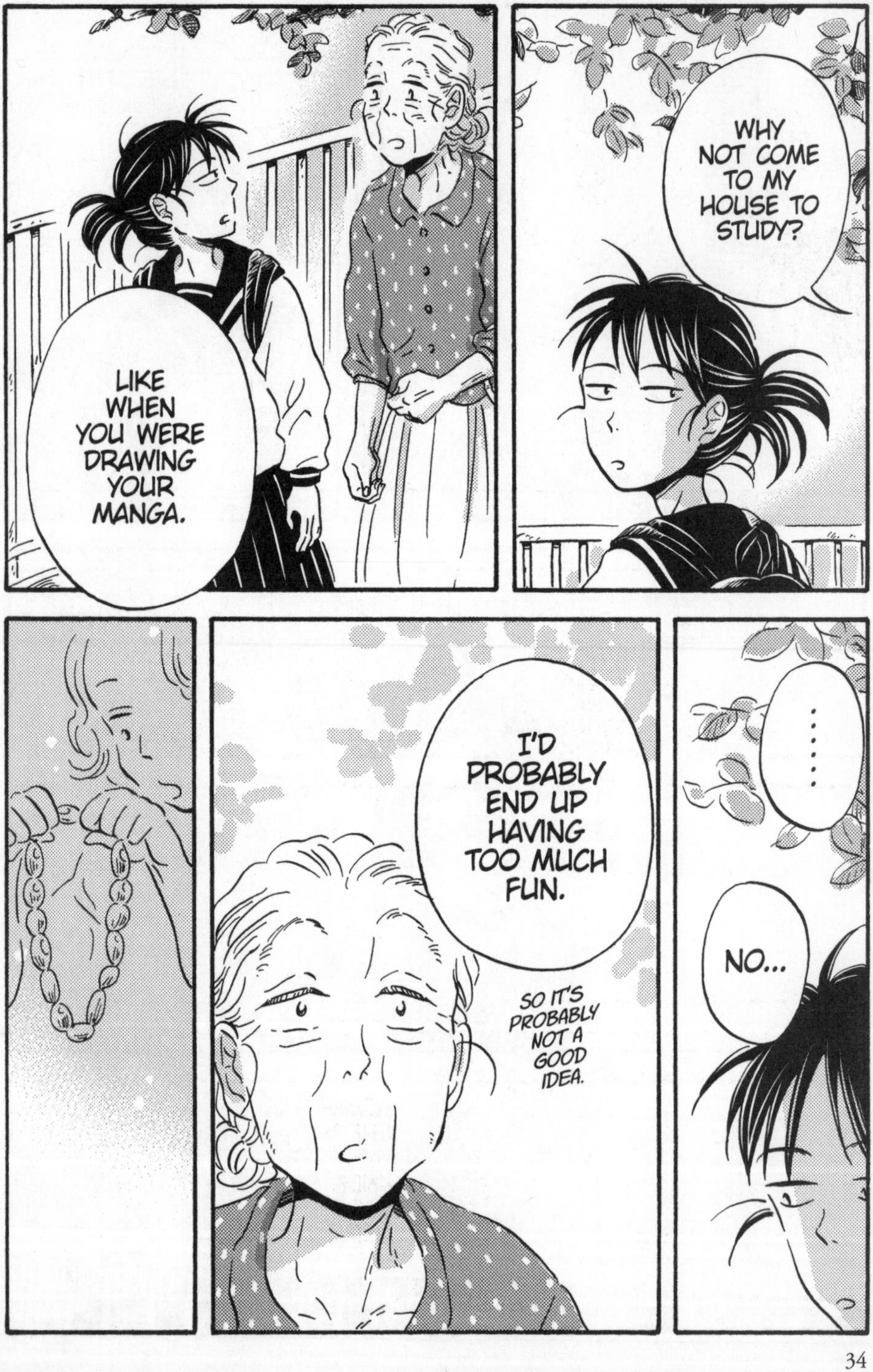
WHY NOT COME TO MY HOUSE TO STUDY?
LIKE WHEN YOU WERE DRAWING YOUR MANGA.
......
NO...
I'D PROBABLY END UP HAVING TOO MUCH FUN.
SO IT'S PROBABLY NOT A GOOD IDEA.

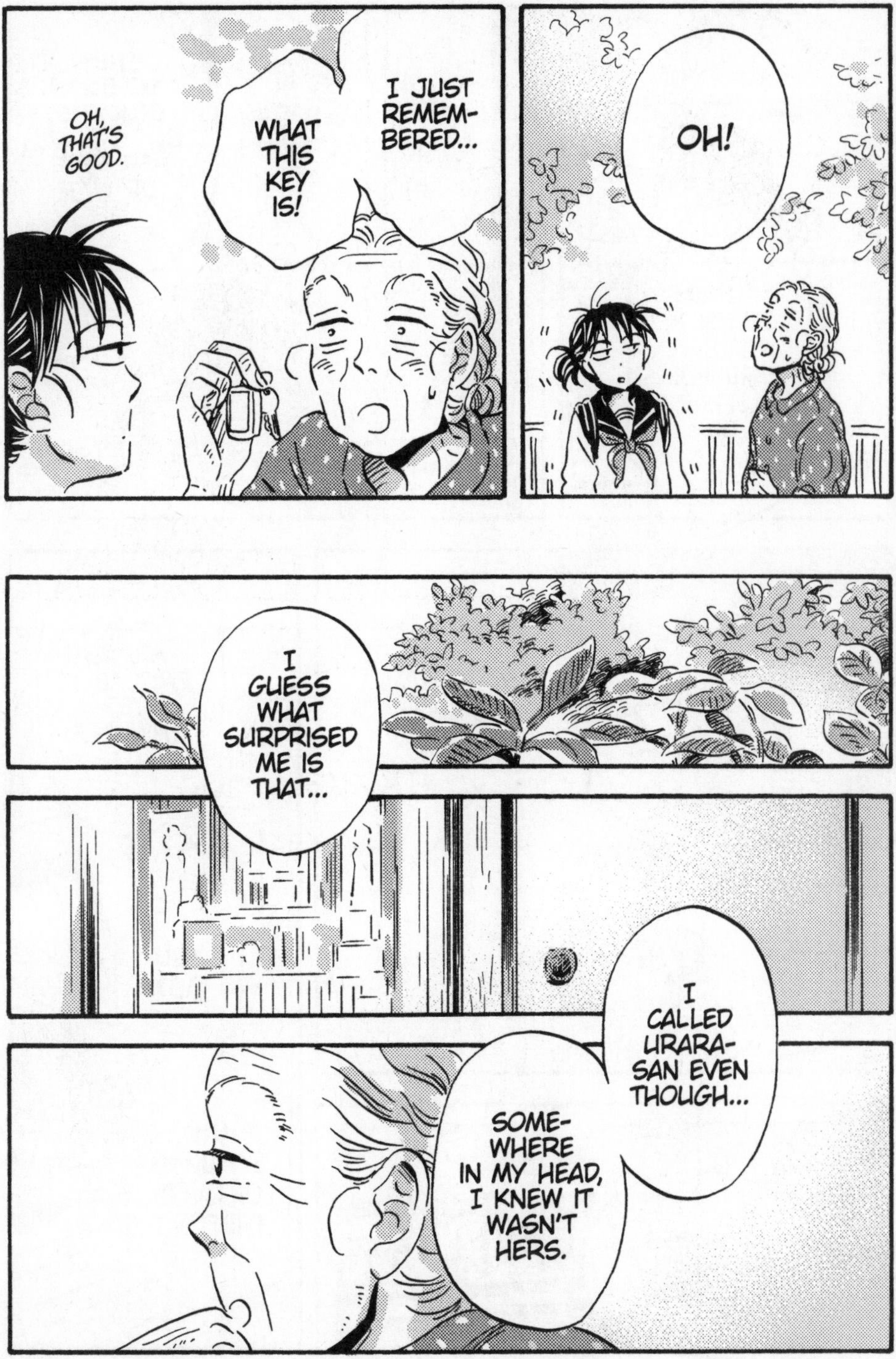
OH!
I JUST REMEMBERED... WHAT THIS KEY IS!
OH, THAT'S GOOD.
I GUESS WHAT SURPRISED ME IS THAT...
I CALLED URARA-SAN EVEN THOUGH...
SOMEWHERE IN MY HEAD, I KNEW IT WASN'T HERS.

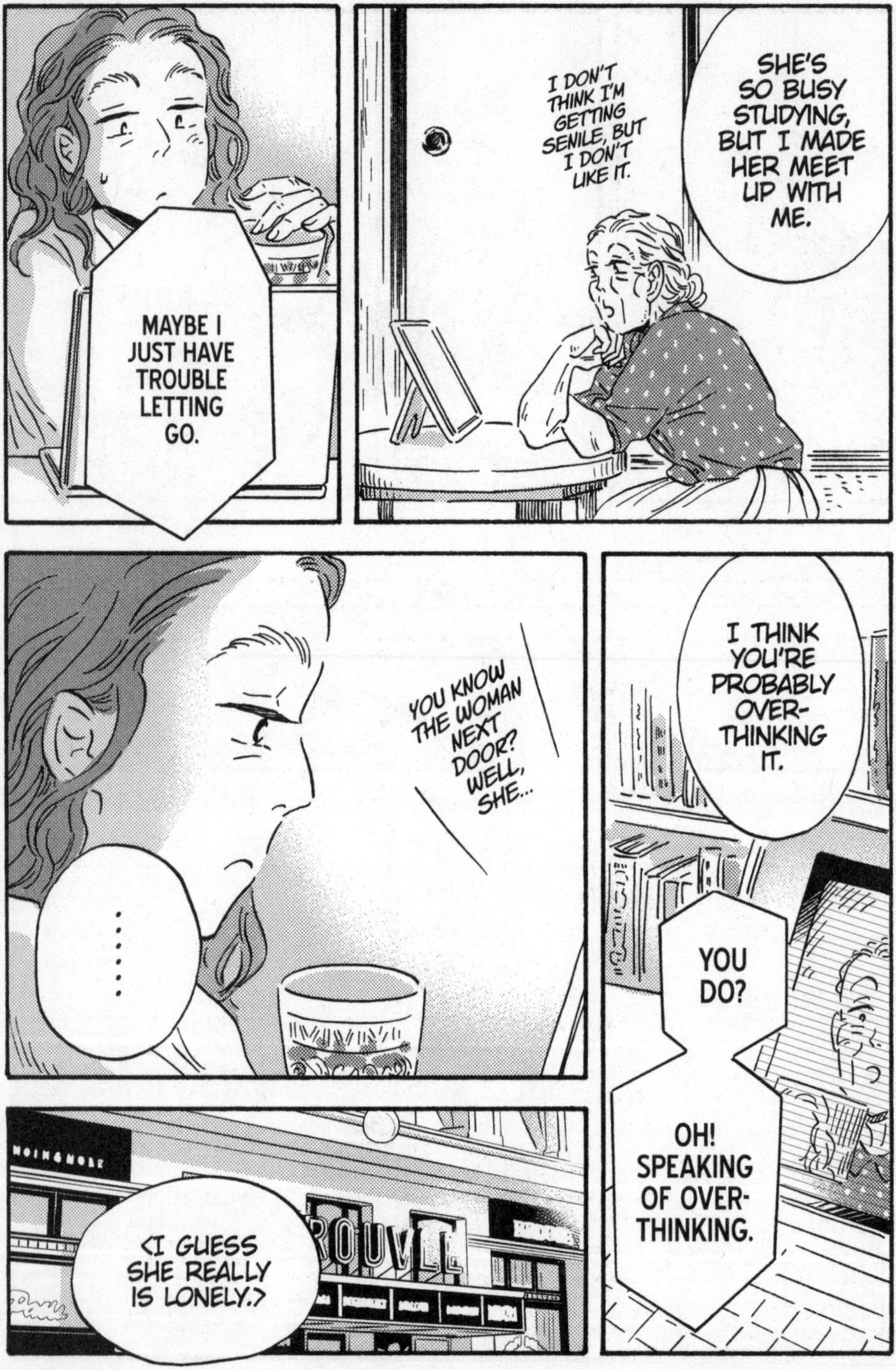
SHE'S SO BUSY STUDYING, BUT I MADE HER MEET UP WITH ME.
I DON'T THINK I'M GETTING SENILE, BUT I DON'T LIKE IT.
MAYBE I JUST HAVE TROUBLE LETTING GO.
I THINK YOU'RE PROBABLY OVER-THINKING IT.
YOU DO?
OH! SPEAKING OF OVER-THINKING.
YOU KNOW THE WOMAN NEXT DOOR? WELL, SHE...
......
<I GUESS SHE REALLY IS LONELY.>

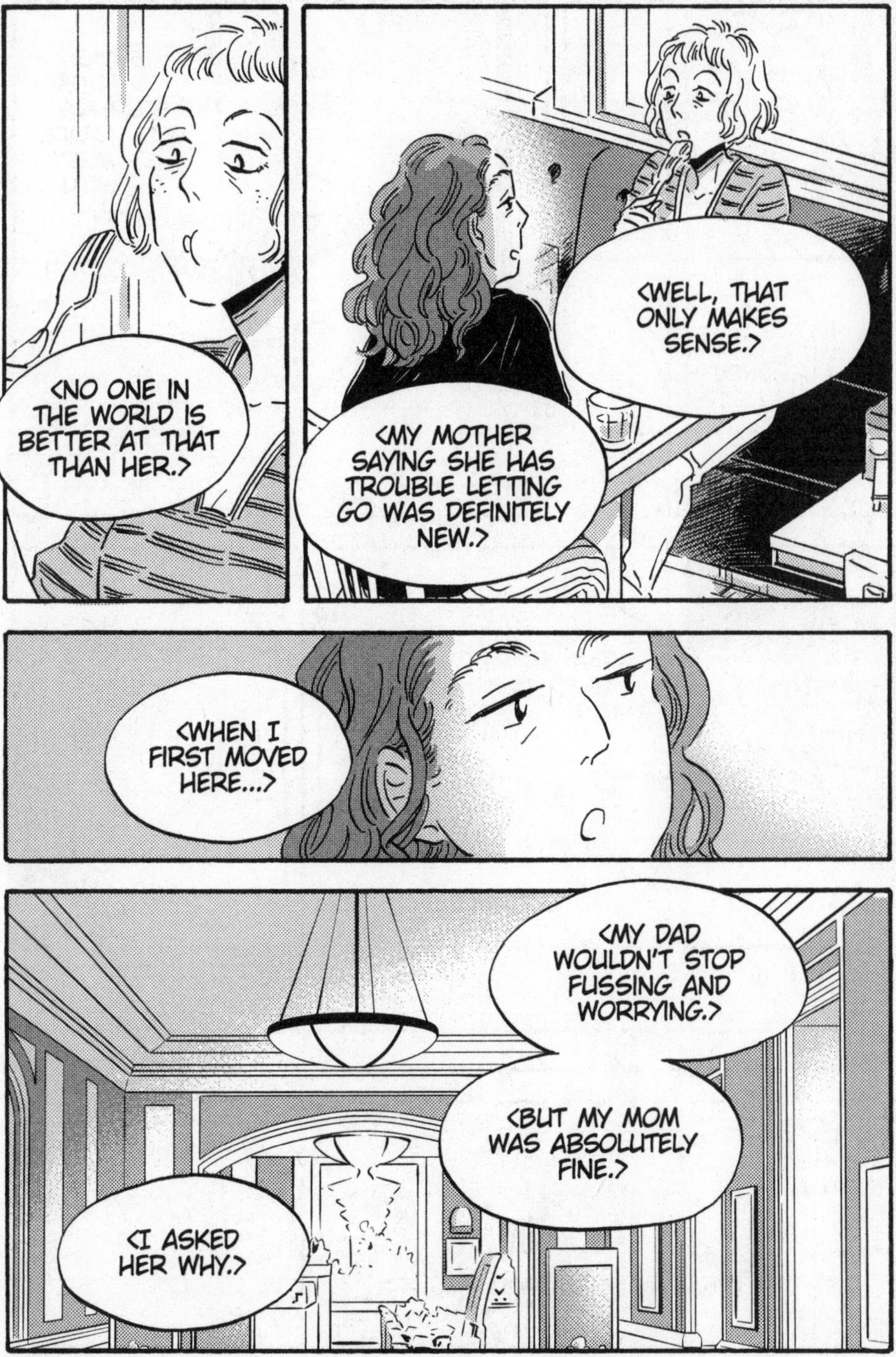
<WELL, THAT ONLY MAKES SENSE.>
<MY MOTHER SAYING SHE HAS TROUBLE LETTING GO WAS DEFINITELY NEW.>
<NO ONE IN THE WORLD IS BETTER AT THAT THAN HER.>
<WHEN I FIRST MOVED HERE...>
<MY DAD WOULDN'T STOP FUSSING AND WORRYING.>
<BUT MY MOM WAS ABSOLUTELY FINE.>
<I ASKED HER WHY.>

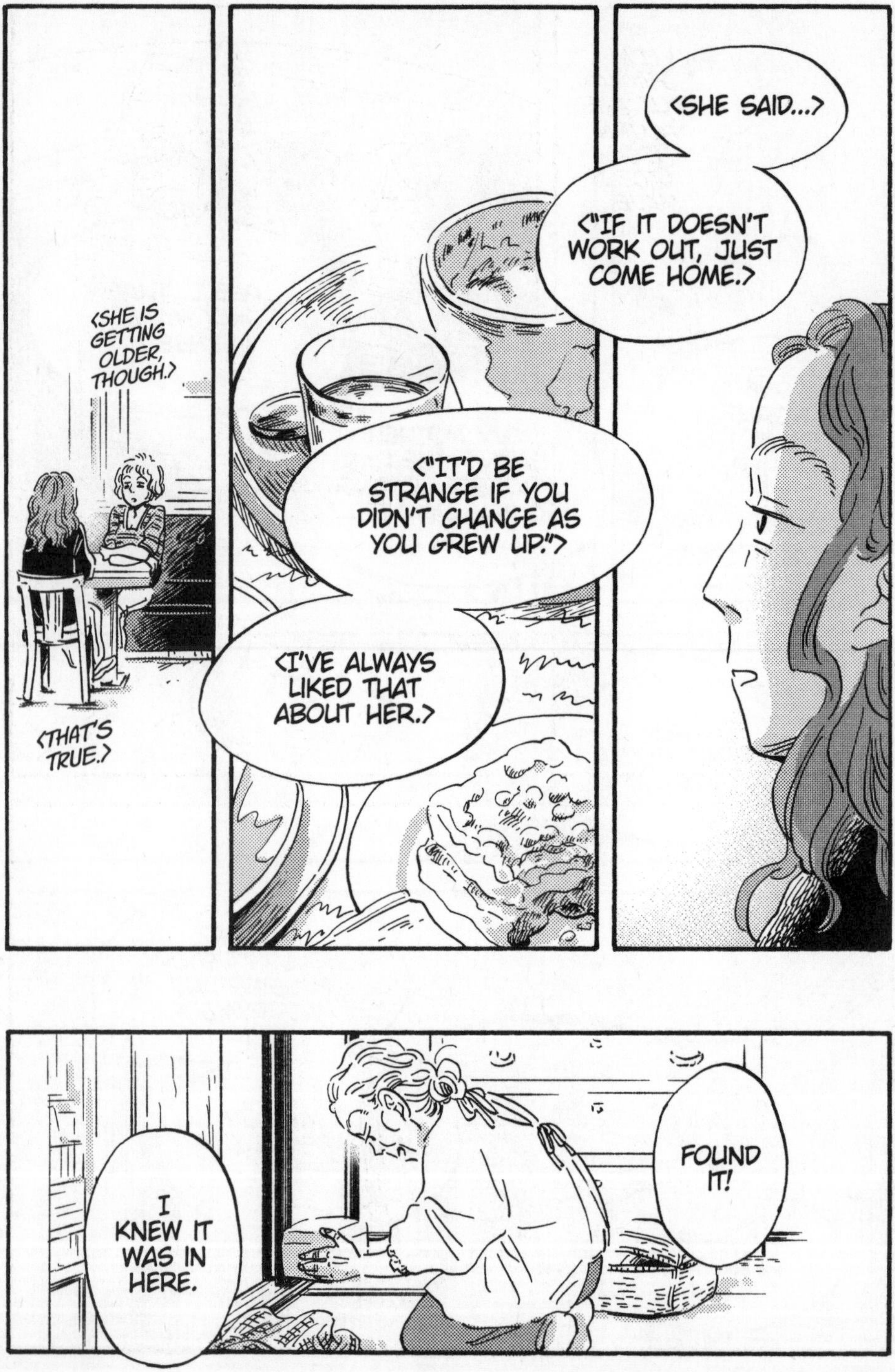
<SHE SAID...>
<"IF IT DOESN'T WORK OUT, JUST COME HOME.>
<"IT'D BE STRANGE IF YOU DIDN'T CHANGE AS YOU GREW UP.">
<I'VE ALWAYS LIKED THAT ABOUT HER.>
<SHE IS GETTING OLDER, THOUGH.>
<THAT'S TRUE.>
FOUND IT!
I KNEW IT WAS IN HERE.

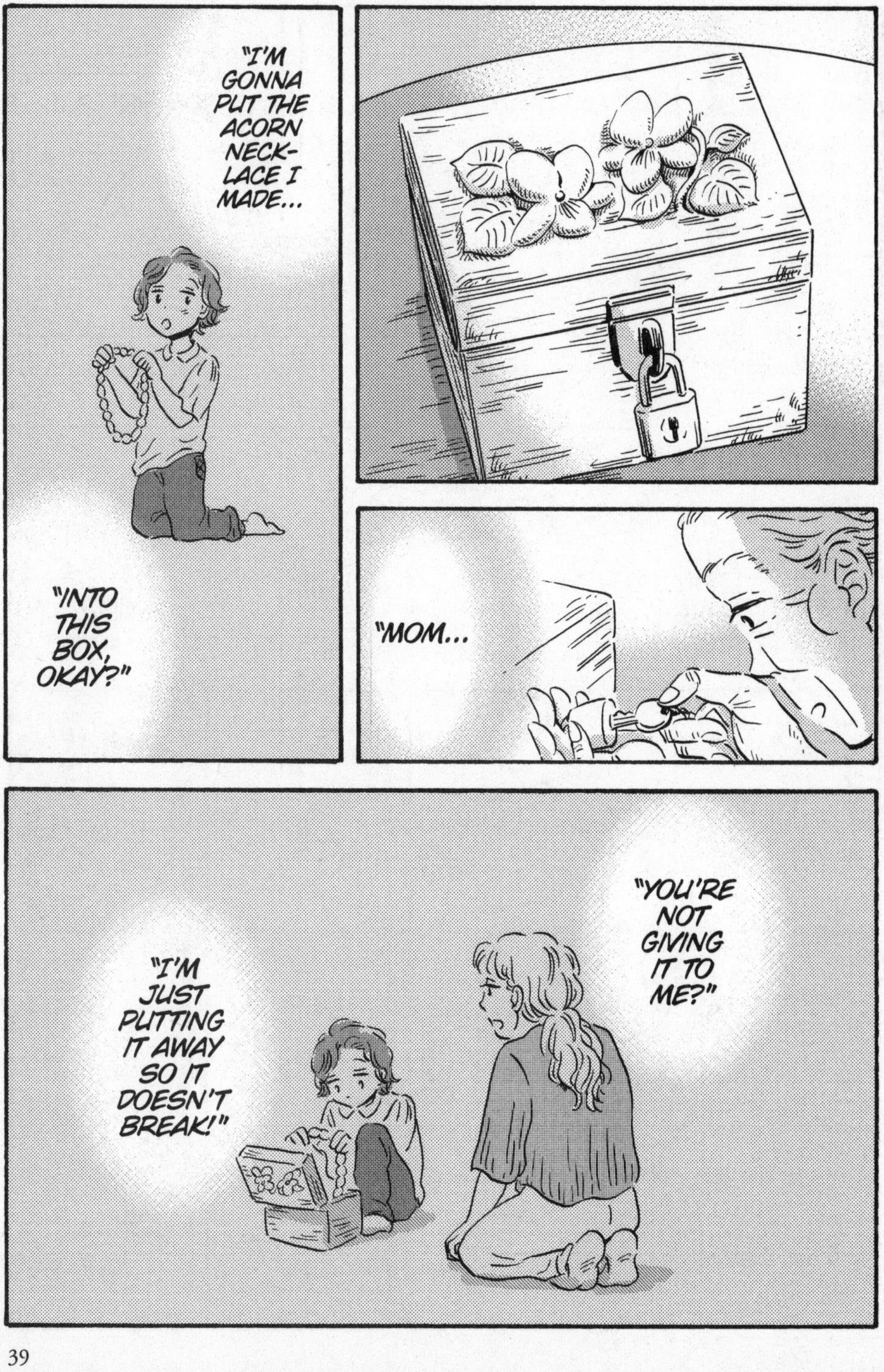
"MOM...
"I'M GONNA PUT THE ACORN NECKLACE I MADE...
"INTO THIS BOX, OKAY?"
"YOU'RE NOT GIVING IT TO ME?"
"I'M JUST PUTTING IT AWAY SO IT DOESN'T BREAK!"

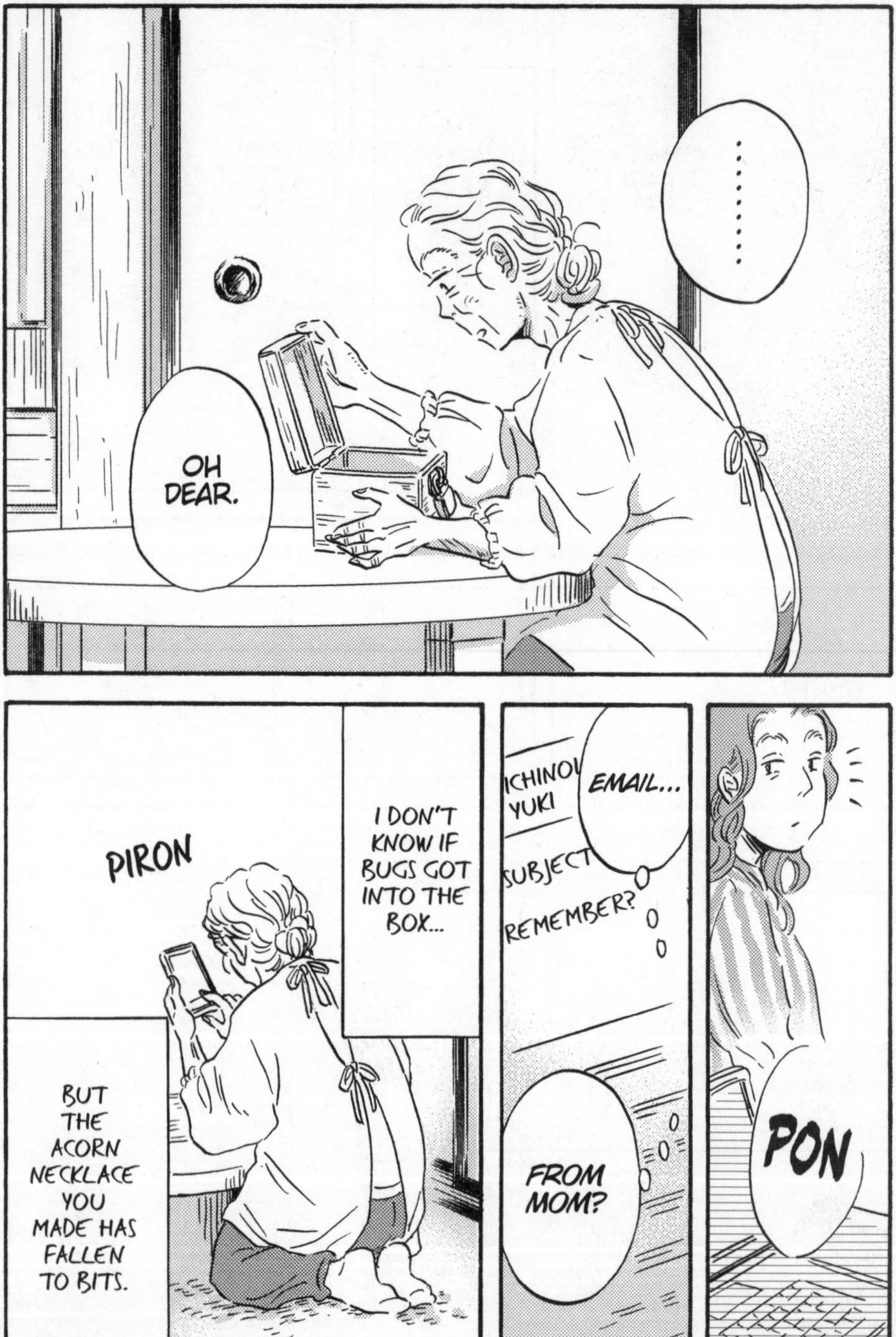
......
OH DEAR.
PON
EMAIL...
ICHINOU
YUKI
SUBJECT
REMEMBER?
FROM MOM?
I DON'T KNOW IF BUGS GOT INTO THE BOX...
PIRON
BUT THE ACORN NECKLACE YOU MADE HAS FALLEN TO BITS.

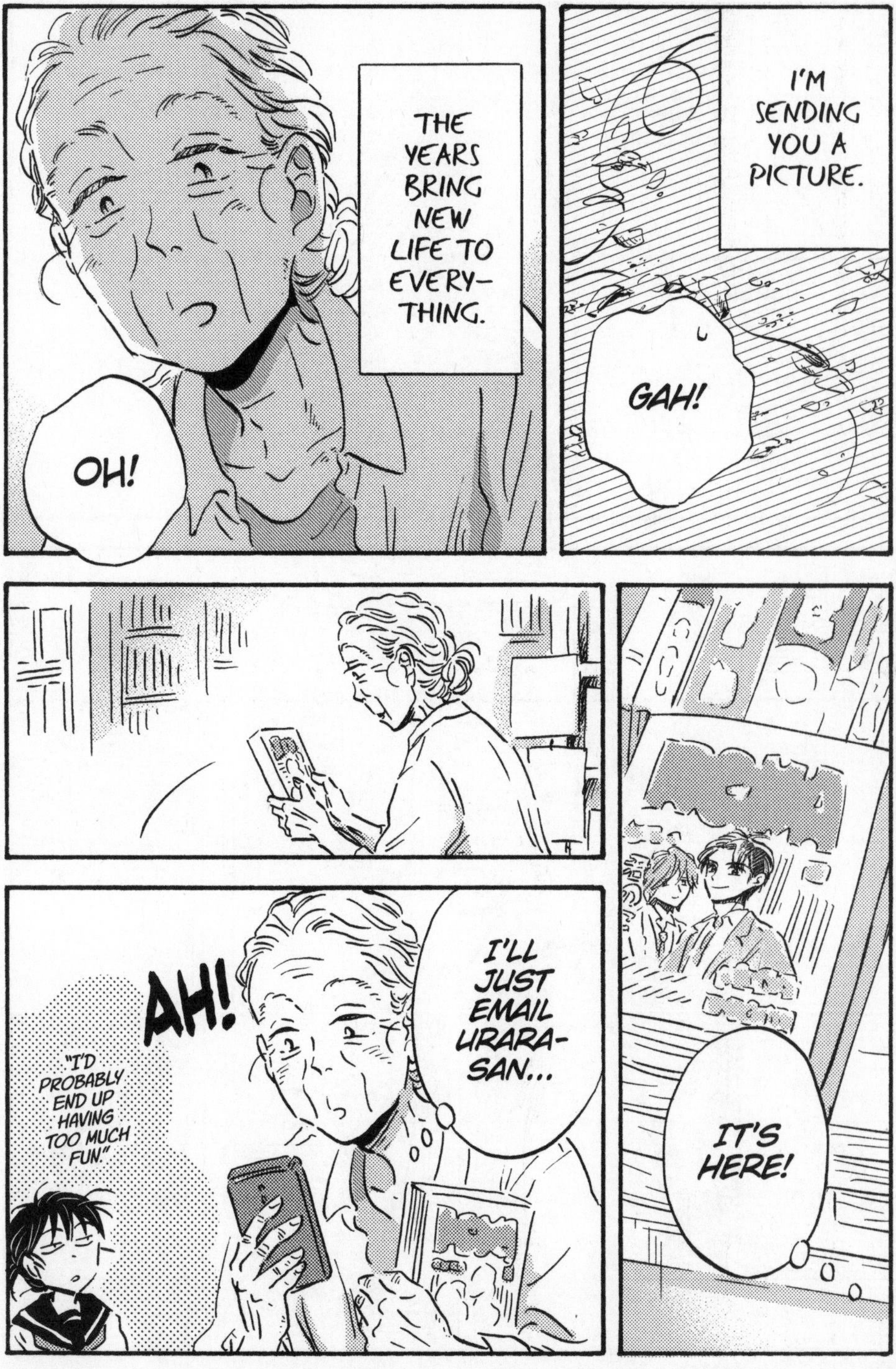
I'M SENDING YOU A PICTURE.
GAH!
THE YEARS BRING NEW LIFE TO EVERY-THING.
OH!
IT'S HERE!
I'LL JUST EMAIL URARA-SAN...
AH!
"I'D PROBABLY END UP HAVING TOO MUCH FUN."

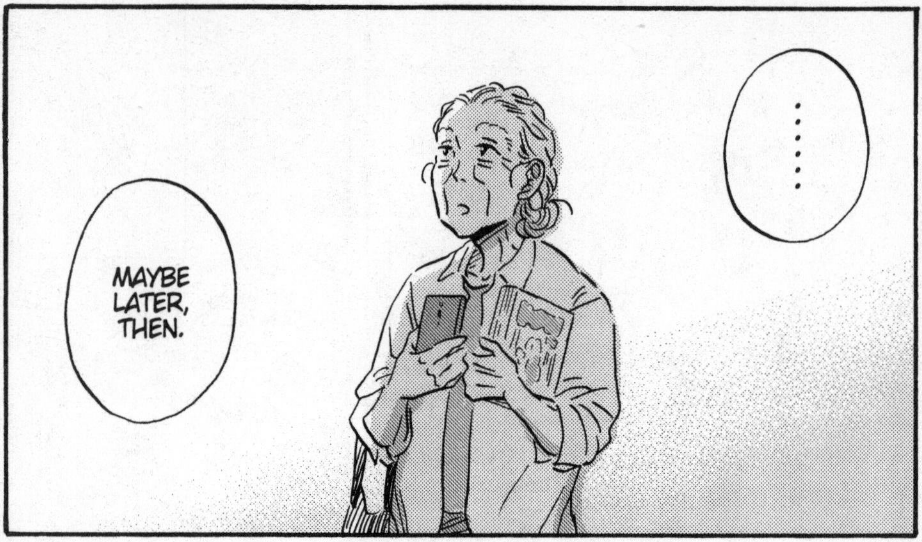
……
MAYBE LATER, THEN.

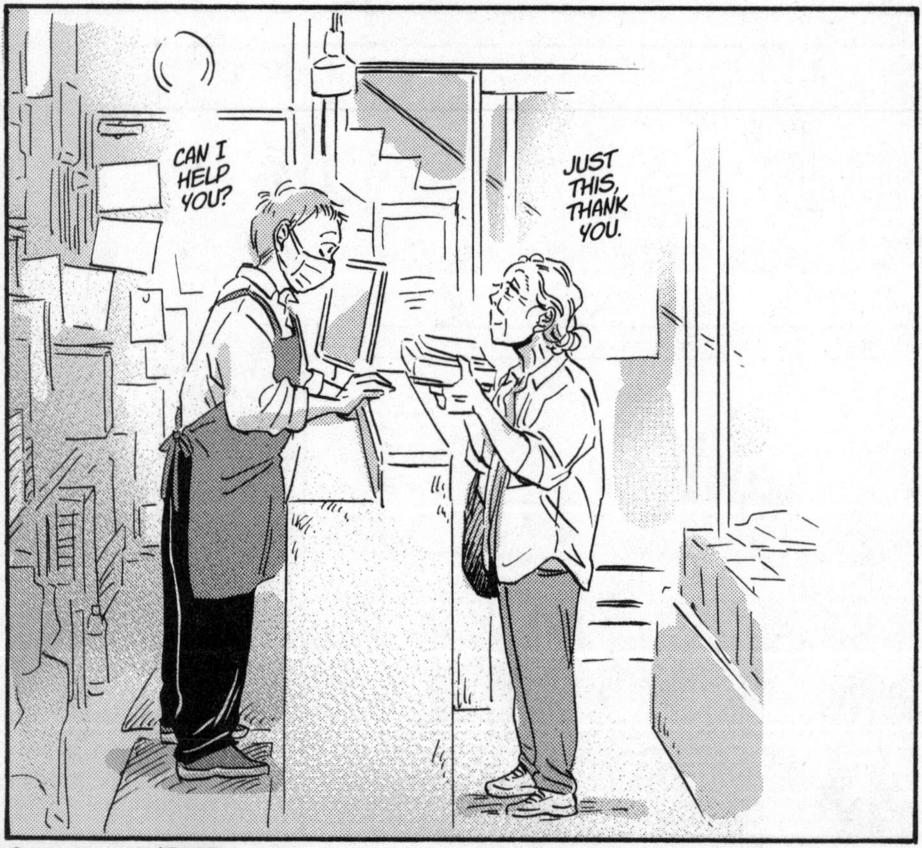
JUST THIS, THANK YOU.
CAN I HELP YOU?

**Chapter 43/END**

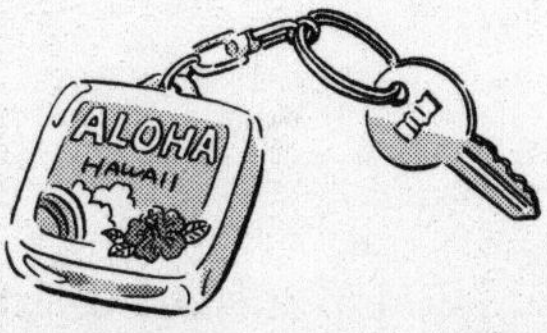
ALOHA
HAWAII

# Chapter 44

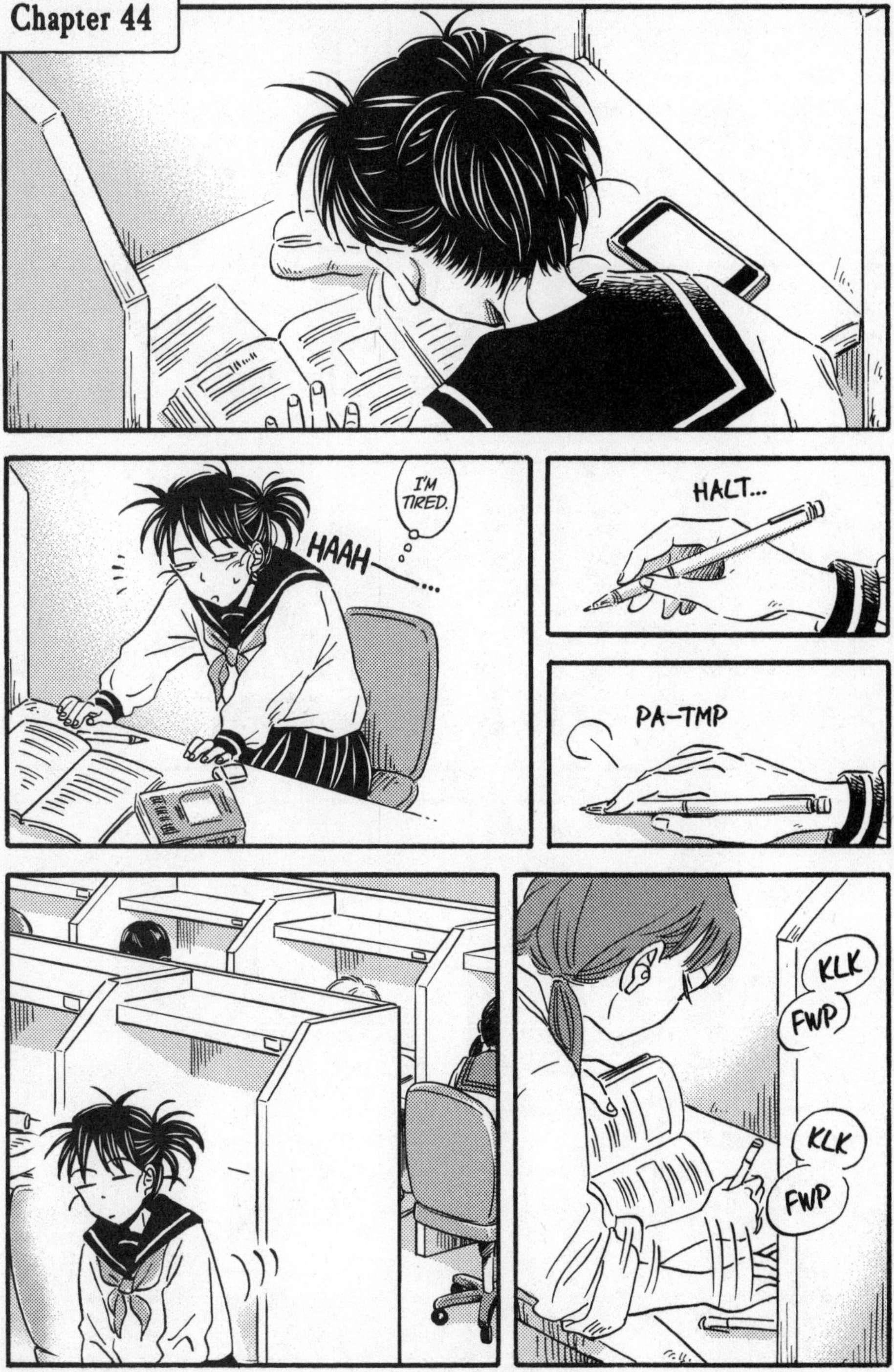

HALT...
PA-TMP
I'M TIRED.
HAAH—...
KLK
FWP
KLK
FWP

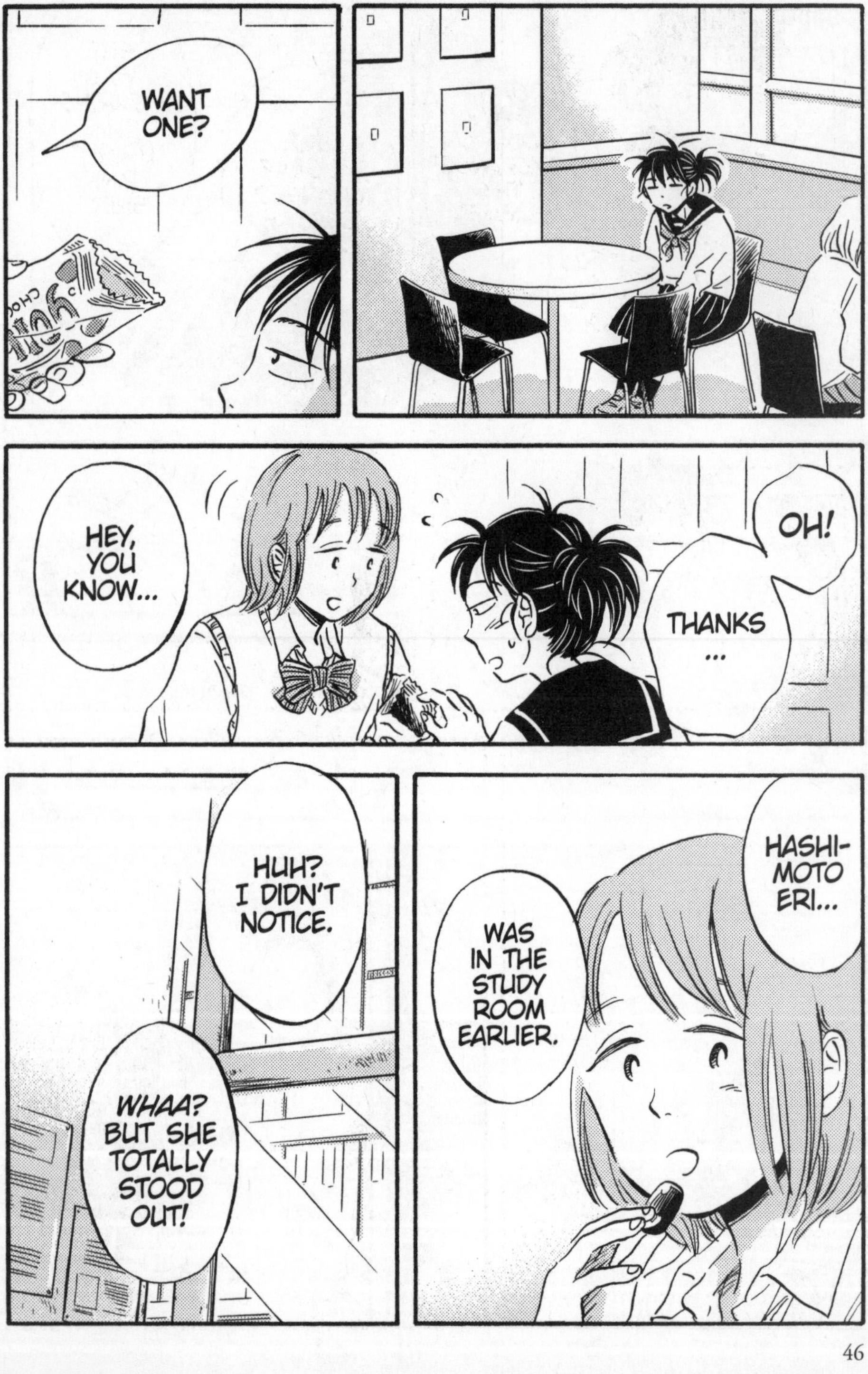
WANT ONE?
OH!
THANKS ...
HEY, YOU KNOW...
HASHI-MOTO ERI...
WAS IN THE STUDY ROOM EARLIER.
HUH? I DIDN'T NOTICE.
WHAA? BUT SHE TOTALLY STOOD OUT!

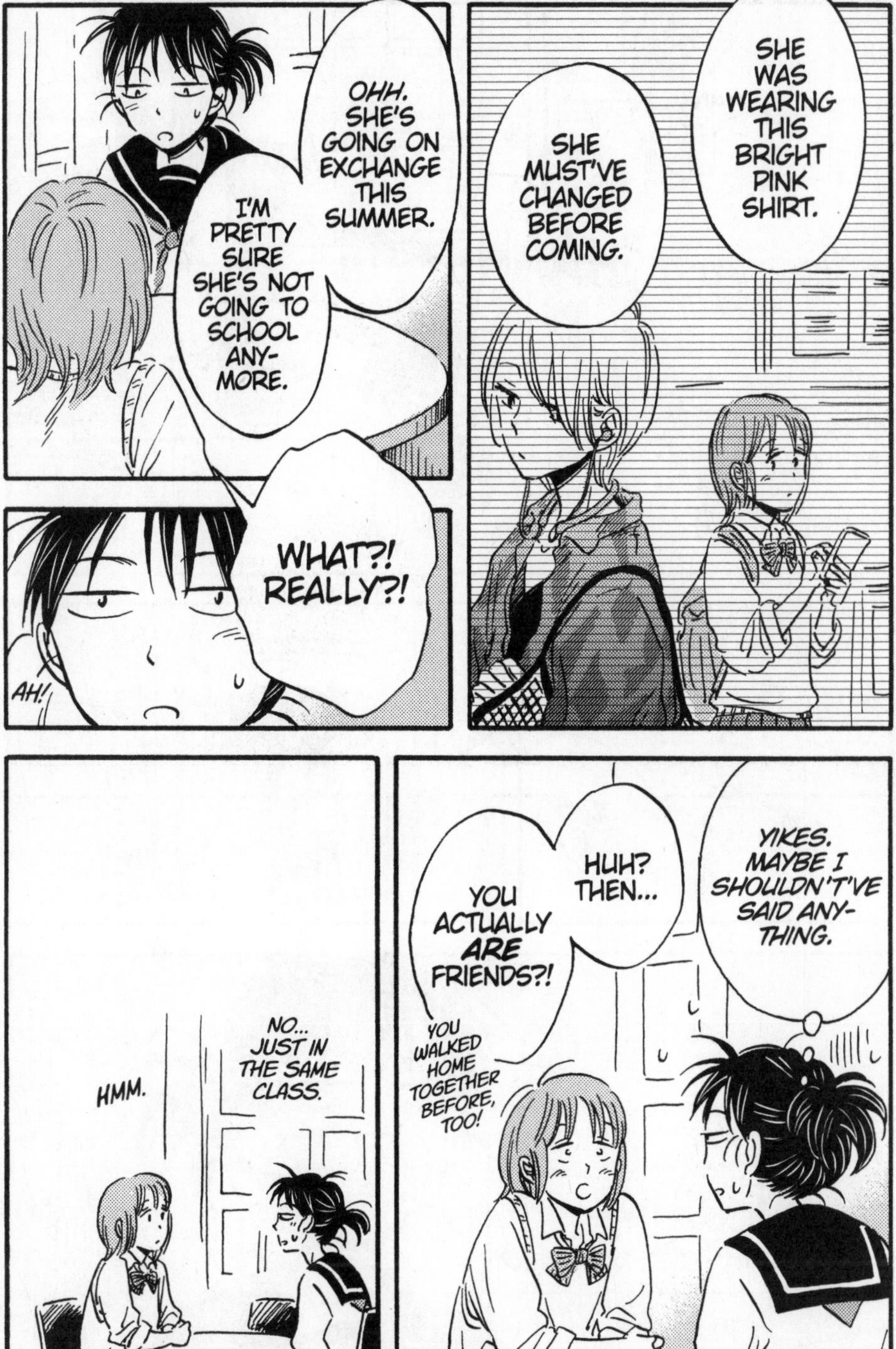
SHE WAS WEARING THIS BRIGHT PINK SHIRT.
SHE MUST'VE CHANGED BEFORE COMING.
OHH. SHE'S GOING ON EXCHANGE THIS SUMMER.
I'M PRETTY SURE SHE'S NOT GOING TO SCHOOL ANY-MORE.
WHAT?! REALLY?!
AH!
YIKES. MAYBE I SHOULDN'T'VE SAID ANY-THING.
HUH? THEN...
YOU ACTUALLY ARE FRIENDS?!
YOU WALKED HOME TOGETHER BEFORE, TOO!
NO... JUST IN THE SAME CLASS.
HMM.

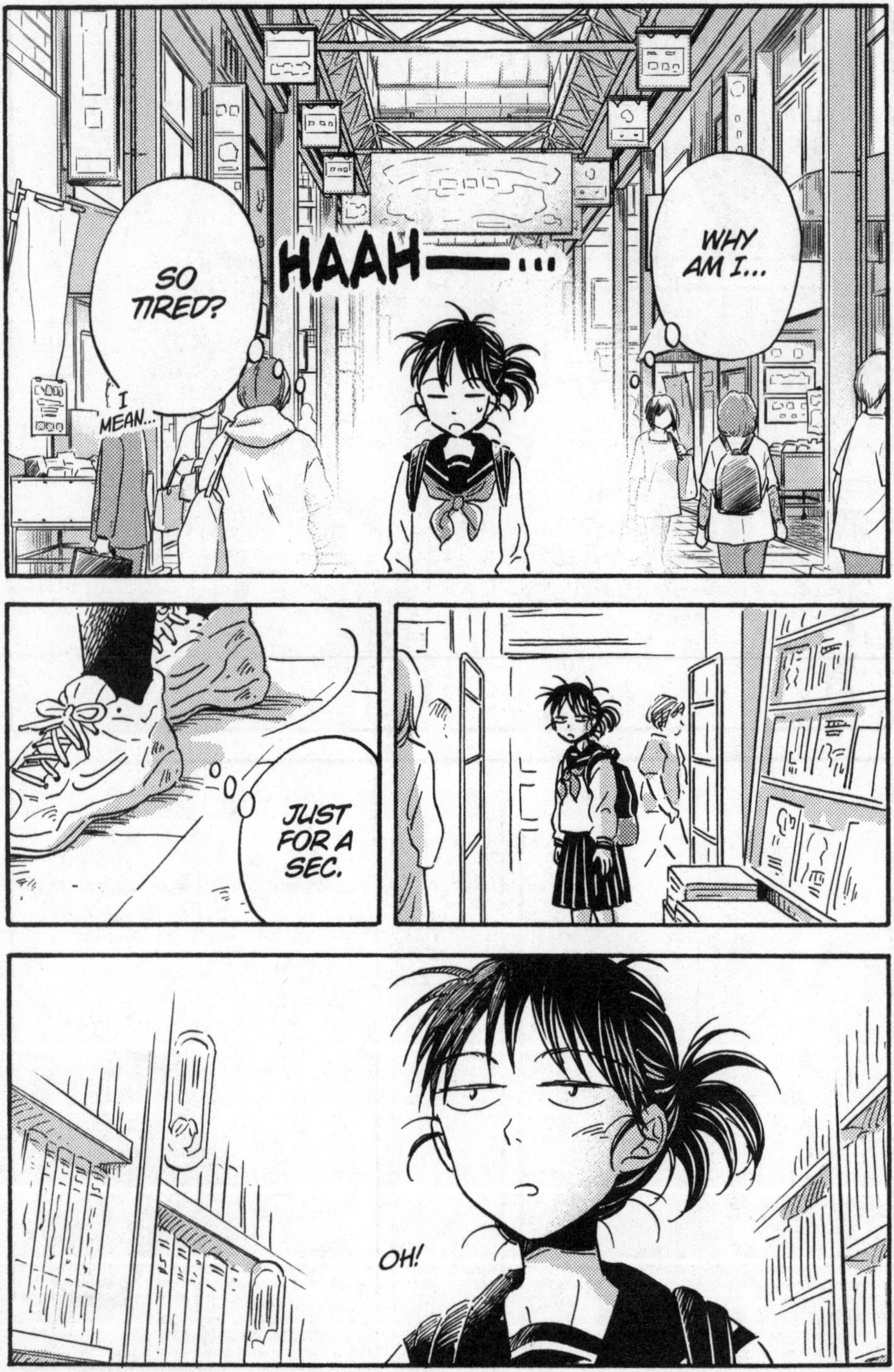
WHY AM I...
HAAH—...
SO TIRED?
I MEAN...
JUST FOR A SEC.
OH!

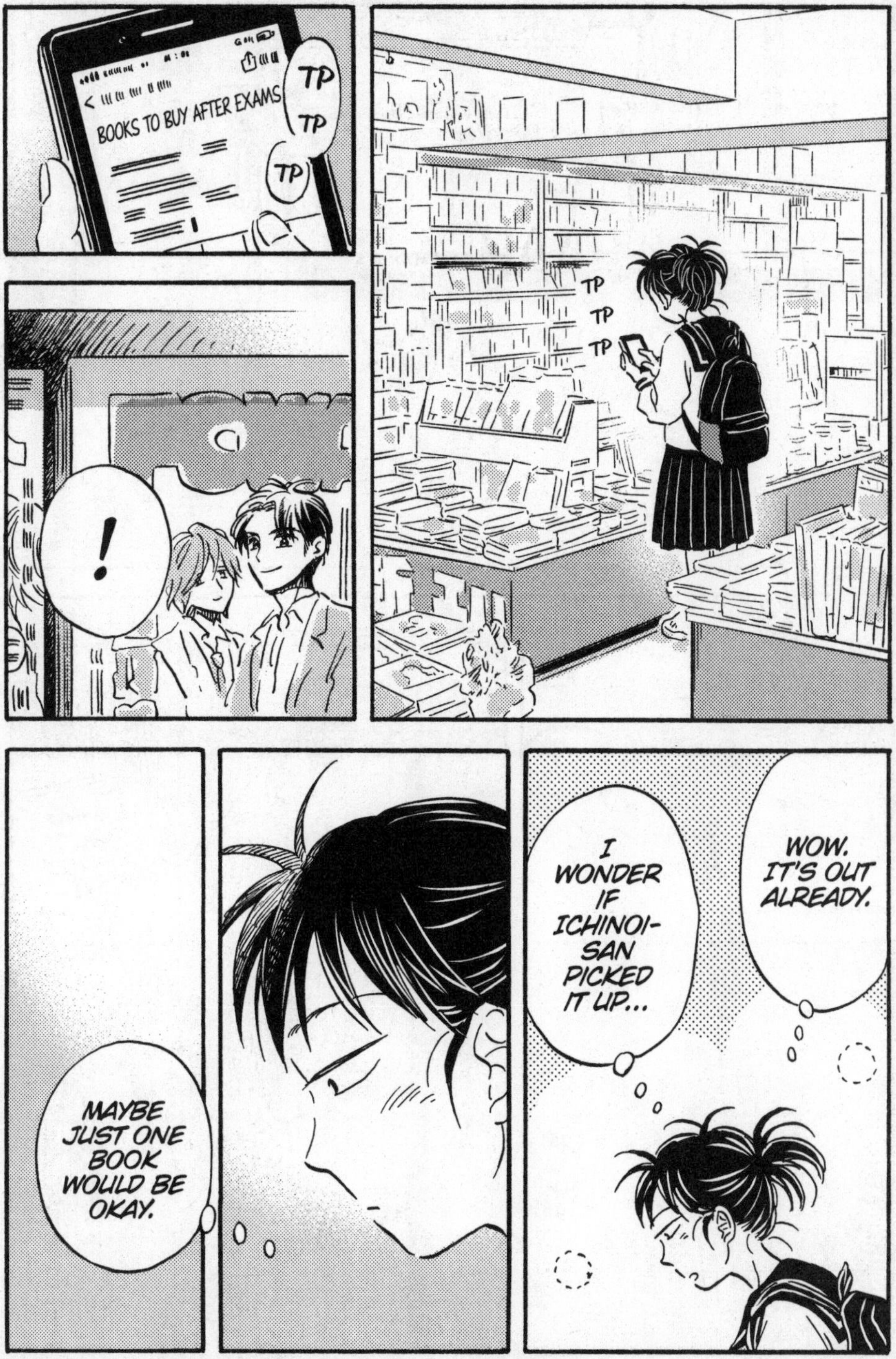
TP
TP
TP
BOOKS TO BUY AFTER EXAMS
TP
TP
TP
!
WOW. IT'S OUT ALREADY.
I WONDER IF ICHINOI-SAN PICKED IT UP...
MAYBE JUST ONE BOOK WOULD BE OKAY.

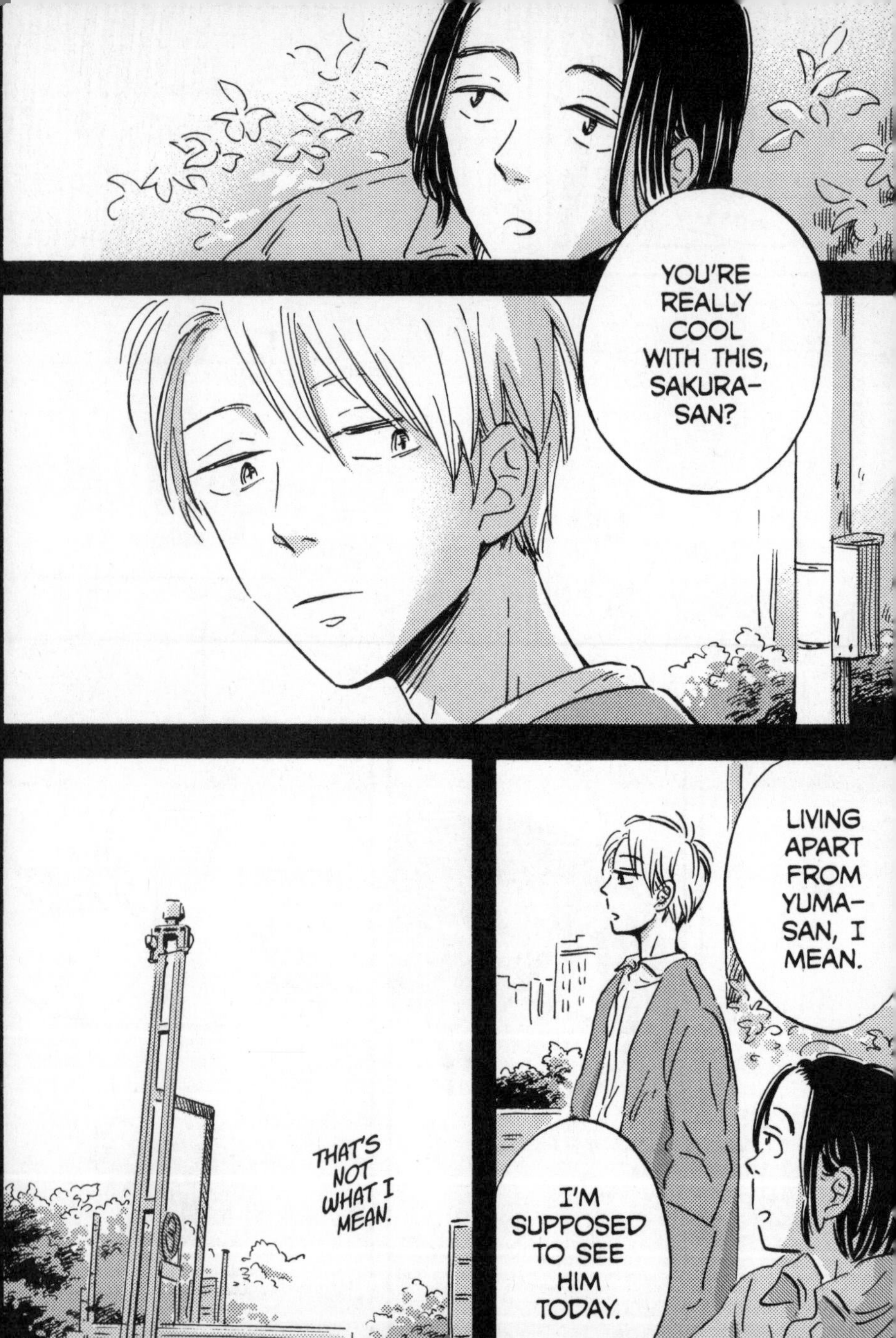
YOU'RE REALLY COOL WITH THIS, SAKURA-SAN?
LIVING APART FROM YUMA-SAN, I MEAN.
I'M SUPPOSED TO SEE HIM TODAY.
THAT'S NOT WHAT I MEAN.

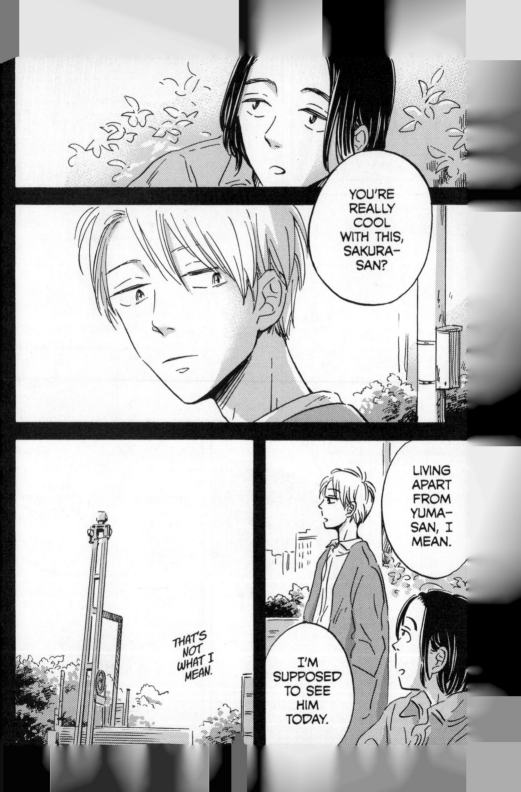

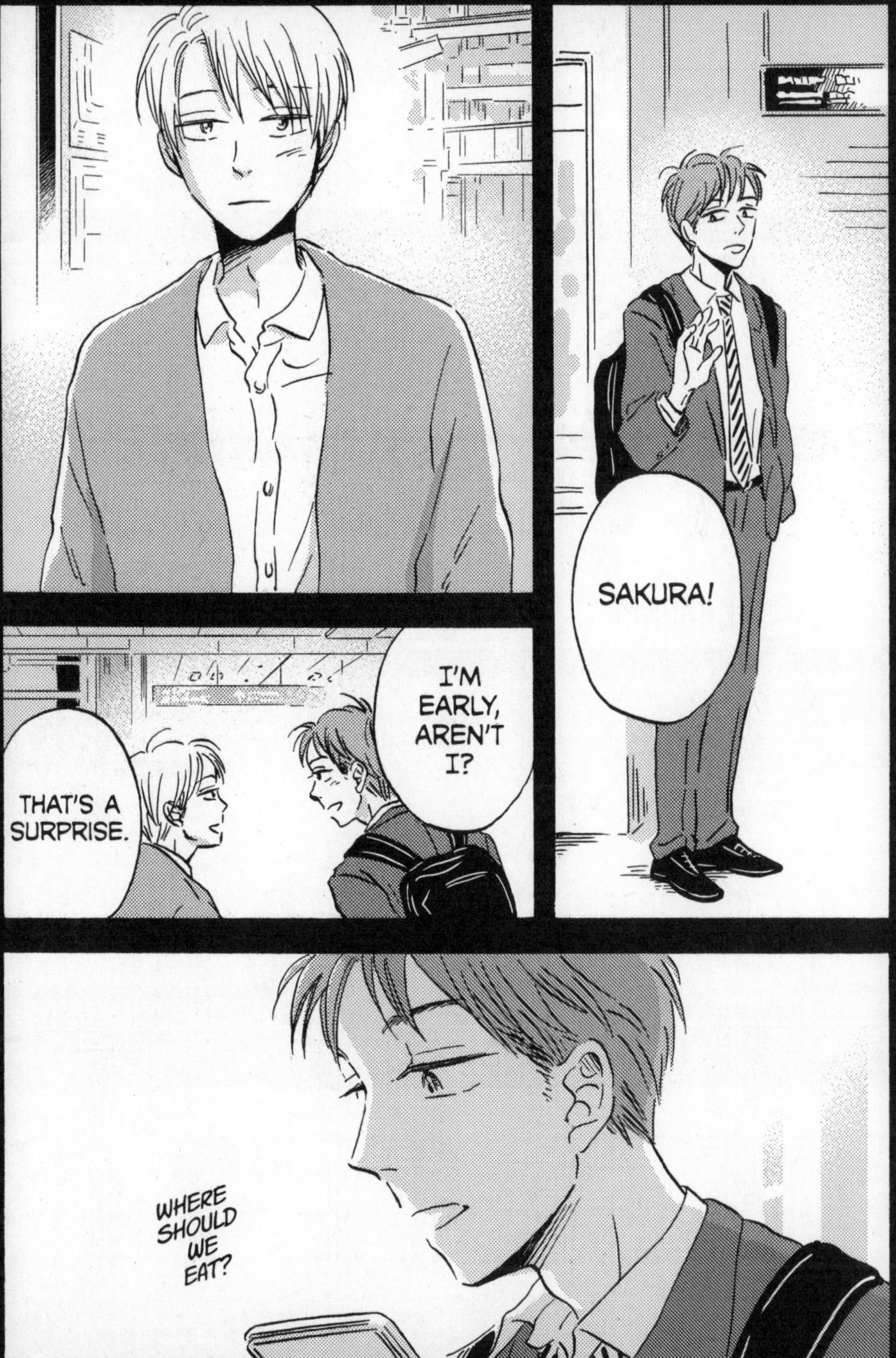
SAKURA!
I'M EARLY, AREN'T I?
THAT'S A SURPRISE.
WHERE SHOULD WE EAT?

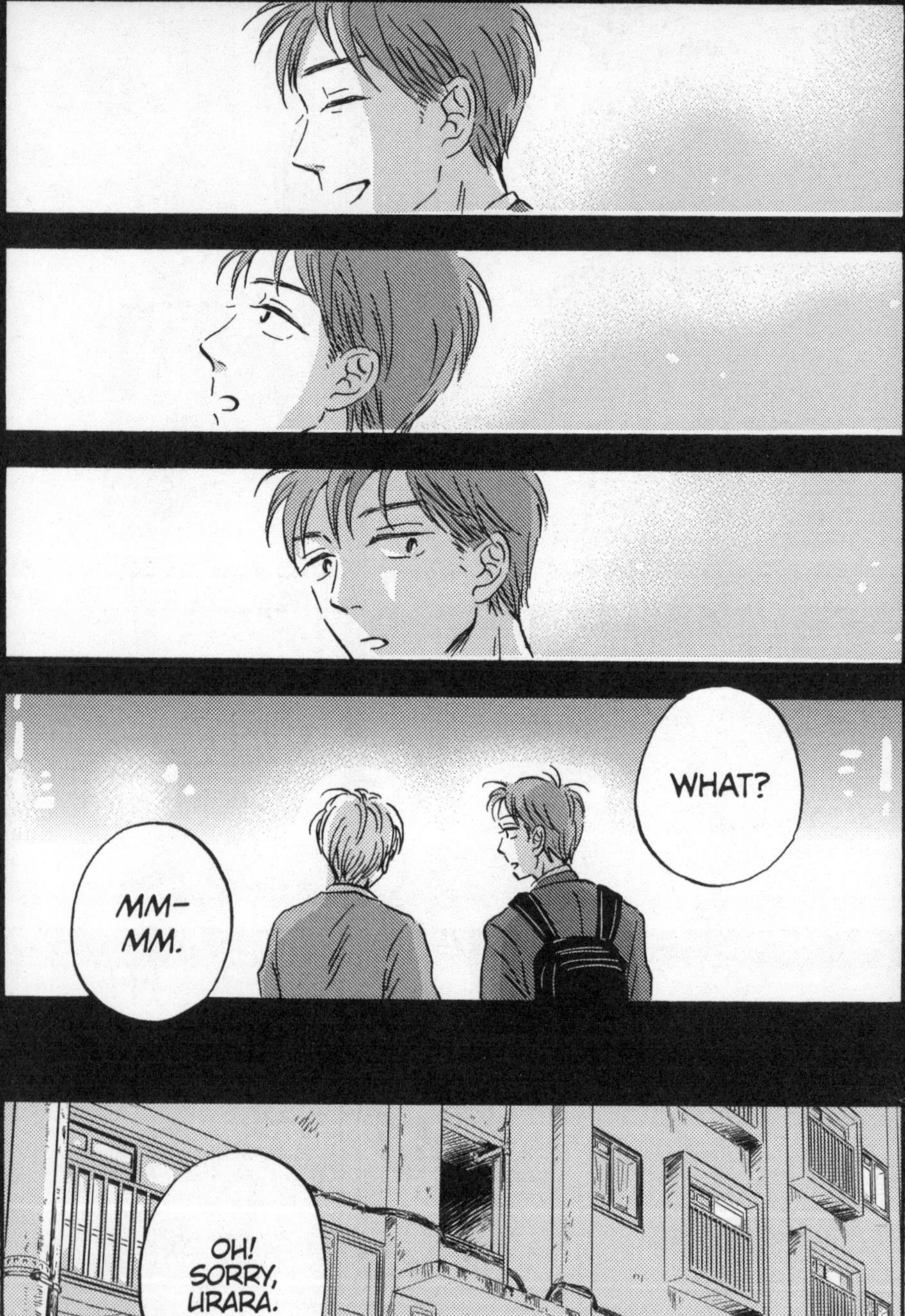
WHAT?
MM-MM.
OH! SORRY, URARA.

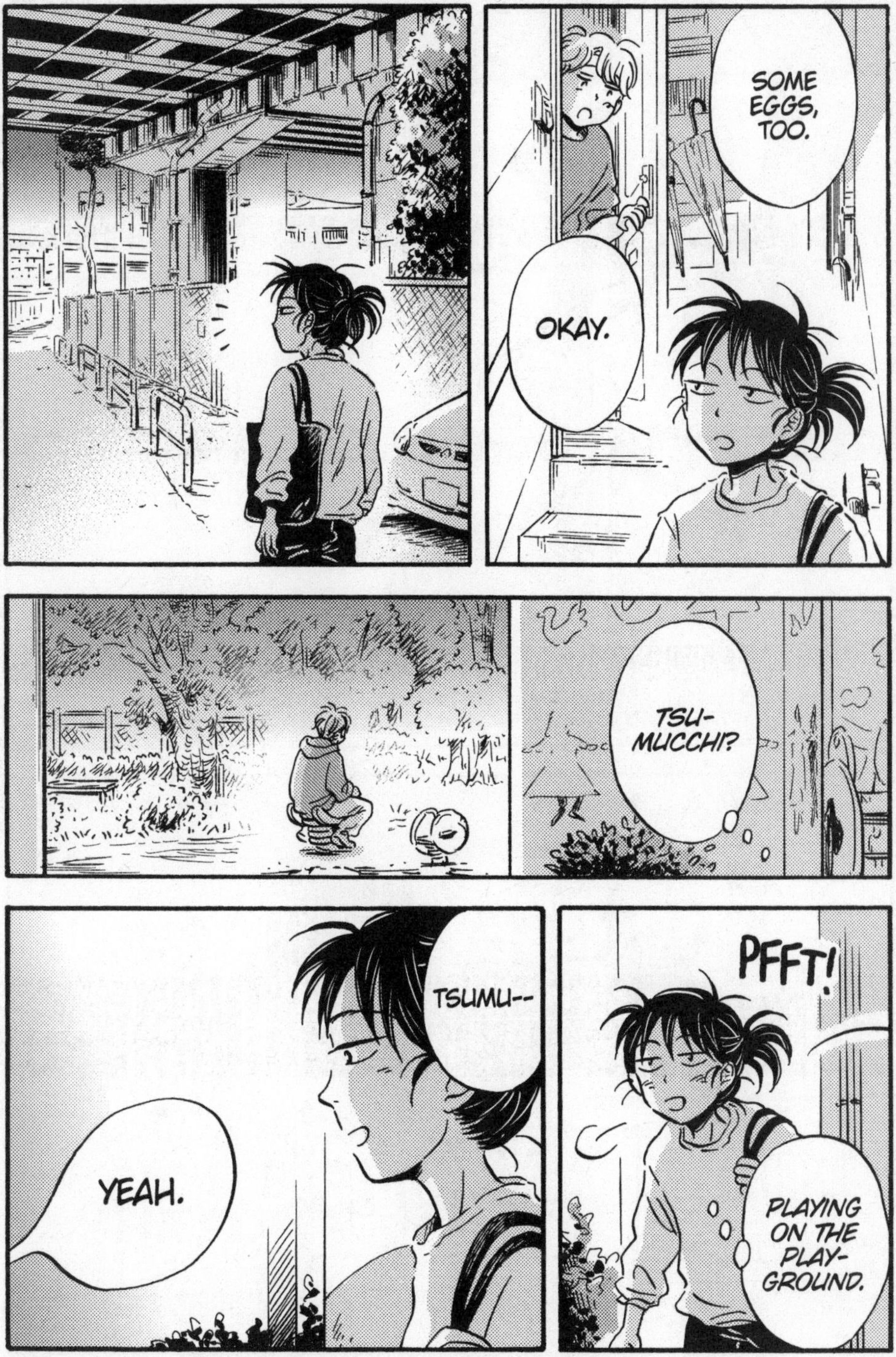
SOME EGGS, TOO.
OKAY.
TSU-MUCCHI?
PFFT!
PLAYING ON THE PLAY-GROUND.
TSUMU--
YEAH.

OH, HE'S ON THE PHONE.

I'VE...

IT'S OKAY.

RIGHT.

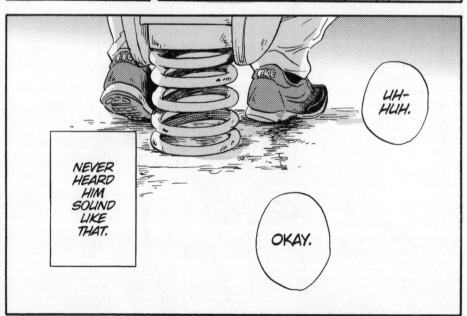

NEVER HEARD HIM SOUND LIKE THAT.

UH-HUH.

OKAY.

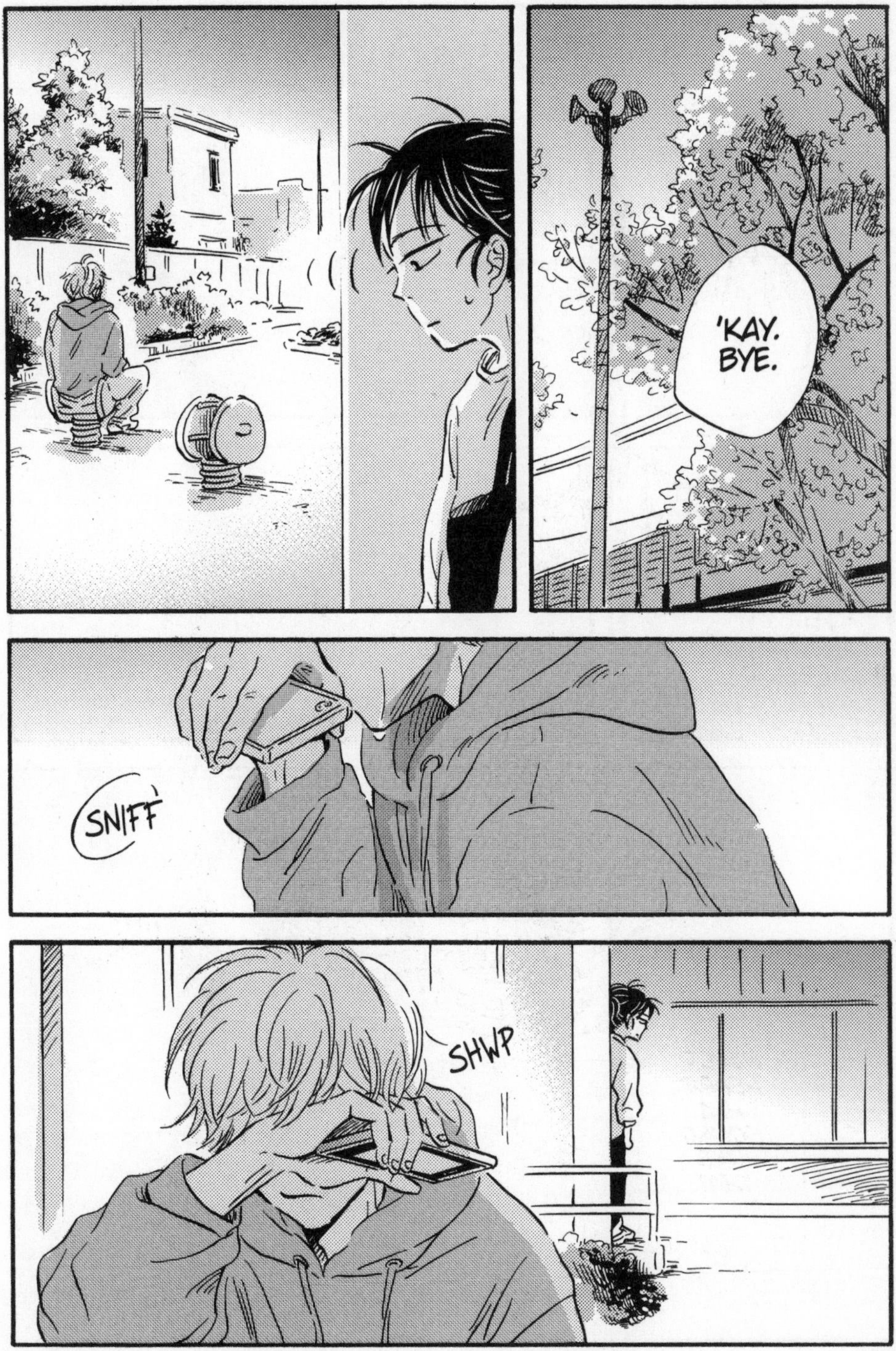
'KAY.
BYE.
SNIFF
SHWP

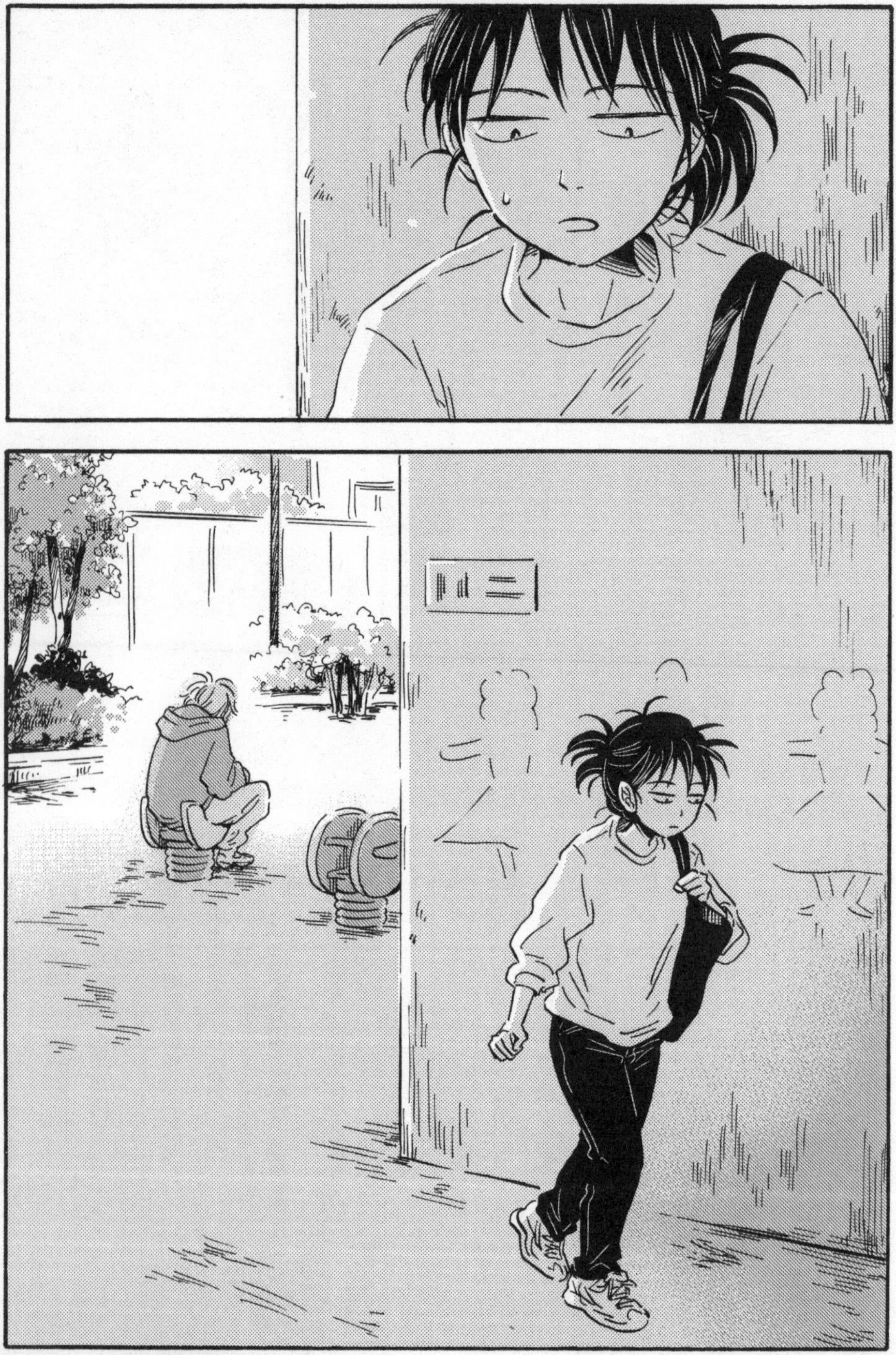

Chapter 44/END

PL metamorphosis

## Chapter 45

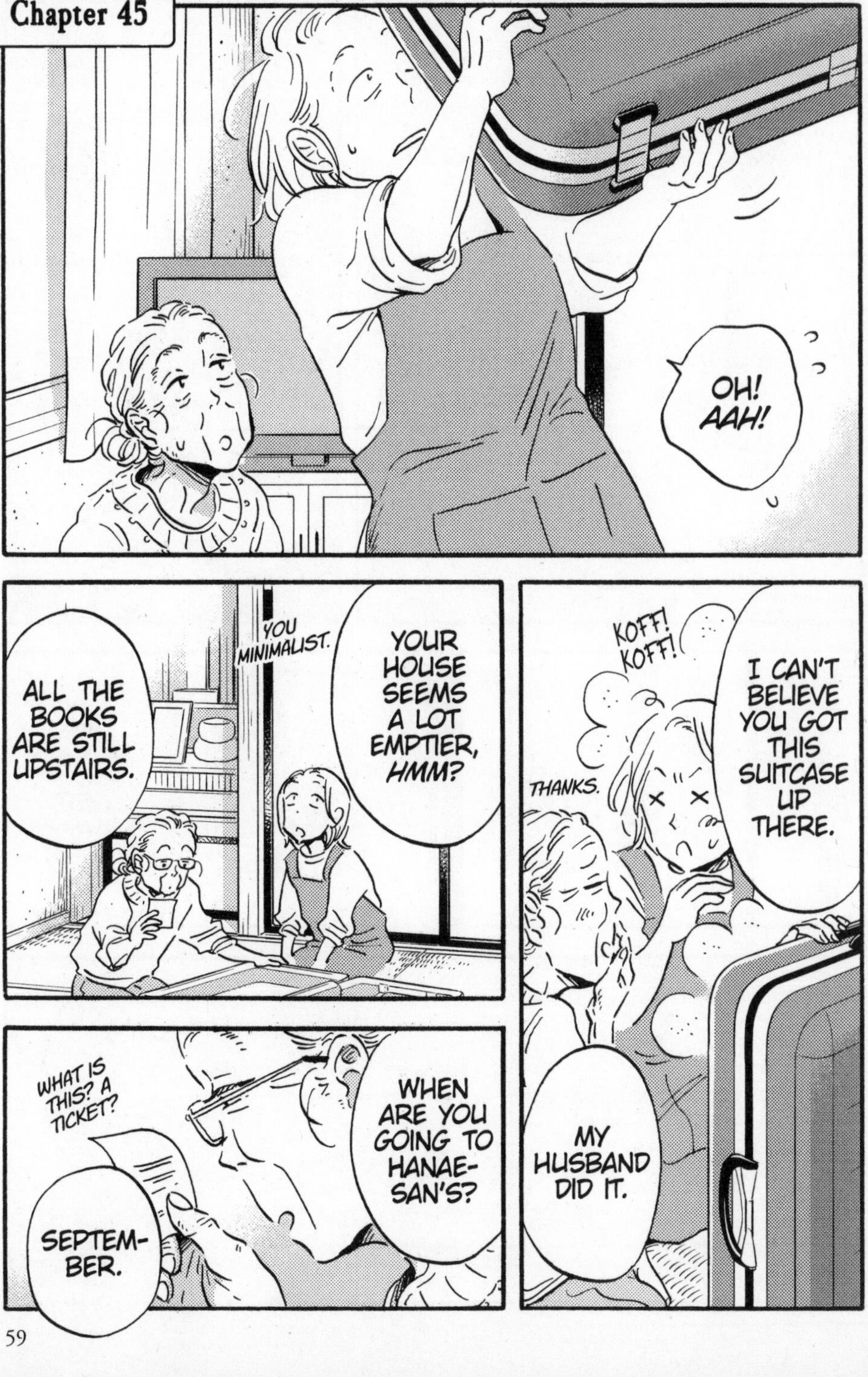
OH! AAH!
I CAN'T BELIEVE YOU GOT THIS SUITCASE UP THERE.
KOFF! KOFF!
THANKS.
MY HUSBAND DID IT.
YOUR HOUSE SEEMS A LOT EMPTIER, HMM?
YOU MINIMALIST.
ALL THE BOOKS ARE STILL UPSTAIRS.
WHEN ARE YOU GOING TO HANAE-SAN'S?
WHAT IS THIS? A TICKET?
SEPTEMBER.

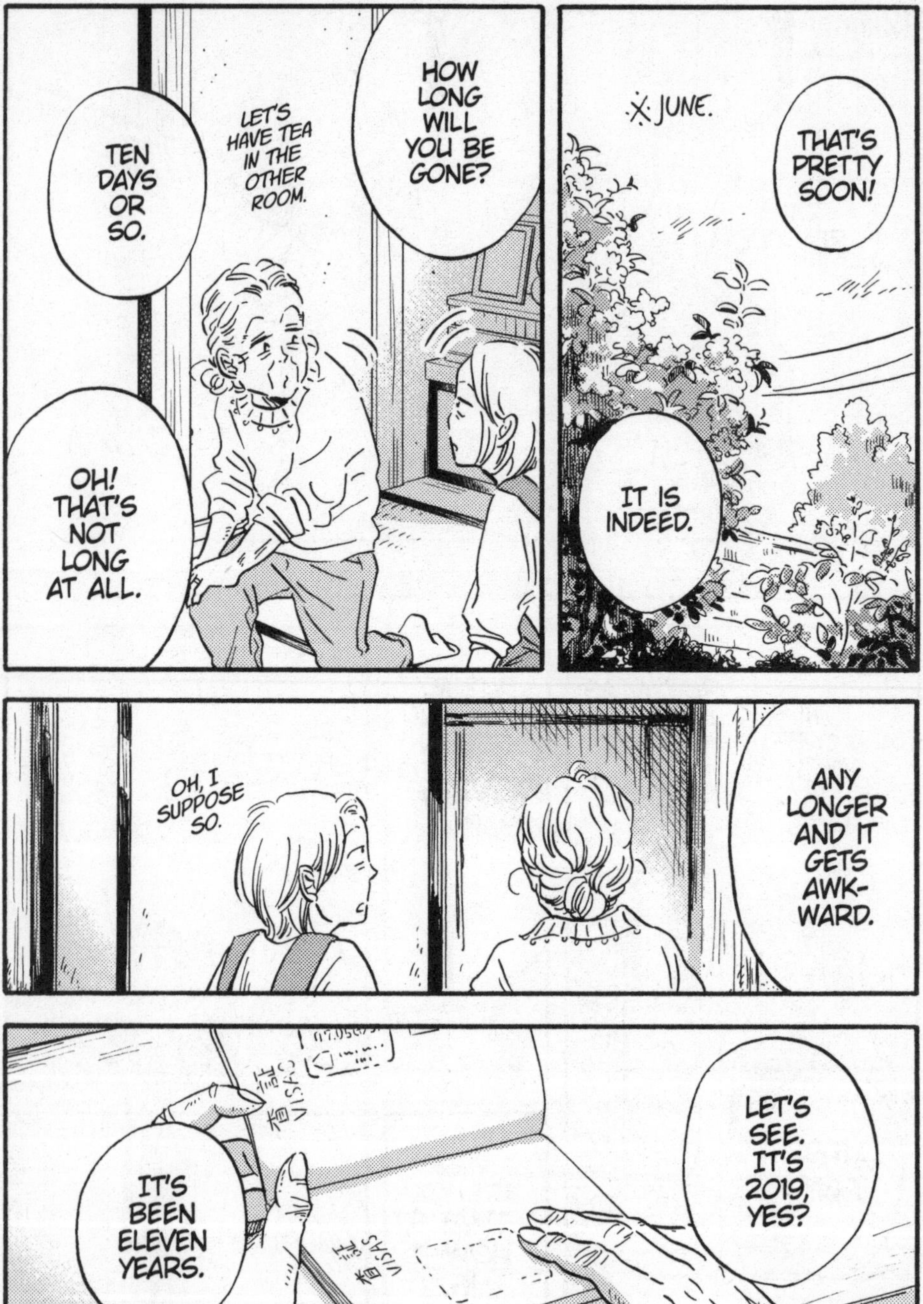
THAT'S PRETTY SOON!
※ JUNE.
IT IS INDEED.
HOW LONG WILL YOU BE GONE?
LET'S HAVE TEA IN THE OTHER ROOM.
TEN DAYS OR SO.
OH! THAT'S NOT LONG AT ALL.
ANY LONGER AND IT GETS AWK-WARD.
OH, I SUPPOSE SO.
LET'S SEE. IT'S 2019, YES?
査証 VISAS
IT'S BEEN ELEVEN YEARS.
査証 VISAS

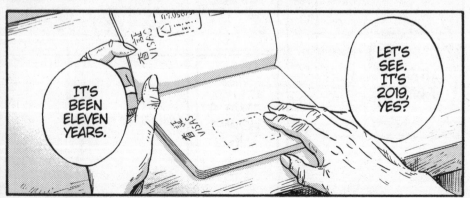

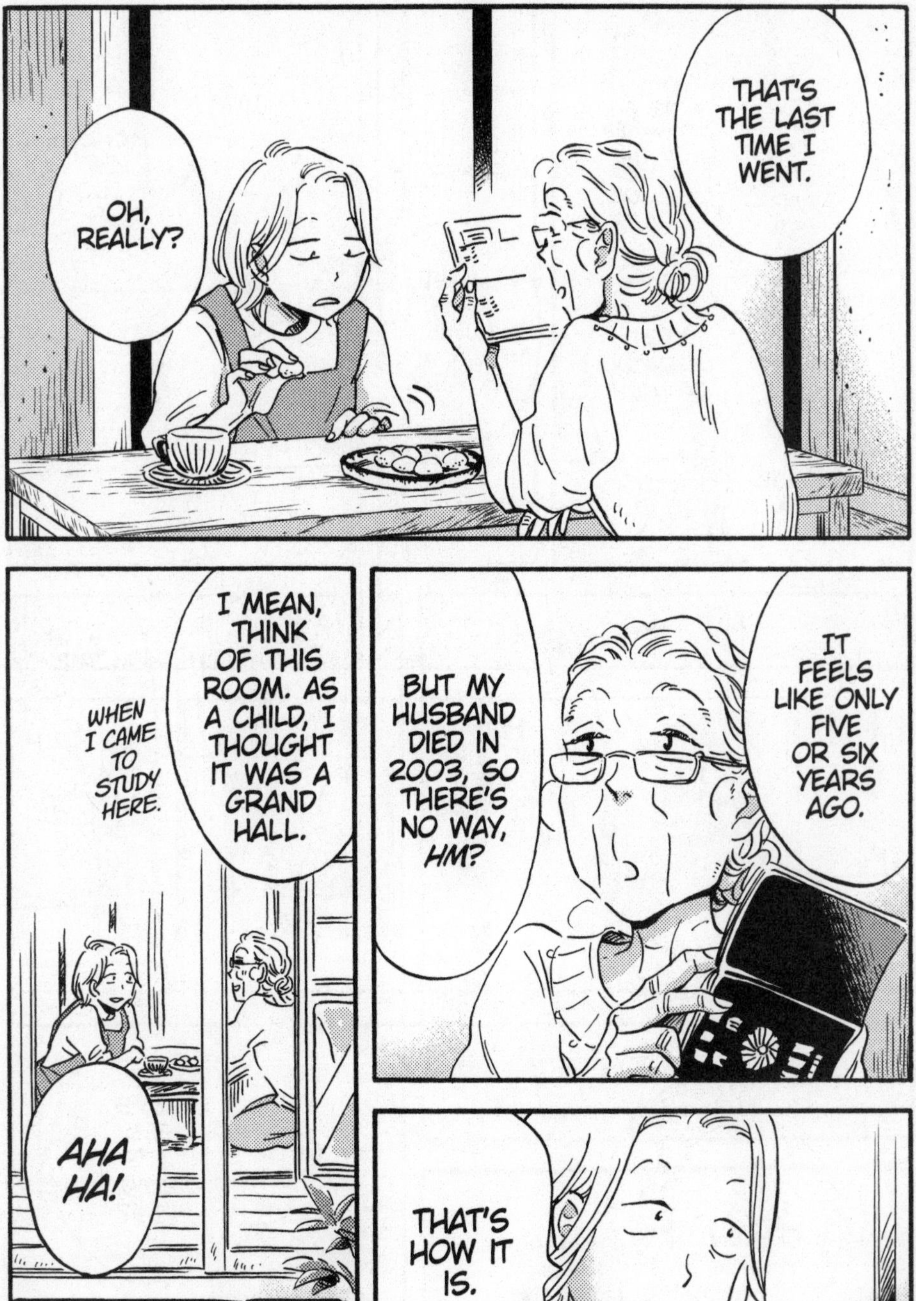
THAT'S THE LAST TIME I WENT.
OH, REALLY?
IT FEELS LIKE ONLY FIVE OR SIX YEARS AGO.
BUT MY HUSBAND DIED IN 2003, SO THERE'S NO WAY, *HM?*
THAT'S HOW IT IS.
I MEAN, THINK OF THIS ROOM. AS A CHILD, I THOUGHT IT WAS A GRAND HALL.
WHEN I CAME TO STUDY HERE.
*AHA HA!*

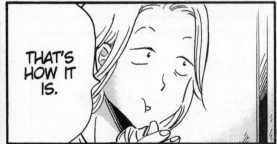

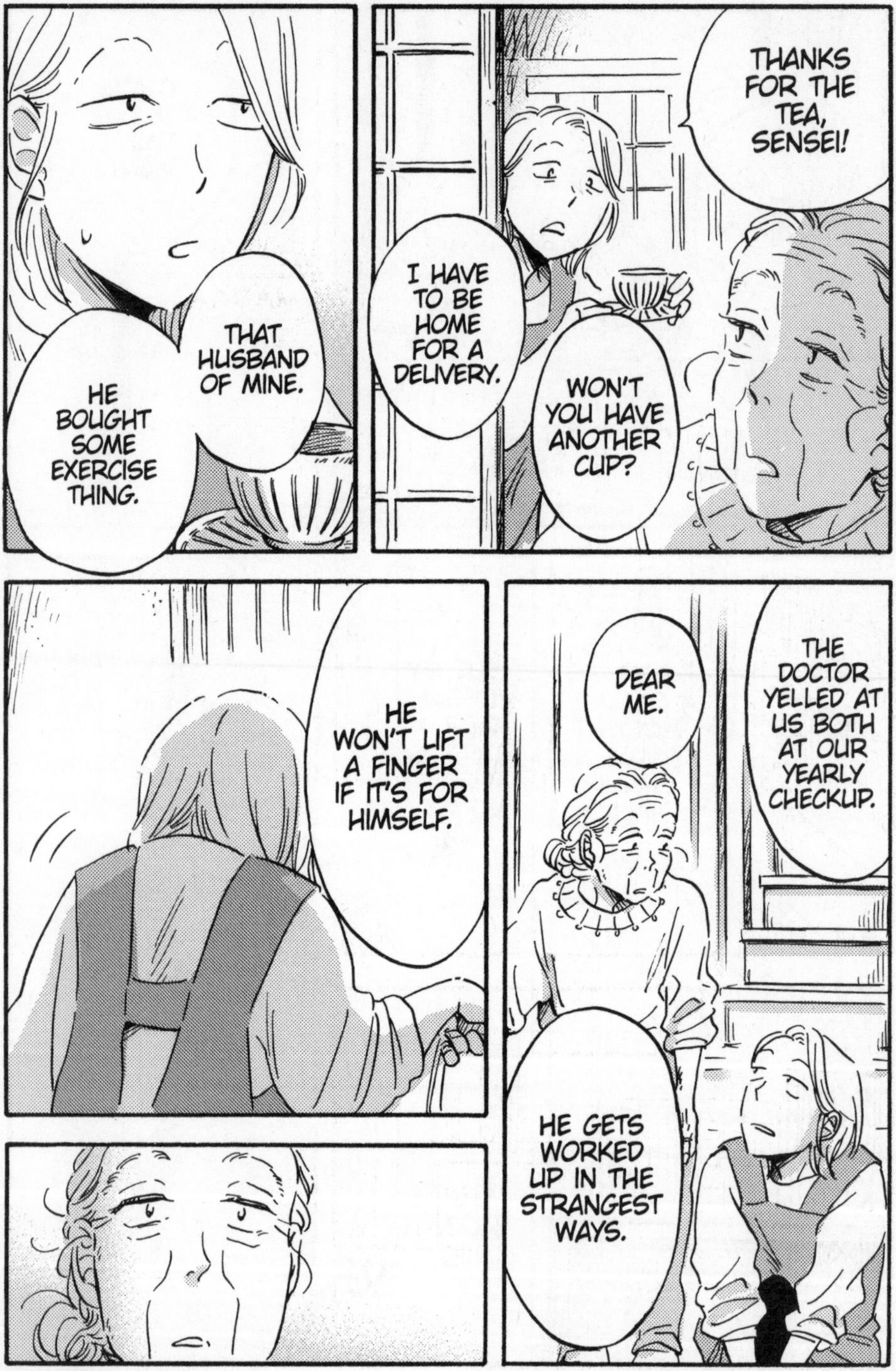
THANKS FOR THE TEA, SENSEI!
WON'T YOU HAVE ANOTHER CUP?
I HAVE TO BE HOME FOR A DELIVERY.
THAT HUSBAND OF MINE.
HE BOUGHT SOME EXERCISE THING.
THE DOCTOR YELLED AT US BOTH AT OUR YEARLY CHECKUP.
DEAR ME.
HE GETS WORKED UP IN THE STRANGEST WAYS.
HE WON'T LIFT A FINGER IF IT'S FOR HIMSELF.

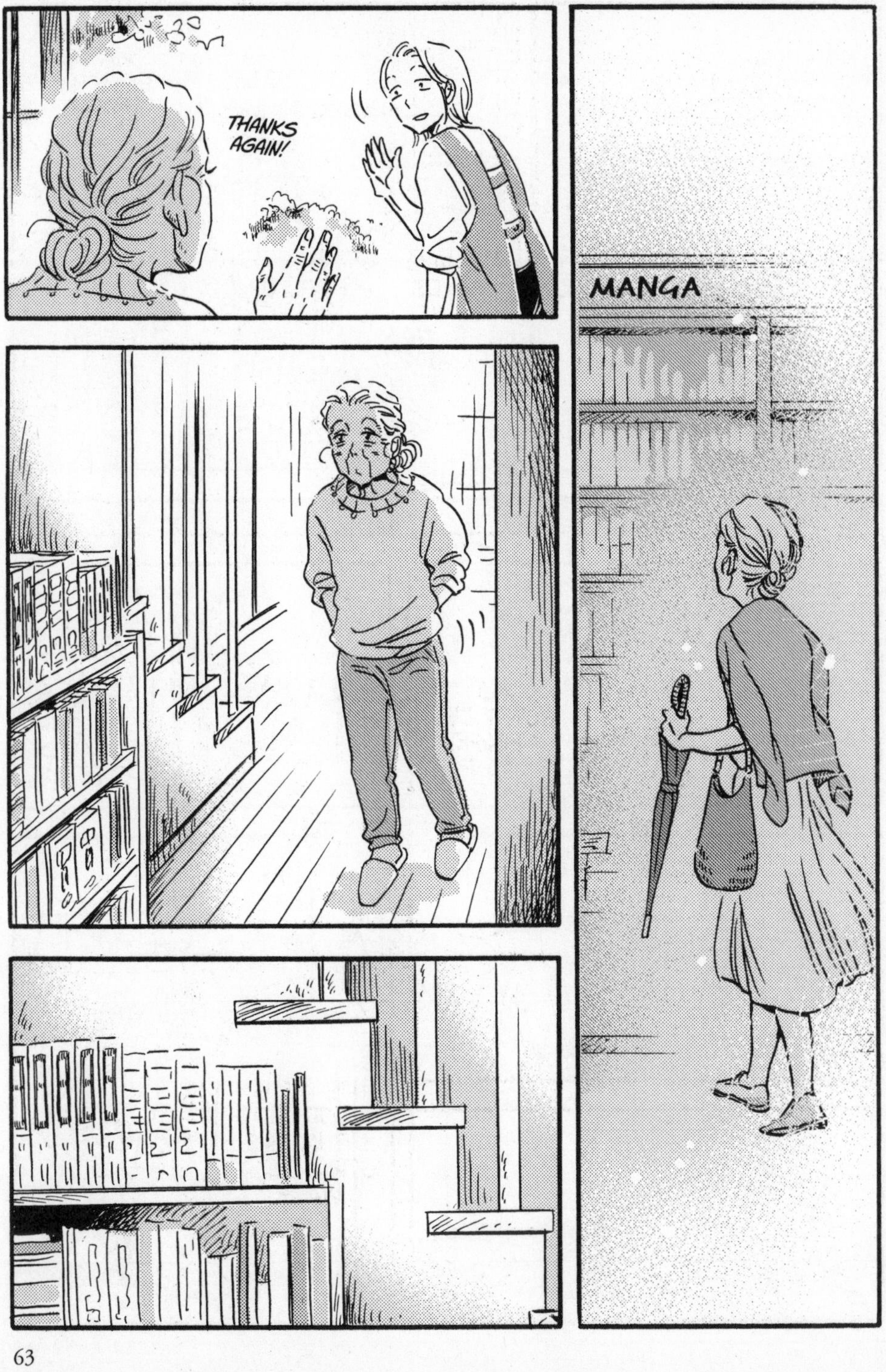
MANGA
THANKS AGAIN!

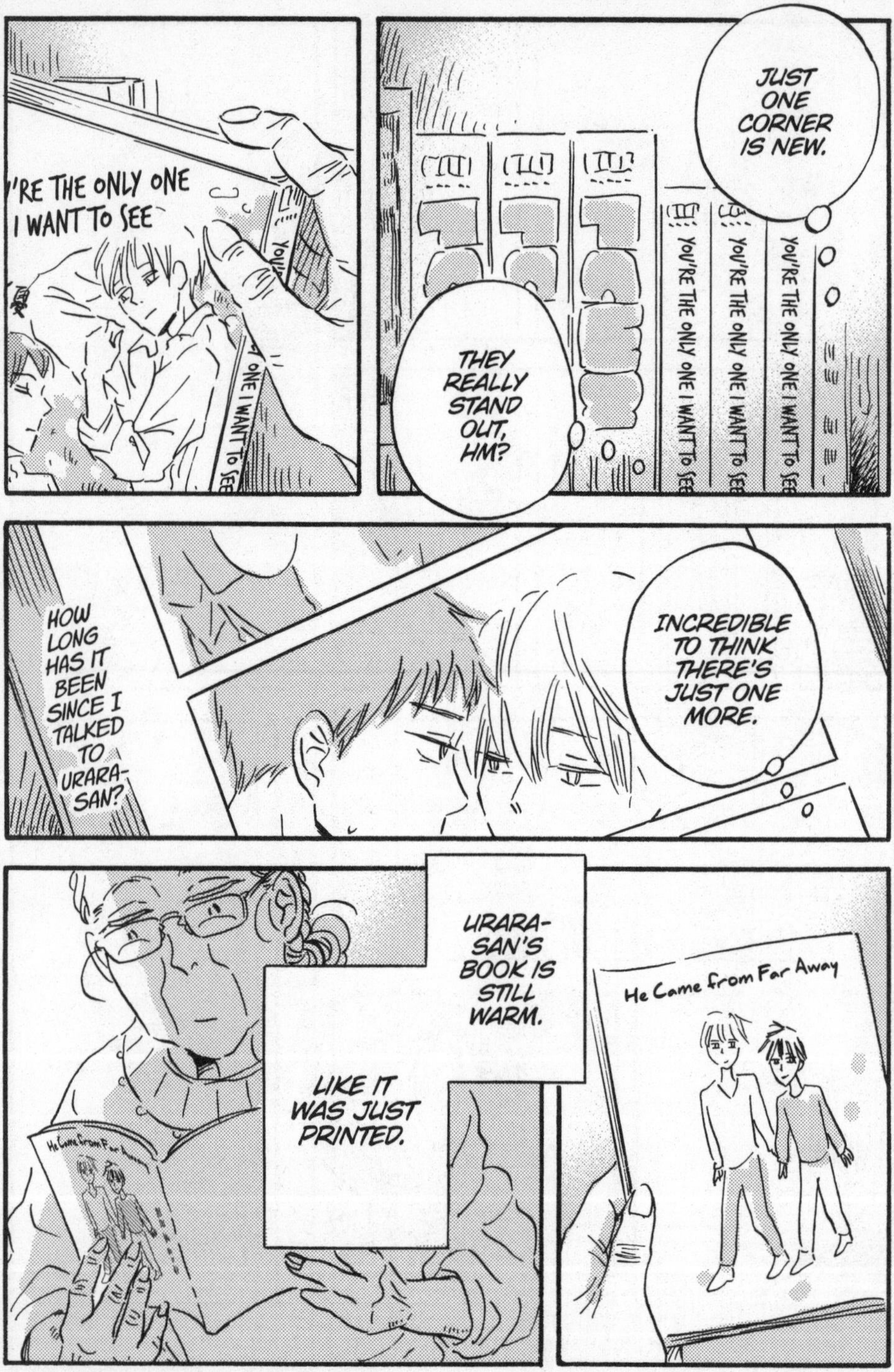
JUST ONE CORNER IS NEW.
THEY REALLY STAND OUT, HM?
YOU'RE THE ONLY ONE I WANT TO SEE
YOU'RE THE ONLY ONE I WANT TO SEE
YOU'RE THE ONLY ONE I WANT TO SEE
'RE THE ONLY ONE I WANT TO SEE
INCREDIBLE TO THINK THERE'S JUST ONE MORE.
HOW LONG HAS IT BEEN SINCE I TALKED TO URARA-SAN?
He Came from Far Away
URARA-SAN'S BOOK IS STILL WARM.
LIKE IT WAS JUST PRINTED.

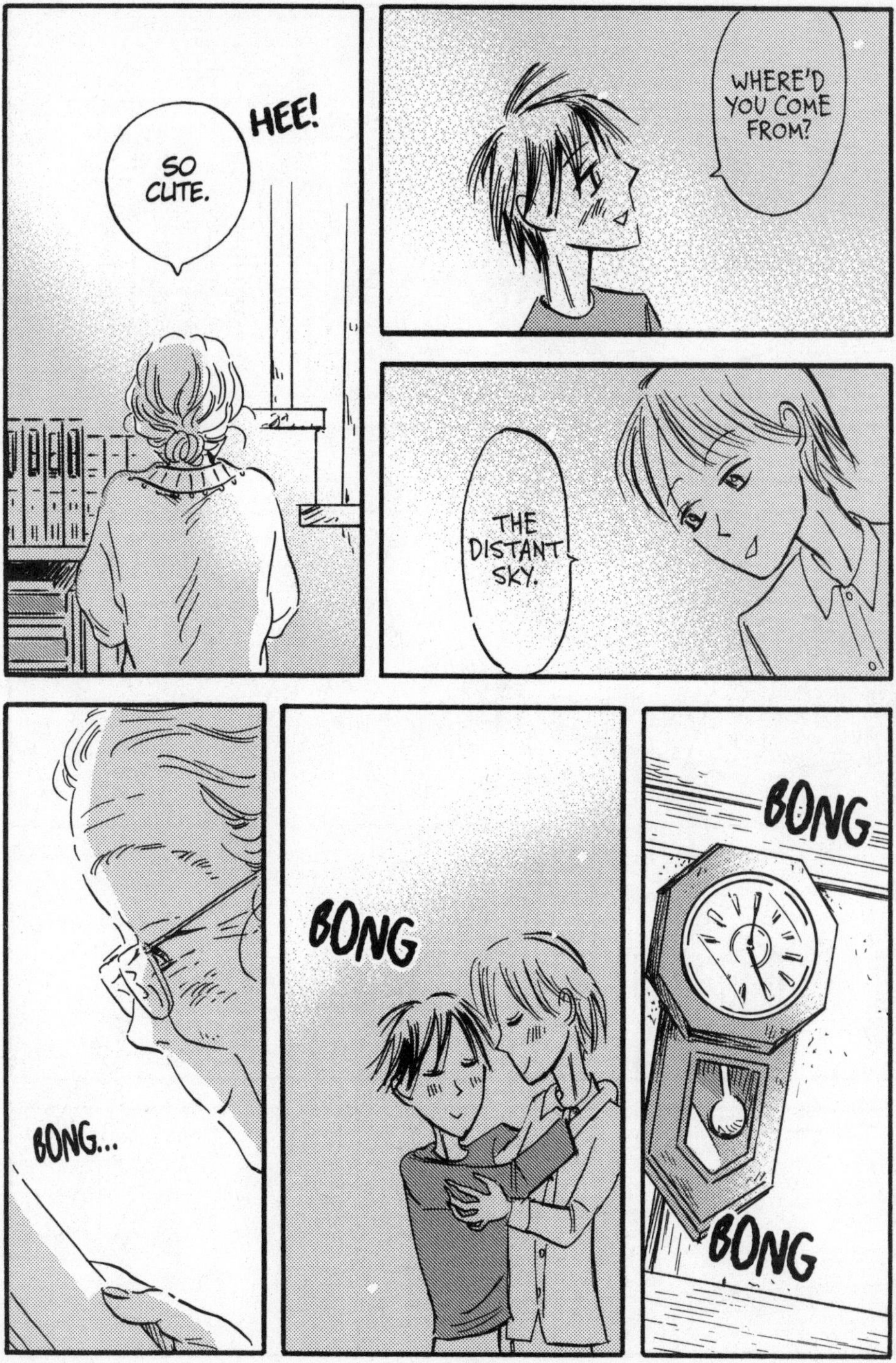
WHERE'D YOU COME FROM?
THE DISTANT SKY.
SO CUTE.
HEE!
BONG
BONG
BONG
BONG...

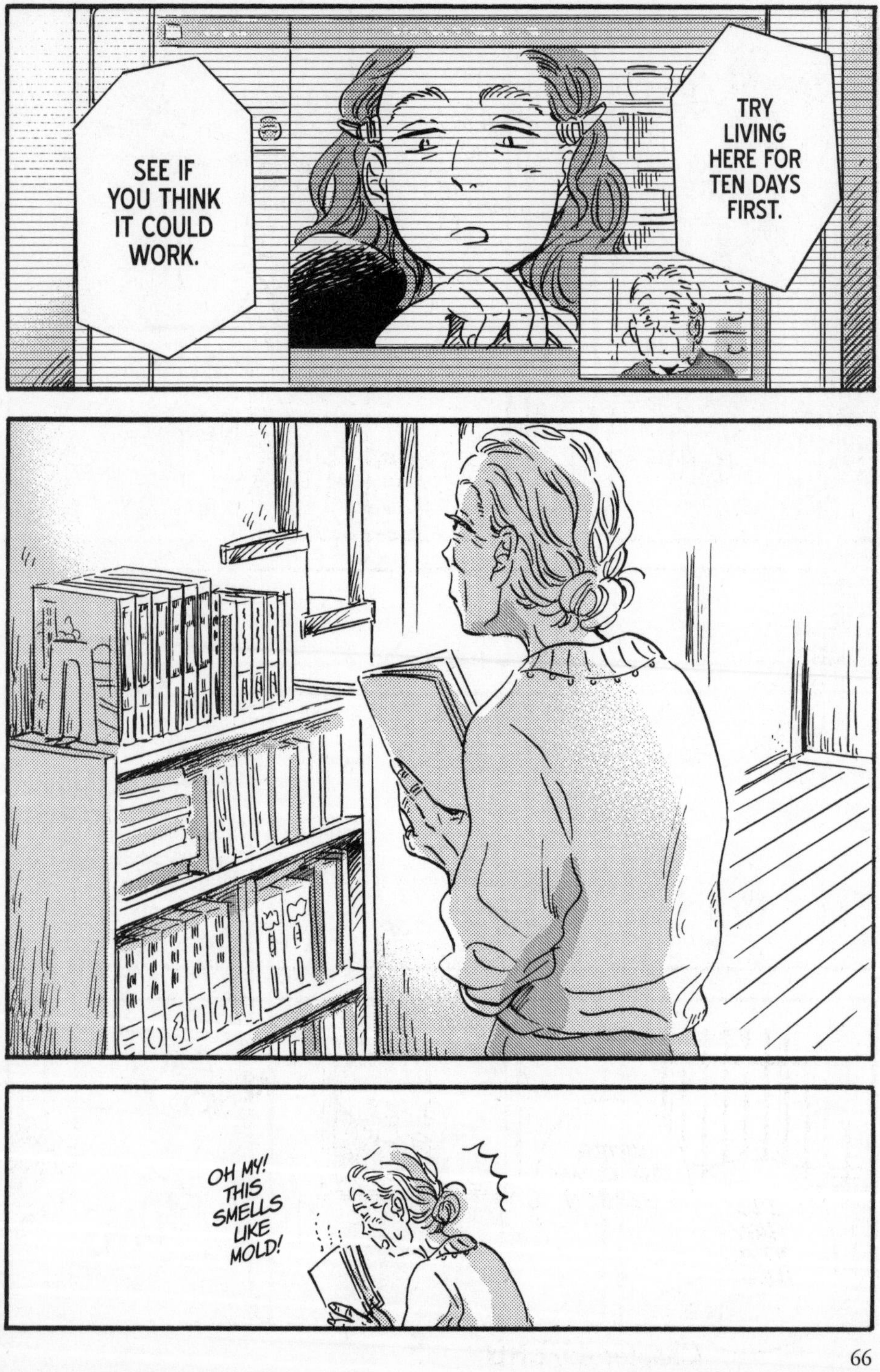
TRY LIVING HERE FOR TEN DAYS FIRST.
SEE IF YOU THINK IT COULD WORK.
OH MY! THIS SMELLS LIKE MOLD!

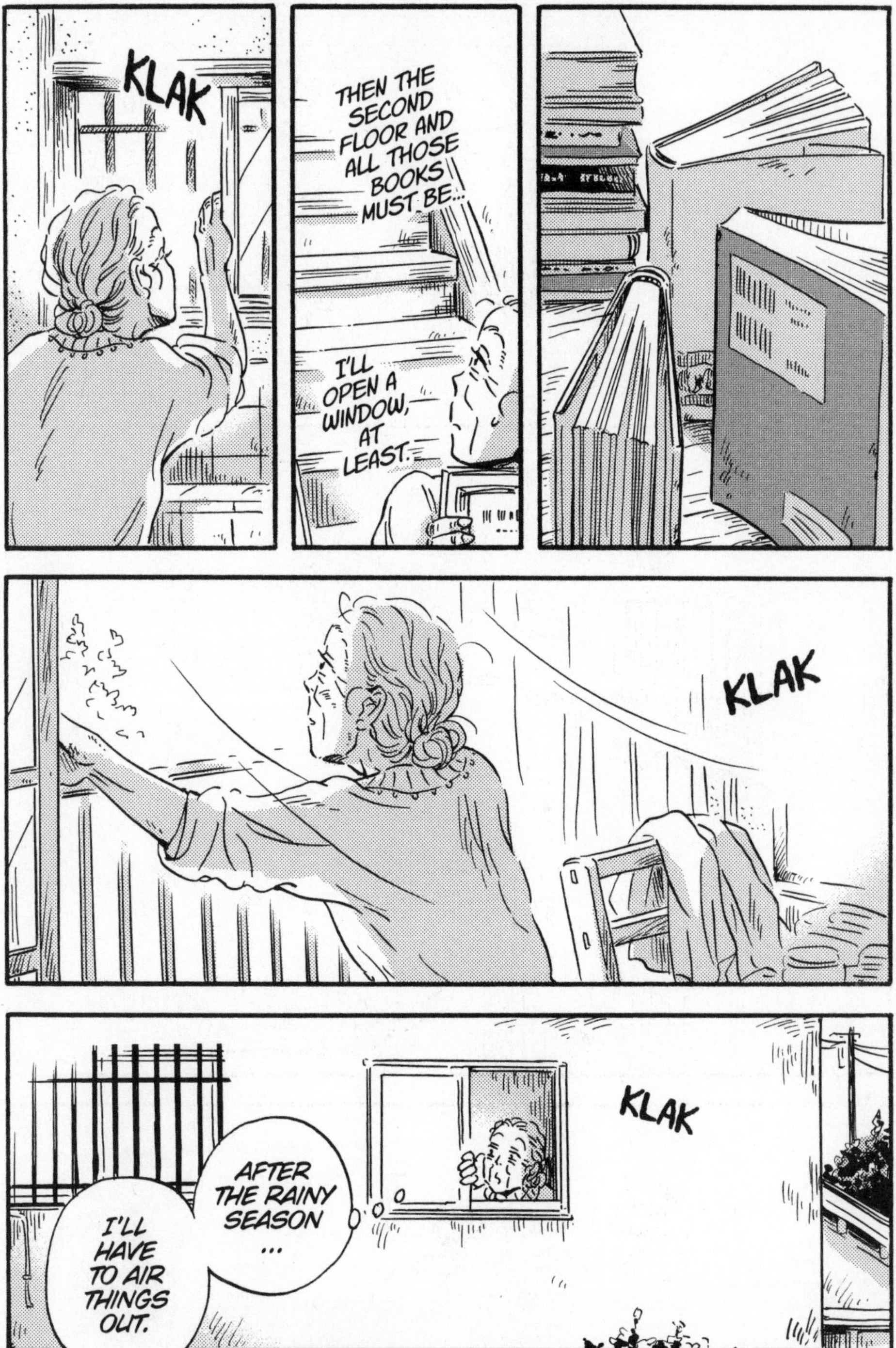
THEN THE SECOND FLOOR AND ALL THOSE BOOKS MUST BE...
I'LL OPEN A WINDOW, AT LEAST.
KLAK
KLAK
KLAK
AFTER THE RAINY SEASON ...
I'LL HAVE TO AIR THINGS OUT.

Chapter 45/END

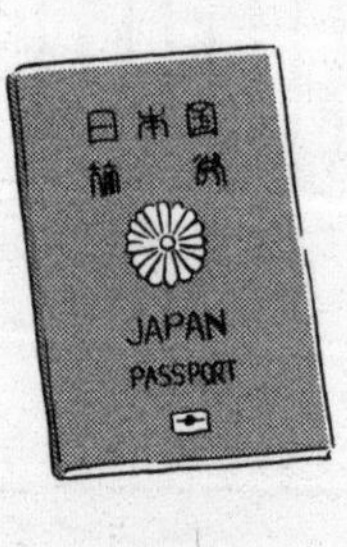
JAPAN
PASSPORT

# Chapter 46

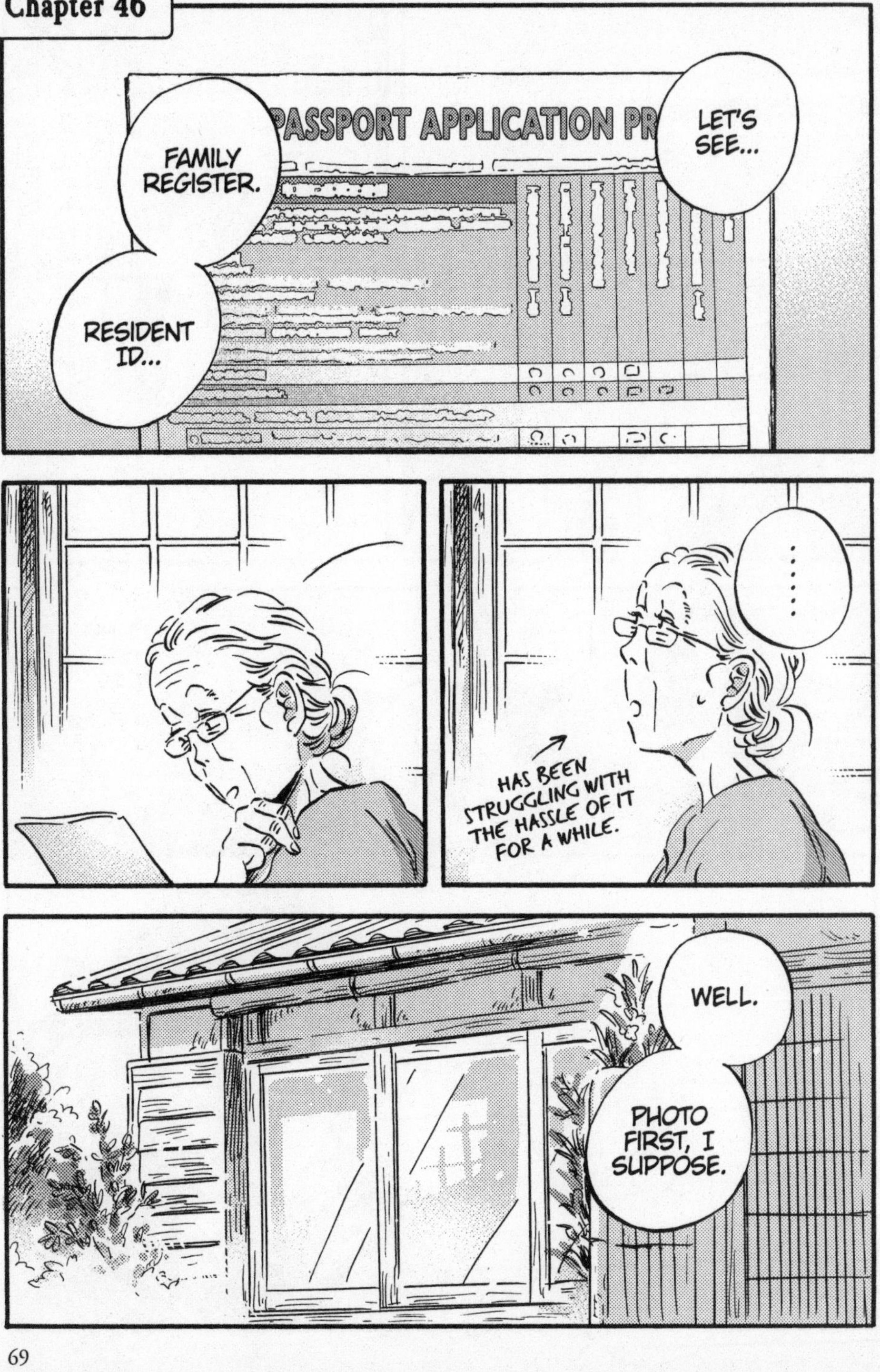

PASSPORT APPLICATION PR
LET'S SEE...
FAMILY REGISTER.
RESIDENT ID...
......
HAS BEEN STRUGGLING WITH THE HASSLE OF IT FOR A WHILE.
WELL.
PHOTO FIRST, I SUPPOSE.

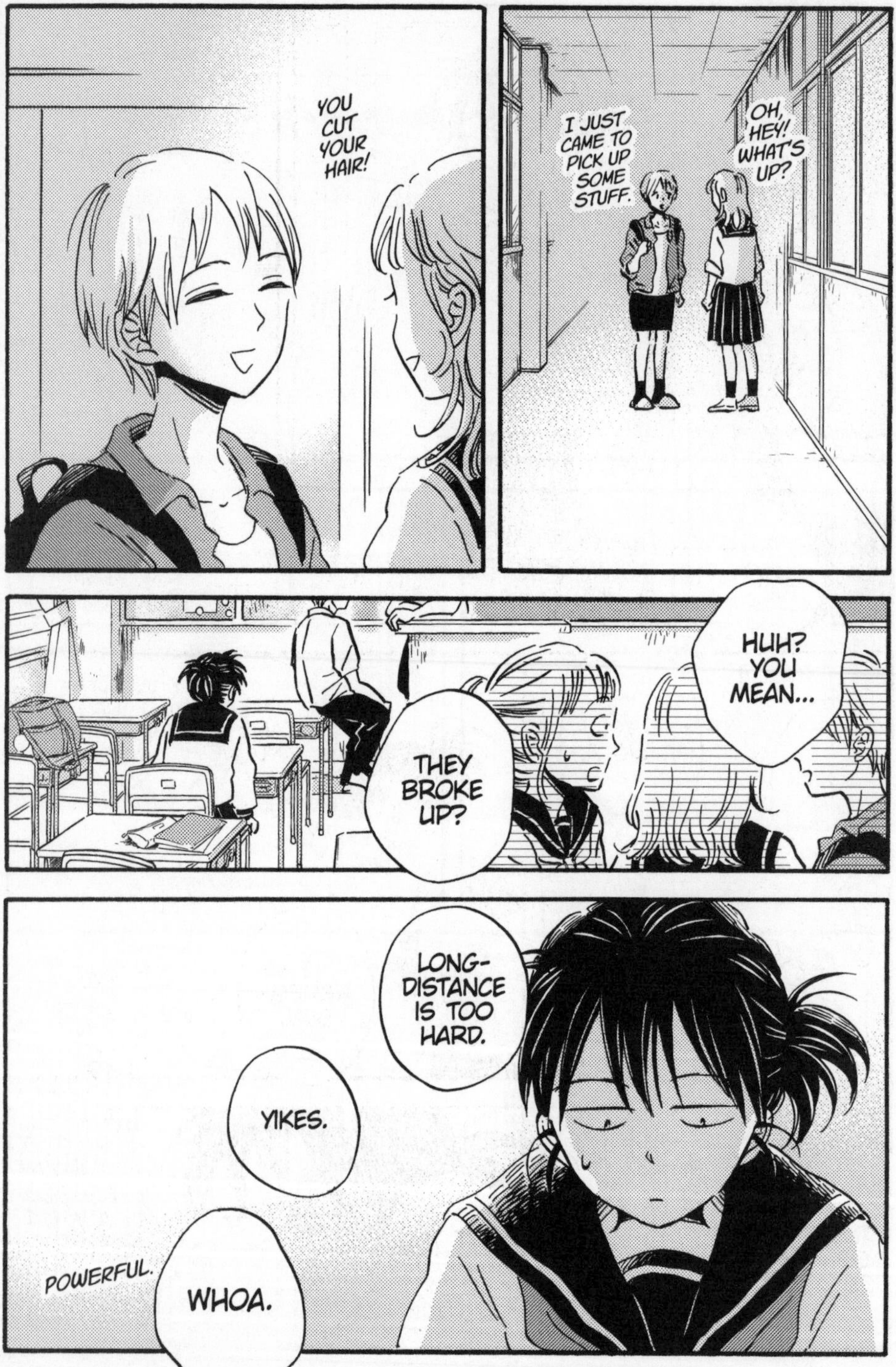
OH, HEY! WHAT'S UP?
I JUST CAME TO PICK UP SOME STUFF.
YOU CUT YOUR HAIR!
HUH? YOU MEAN...
THEY BROKE UP?
LONG-DISTANCE IS TOO HARD.
YIKES.
WHOA.
POWERFUL.

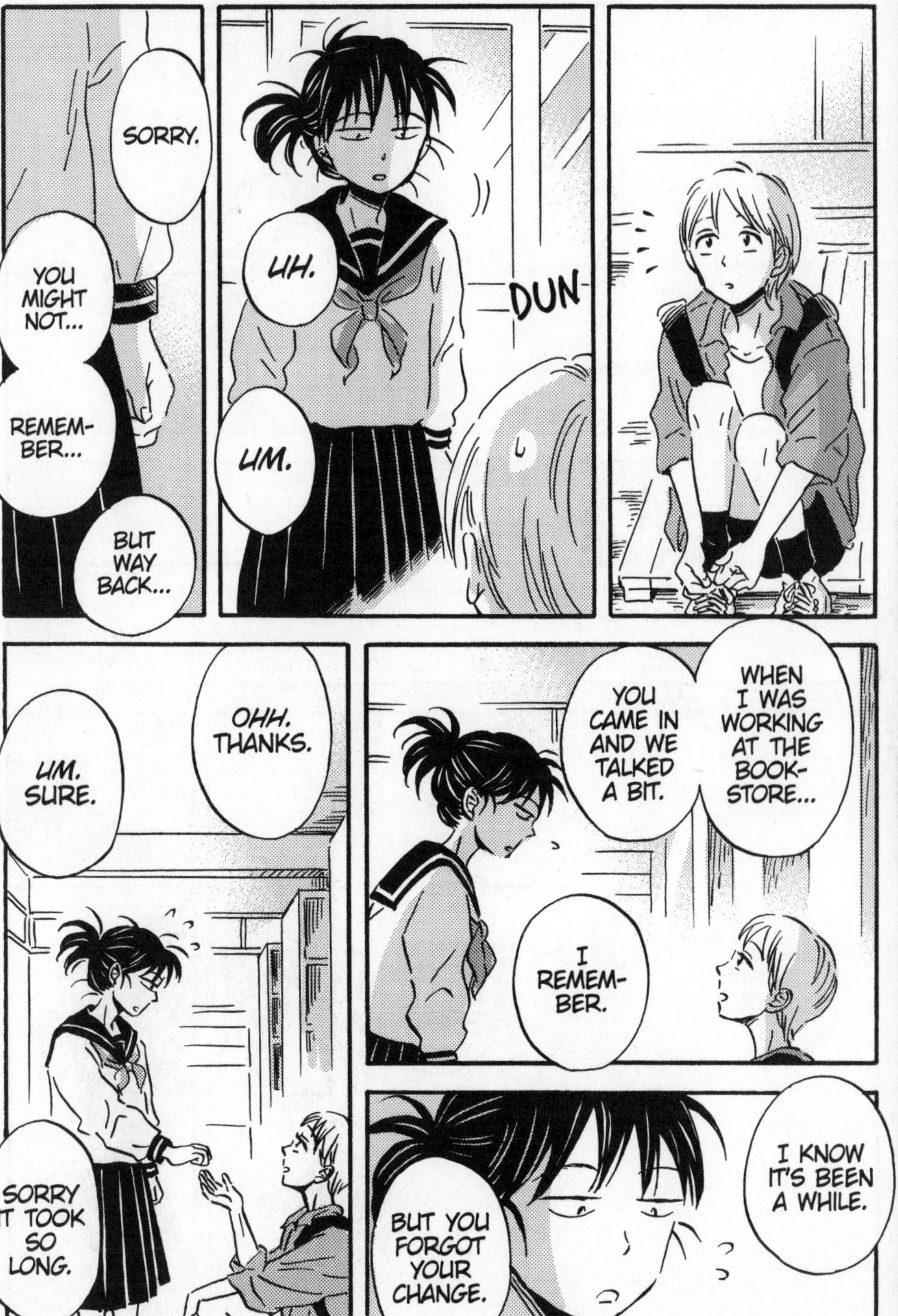
DUN
UH.
UM.
SORRY.
YOU MIGHT NOT...
REMEMBER...
BUT WAY BACK...
WHEN I WAS WORKING AT THE BOOKSTORE...
YOU CAME IN AND WE TALKED A BIT.
I REMEMBER.
I KNOW IT'S BEEN A WHILE.
BUT YOU FORGOT YOUR CHANGE.
OHH. THANKS.
UM. SURE.
SORRY IT TOOK SO LONG.

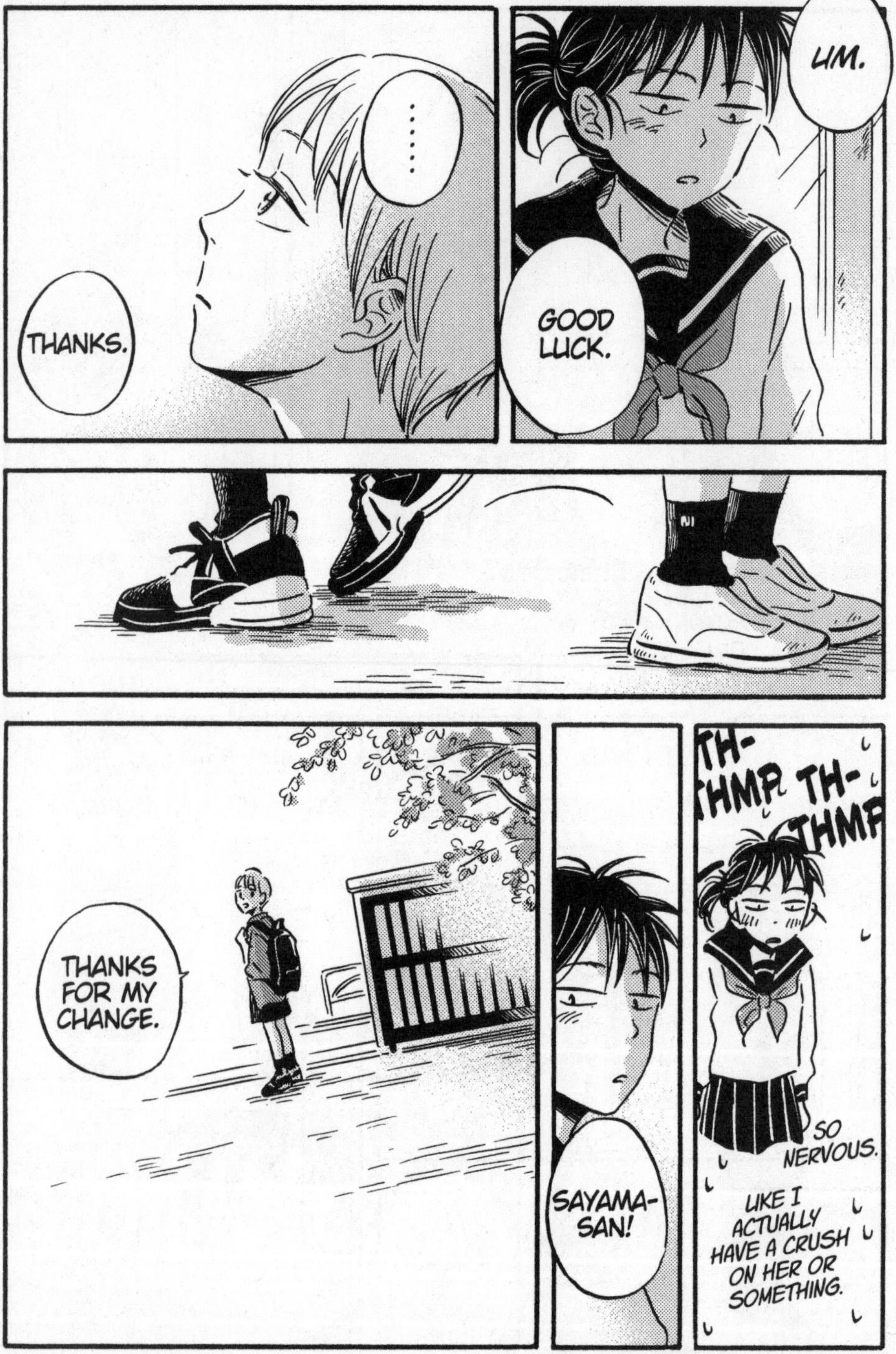
UM.
GOOD LUCK.
......
THANKS.
TH-THMP TH-THMP
SO NERVOUS.
LIKE I ACTUALLY HAVE A CRUSH ON HER OR SOMETHING.
SAYAMA-SAN!
THANKS FOR MY CHANGE.

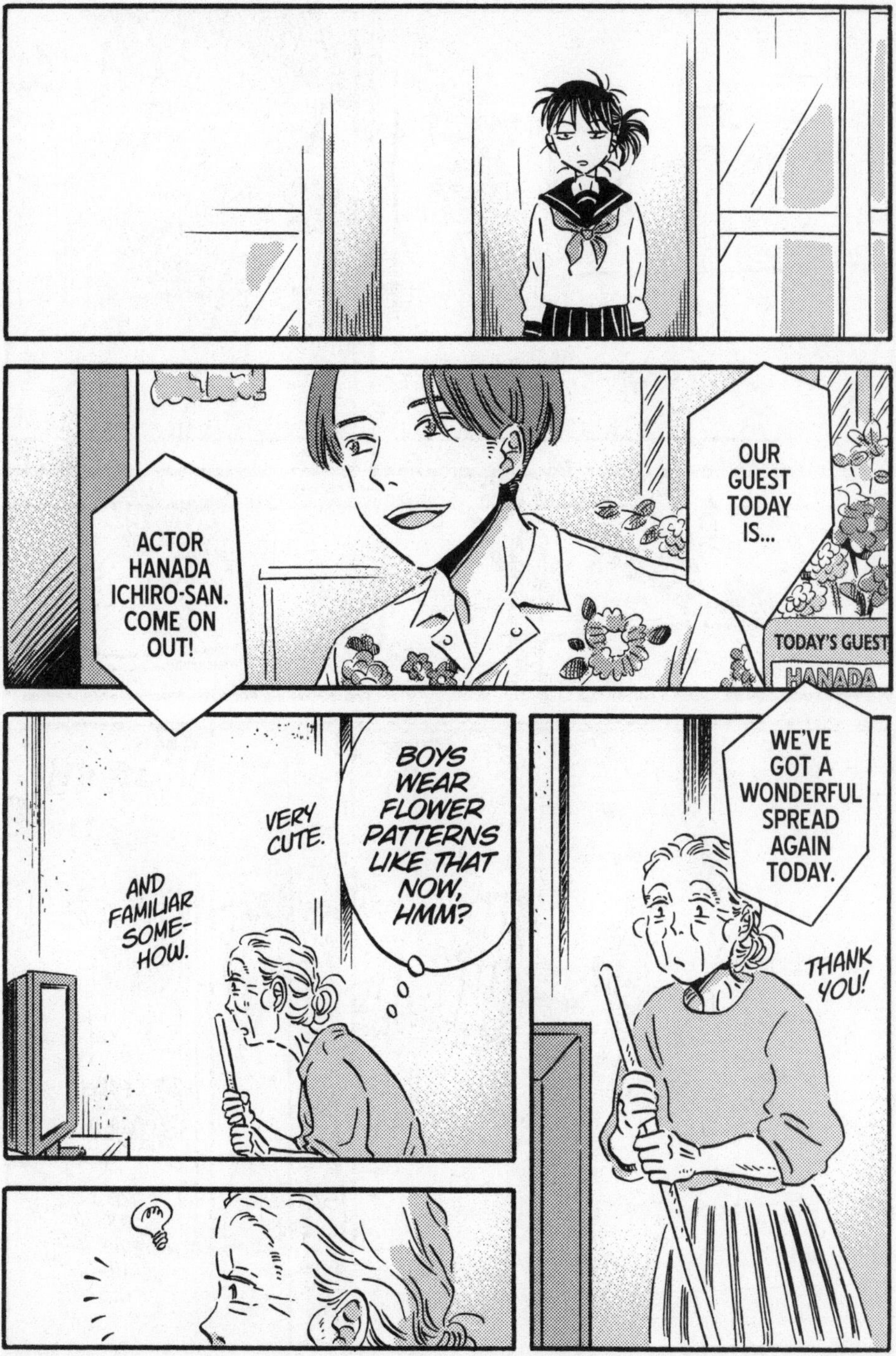
OUR GUEST TODAY IS...
TODAY'S GUEST
HANADA
ACTOR HANADA ICHIRO-SAN. COME ON OUT!
WE'VE GOT A WONDERFUL SPREAD AGAIN TODAY.
THANK YOU!
BOYS WEAR FLOWER PATTERNS LIKE THAT NOW, HMM?
VERY CUTE.
AND FAMILIAR SOME-HOW.

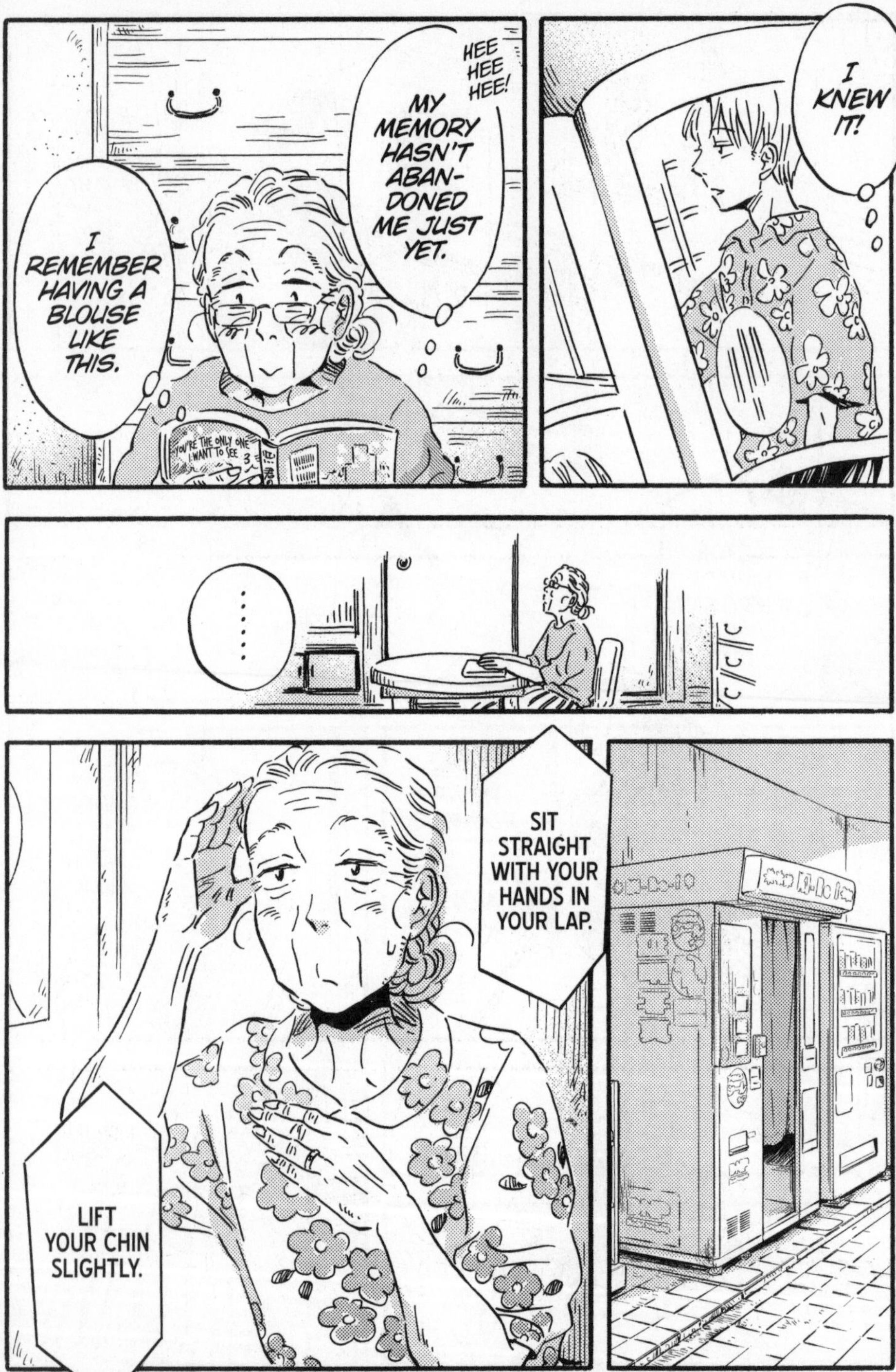
I KNEW IT!
HEE HEE HEE!
MY MEMORY HASN'T ABAN-DONED ME JUST YET.
I REMEMBER HAVING A BLOUSE LIKE THIS.
YOU'RE THE ONLY ONE I WANT TO SEE 3
......
SIT STRAIGHT WITH YOUR HANDS IN YOUR LAP.
LIFT YOUR CHIN SLIGHTLY.

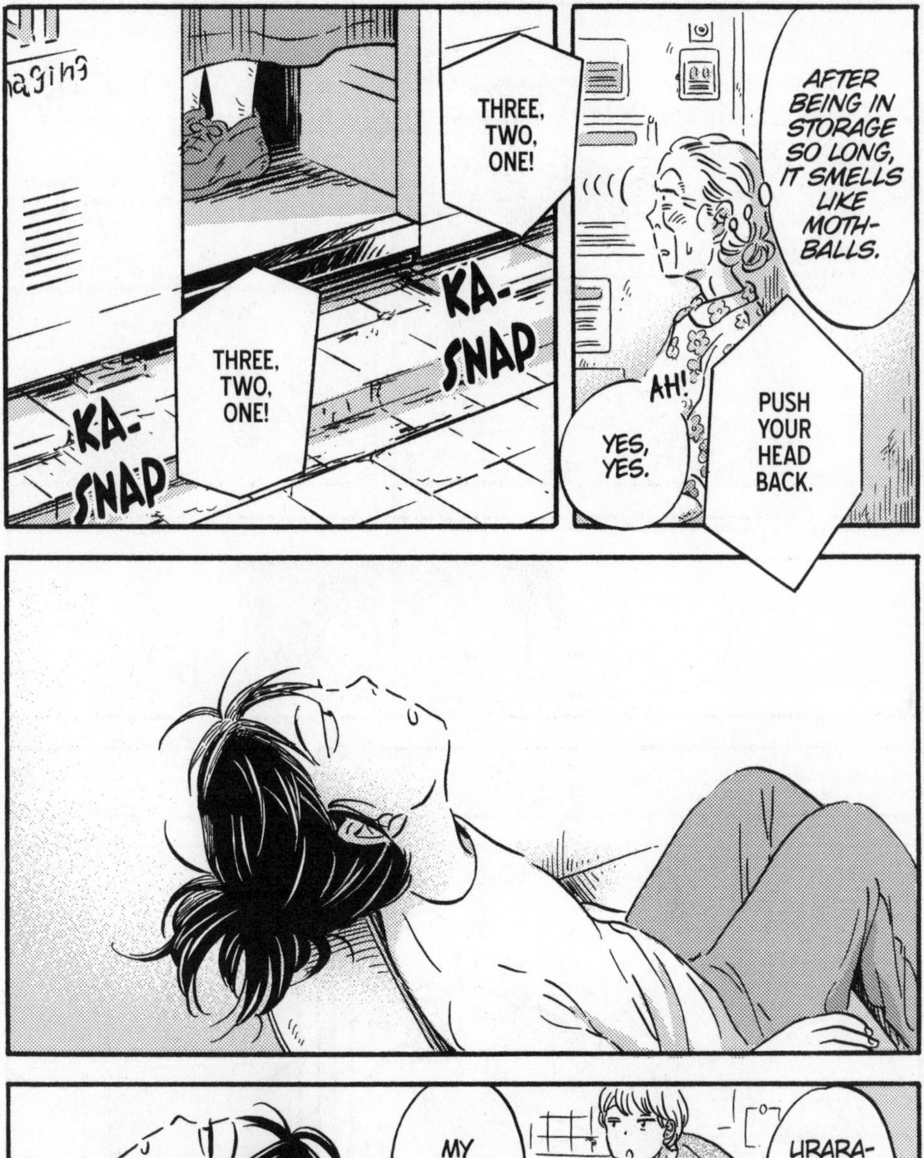
AFTER BEING IN STORAGE SO LONG, IT SMELLS LIKE MOTH-BALLS.
PUSH YOUR HEAD BACK.
AH!
YES, YES.
THREE, TWO, ONE!
KA-SNAP
THREE, TWO, ONE!
KA-SNAP
URARA-SAAAN. GET IT TOGETH-ER.
MY BRAIN IS...
OVER CAPACITY RIGHT NOW.

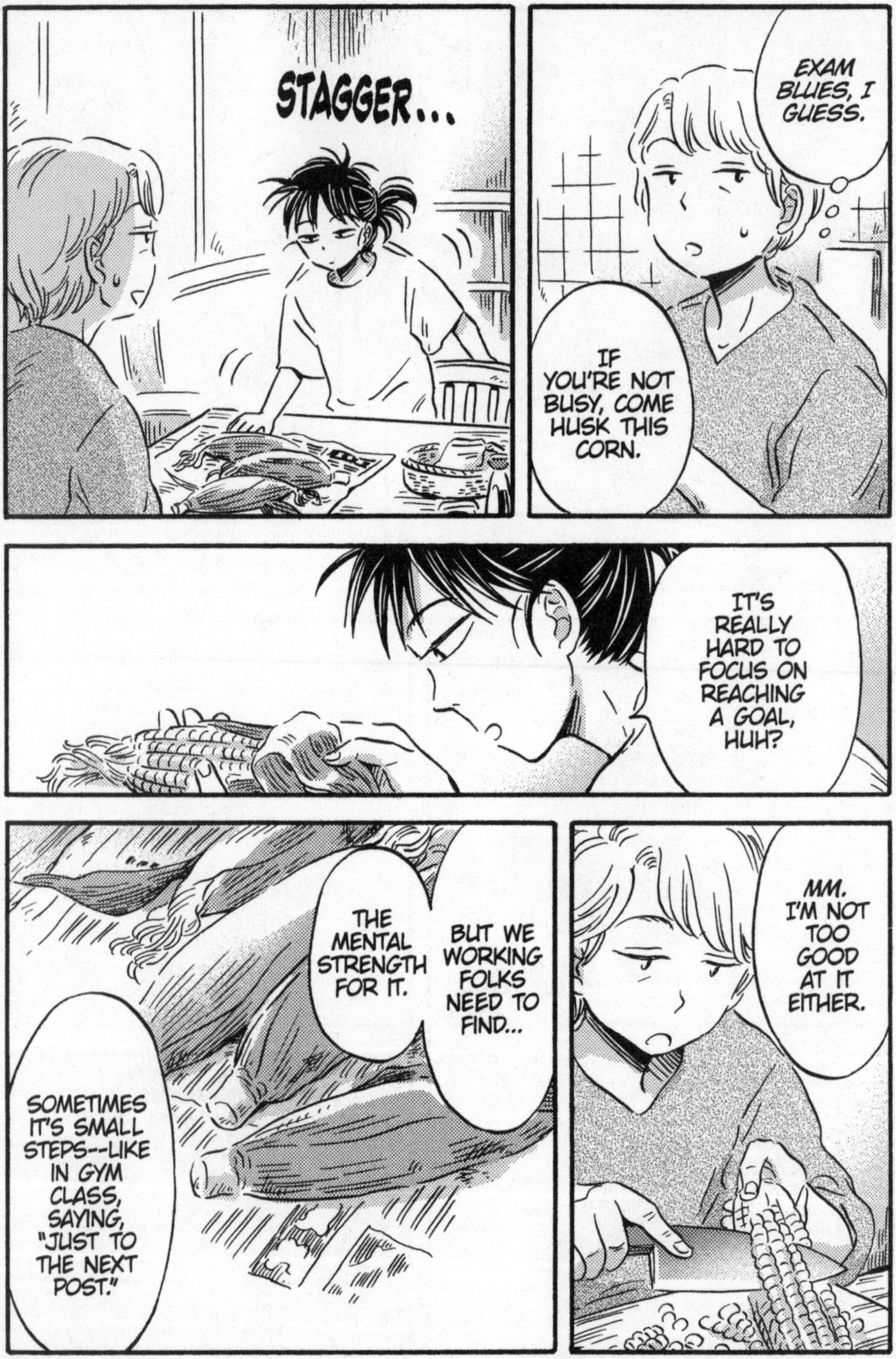
EXAM BLUES, I GUESS.
IF YOU'RE NOT BUSY, COME HUSK THIS CORN.
STAGGER...
IT'S REALLY HARD TO FOCUS ON REACHING A GOAL, HUH?
MM. I'M NOT TOO GOOD AT IT EITHER.
BUT WE WORKING FOLKS NEED TO FIND...
THE MENTAL STRENGTH FOR IT.
SOMETIMES IT'S SMALL STEPS--LIKE IN GYM CLASS, SAYING, "JUST TO THE NEXT POST."

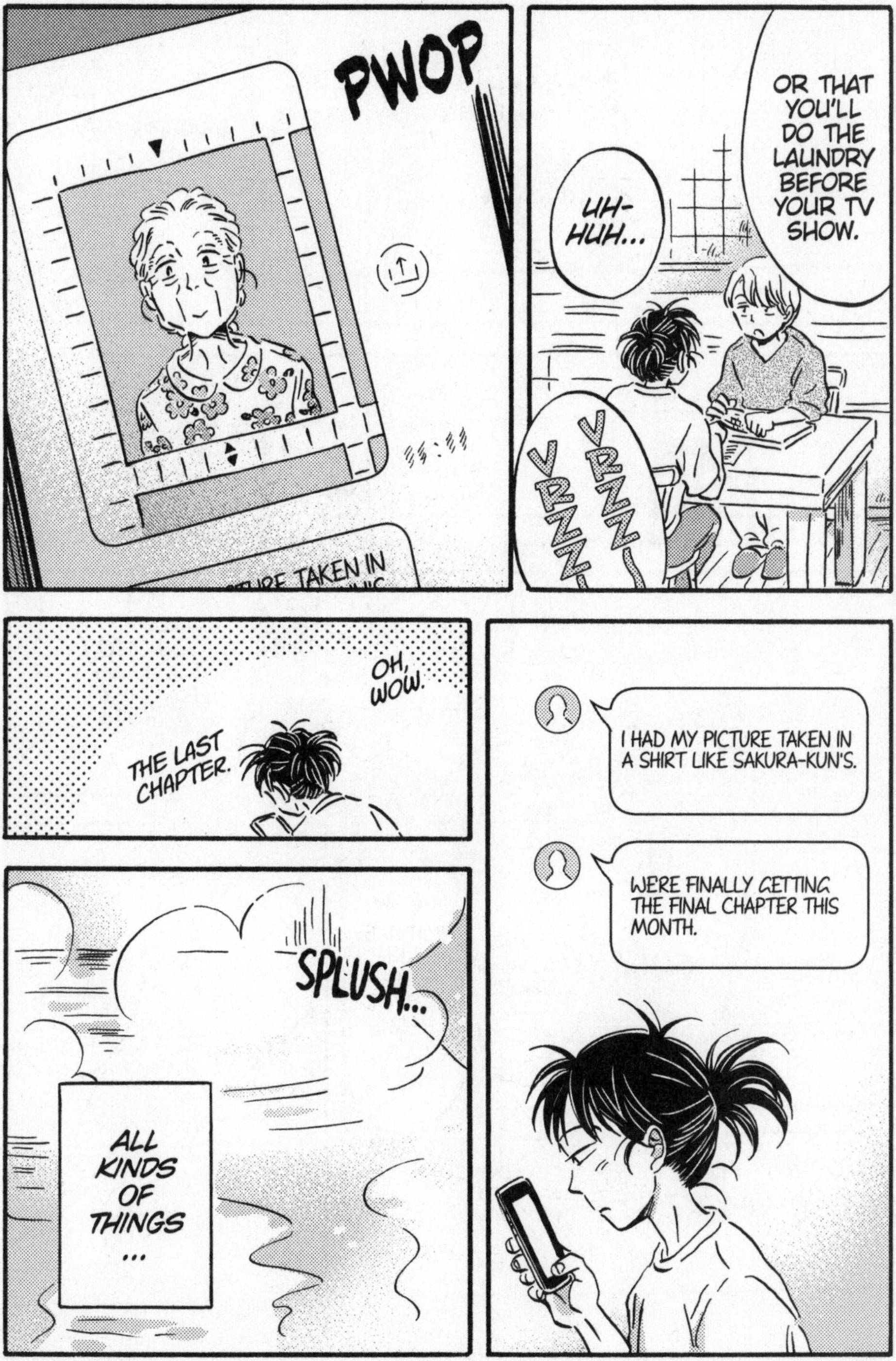
OR THAT YOU'LL DO THE LAUNDRY BEFORE YOUR TV SHOW.
UH-HUH...
VRZZZ VRZZZ
PWOP
I HAD MY PICTURE TAKEN IN A SHIRT LIKE SAKURA-KUN'S.
WE'RE FINALLY GETTING THE FINAL CHAPTER THIS MONTH.
OH, WOW.
THE LAST CHAPTER.
SPLUSH...
ALL KINDS OF THINGS ...

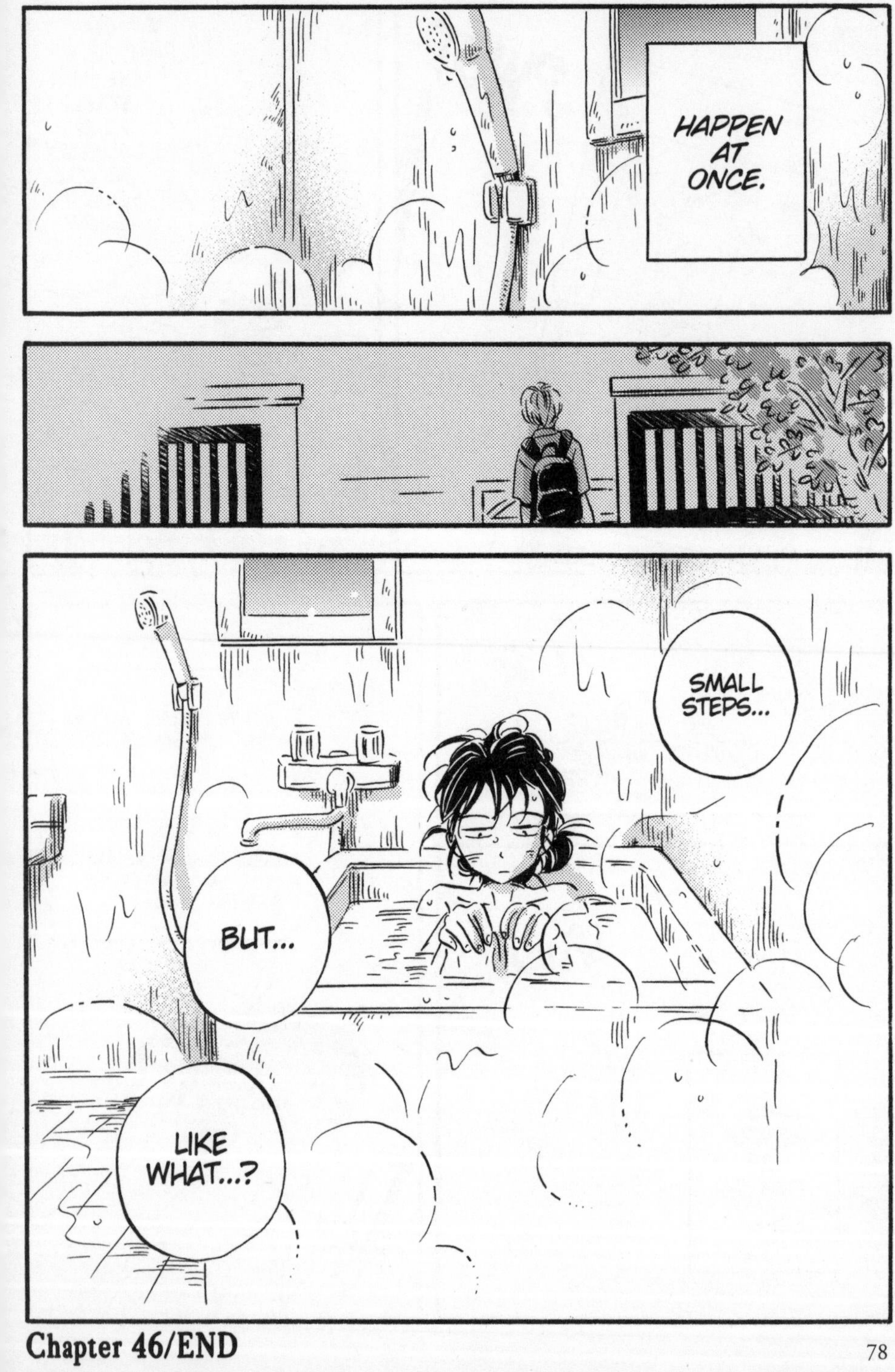
HAPPEN AT ONCE.
SMALL STEPS...
BUT...
LIKE WHAT...?

Chapter 46/END

# Chapter 47

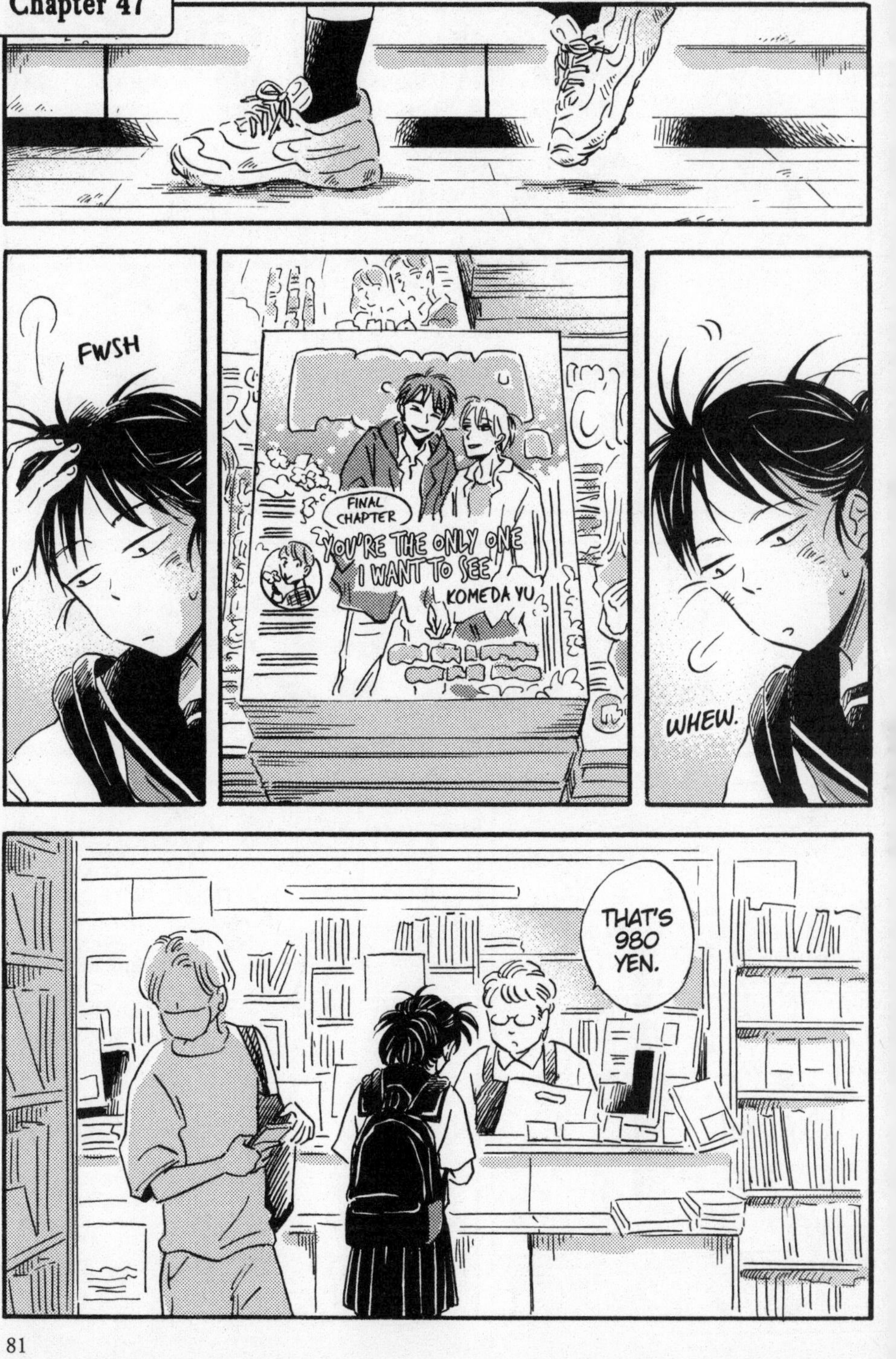
WHEW.
FINAL CHAPTER
YOU'RE THE ONLY ONE I WANT TO SEE
KOMEDA YU
FWSH
THAT'S 980 YEN.

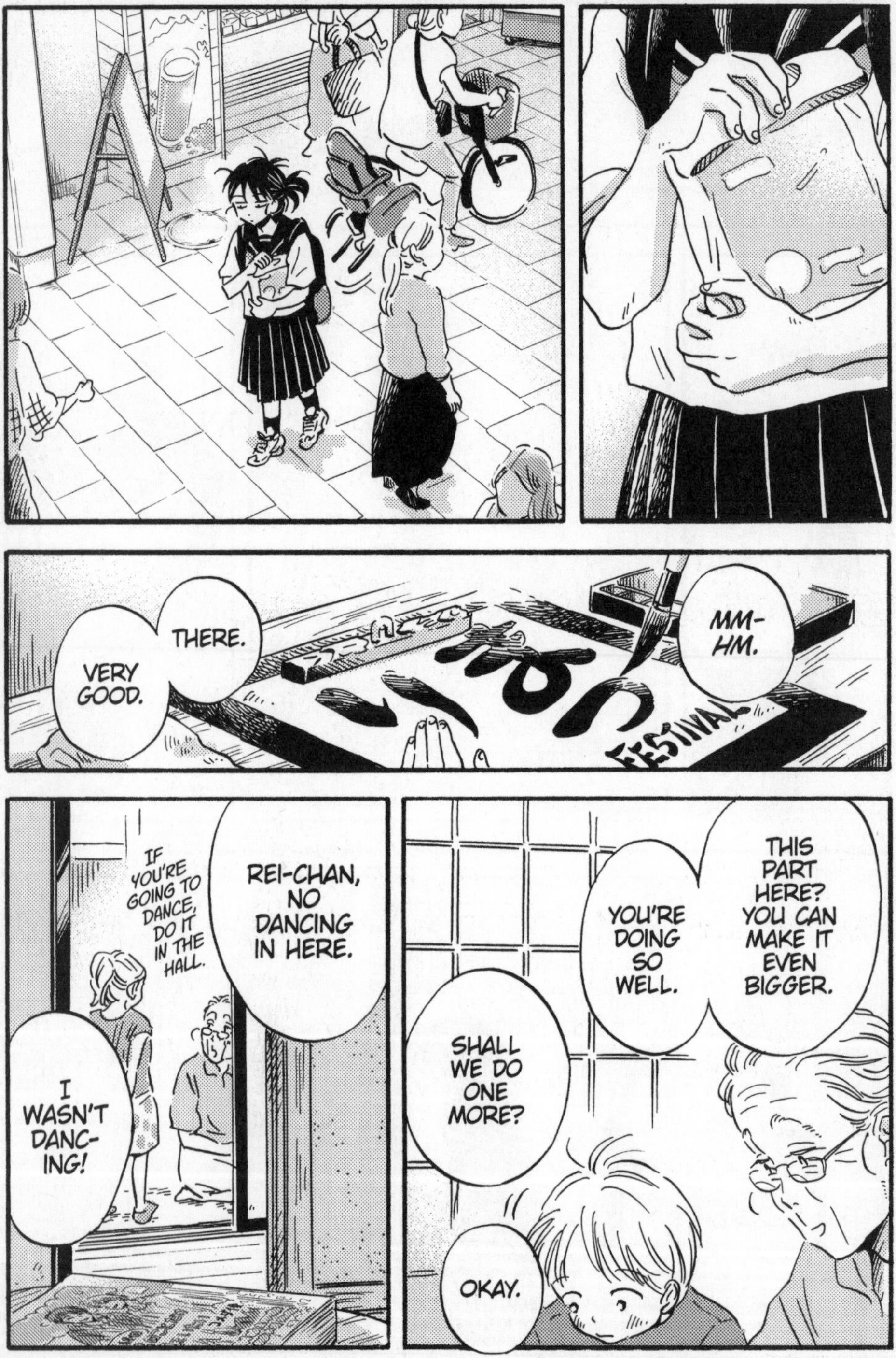
MM-HM.
THERE.
VERY GOOD.
FESTIVAL
THIS PART HERE? YOU CAN MAKE IT EVEN BIGGER.
YOU'RE DOING SO WELL.
SHALL WE DO ONE MORE?
OKAY.
REI-CHAN, NO DANCING IN HERE.
IF YOU'RE GOING TO DANCE, DO IT IN THE HALL.
I WASN'T DANCING!

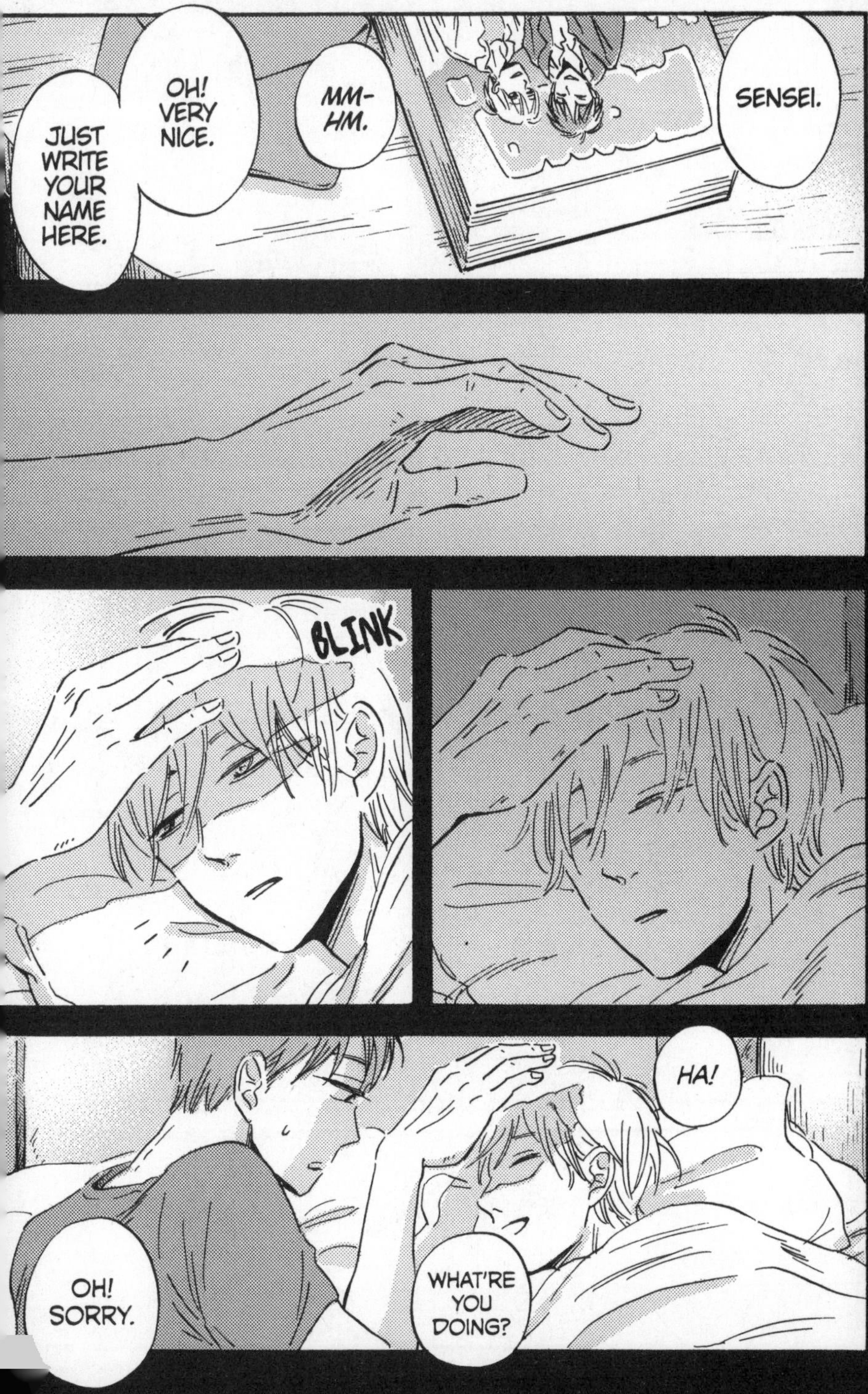
SENSEI.
MM-HM.
OH! VERY NICE.
JUST WRITE YOUR NAME HERE.
BLINK
HA!
WHAT'RE YOU DOING?
OH! SORRY.

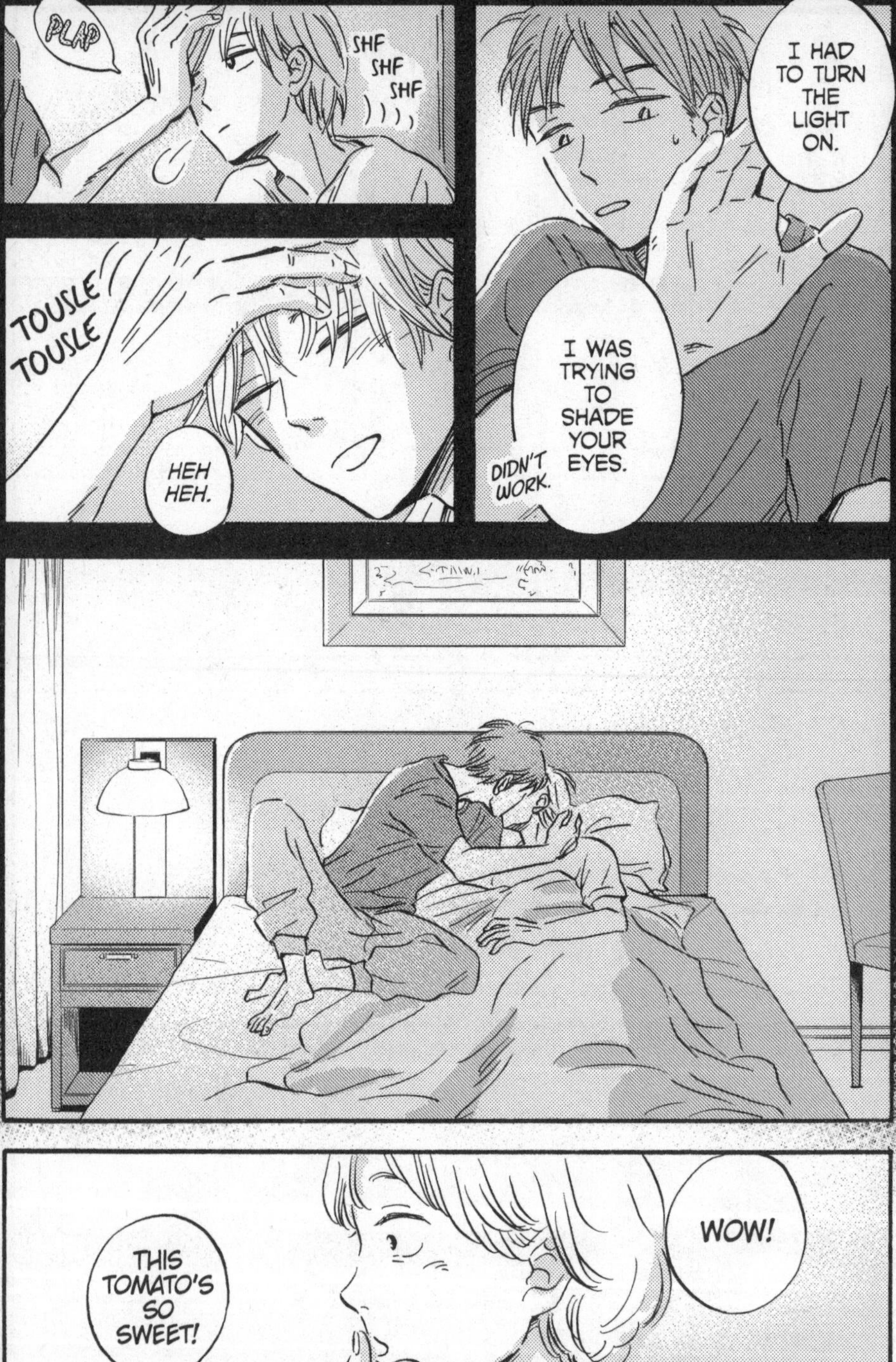
I HAD TO TURN THE LIGHT ON.
I WAS TRYING TO SHADE YOUR EYES.
DIDN'T WORK.
PLAP
SHF SHF SHF
TOUSLE TOUSLE
HEH HEH.
WOW!
THIS TOMATO'S SO SWEET!

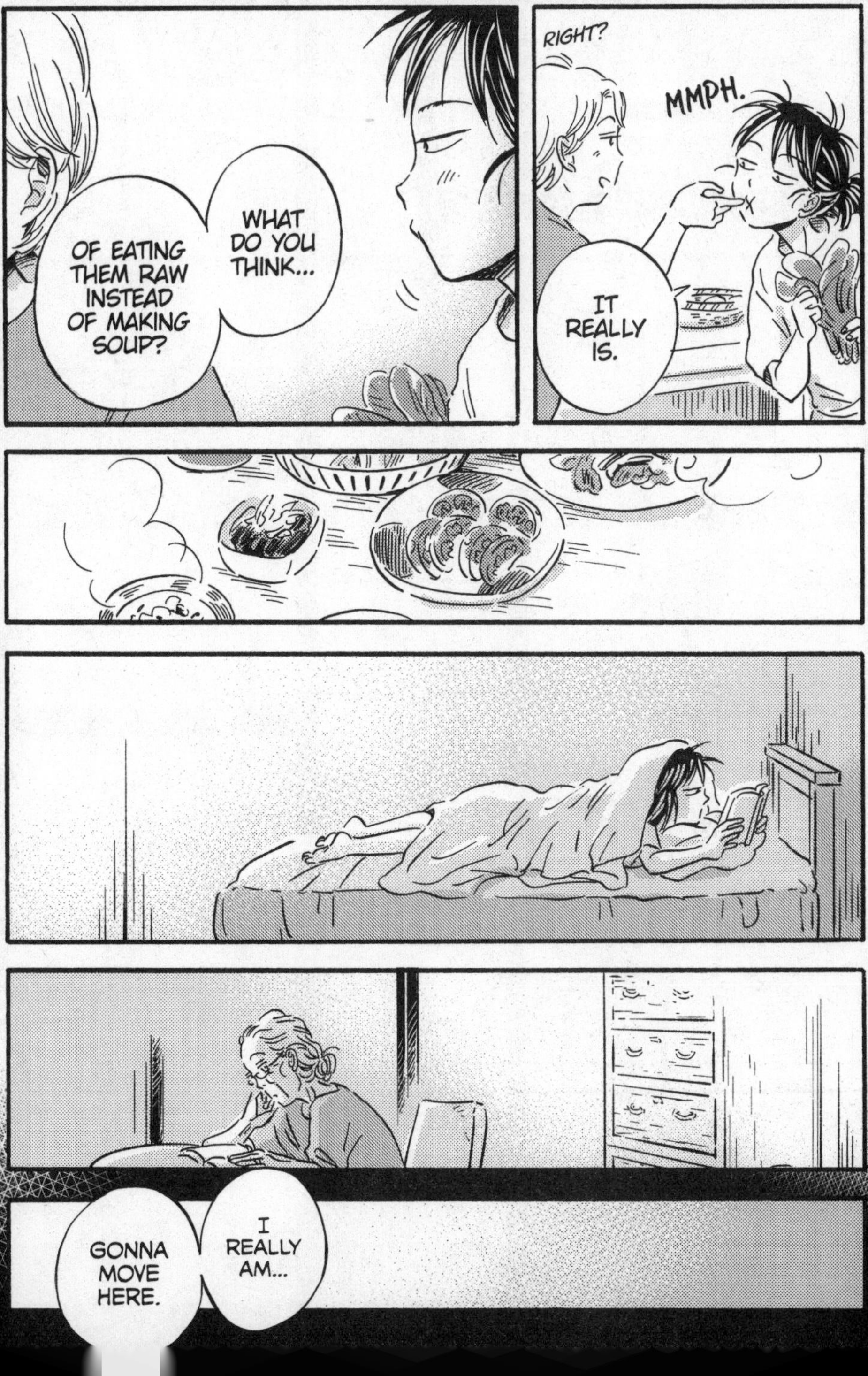
RIGHT?
MMPH.
IT REALLY IS.
WHAT DO YOU THINK...
OF EATING THEM RAW INSTEAD OF MAKING SOUP?
I REALLY AM...
GONNA MOVE HERE.

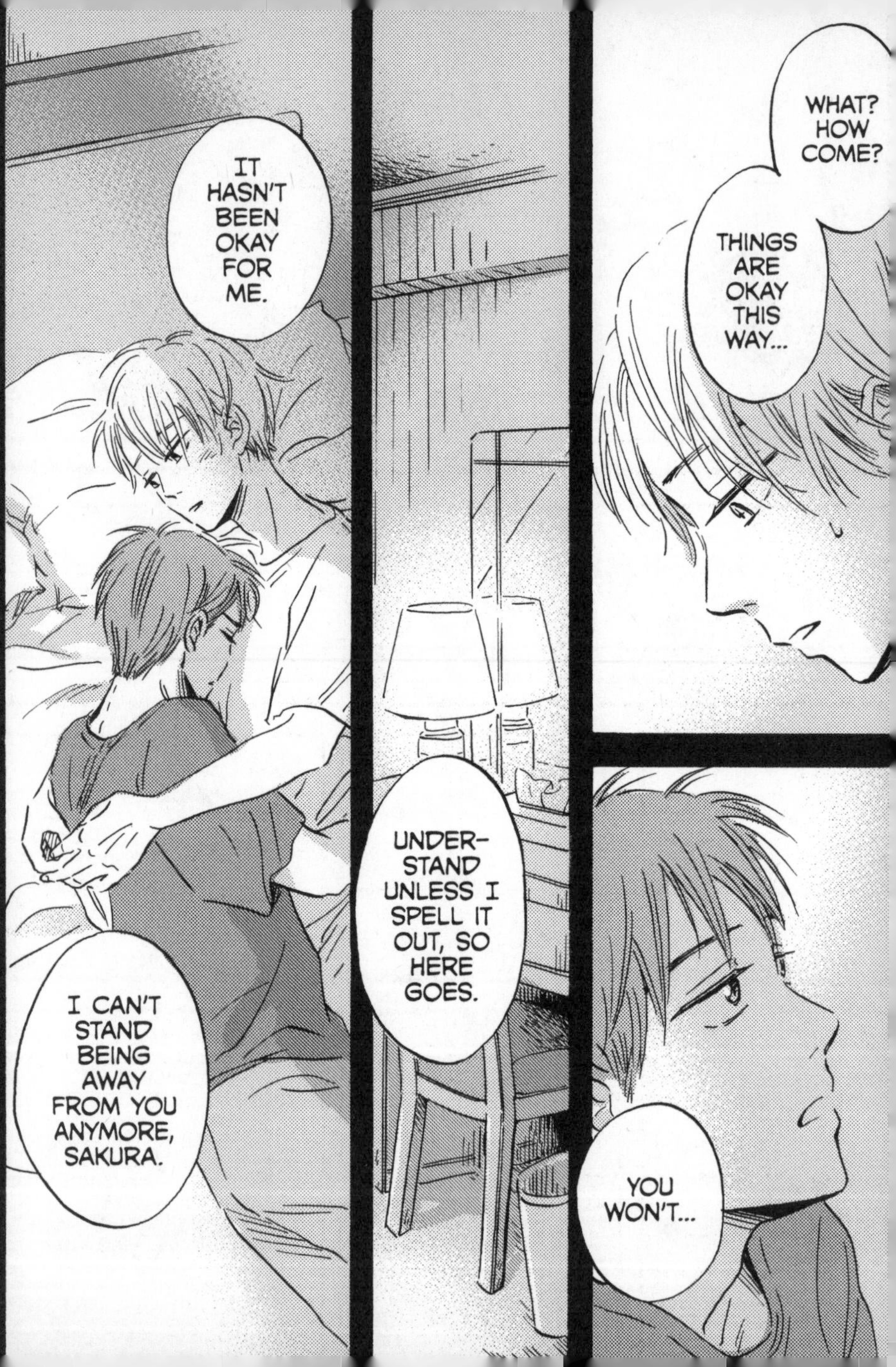
WHAT? HOW COME?
THINGS ARE OKAY THIS WAY...
YOU WON'T...
UNDER-STAND UNLESS I SPELL IT OUT, SO HERE GOES.
IT HASN'T BEEN OKAY FOR ME.
I CAN'T STAND BEING AWAY FROM YOU ANYMORE, SAKURA.

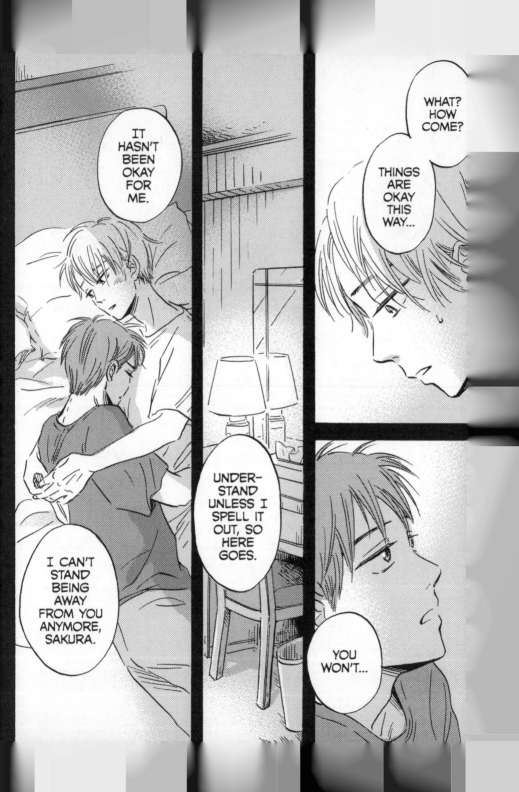

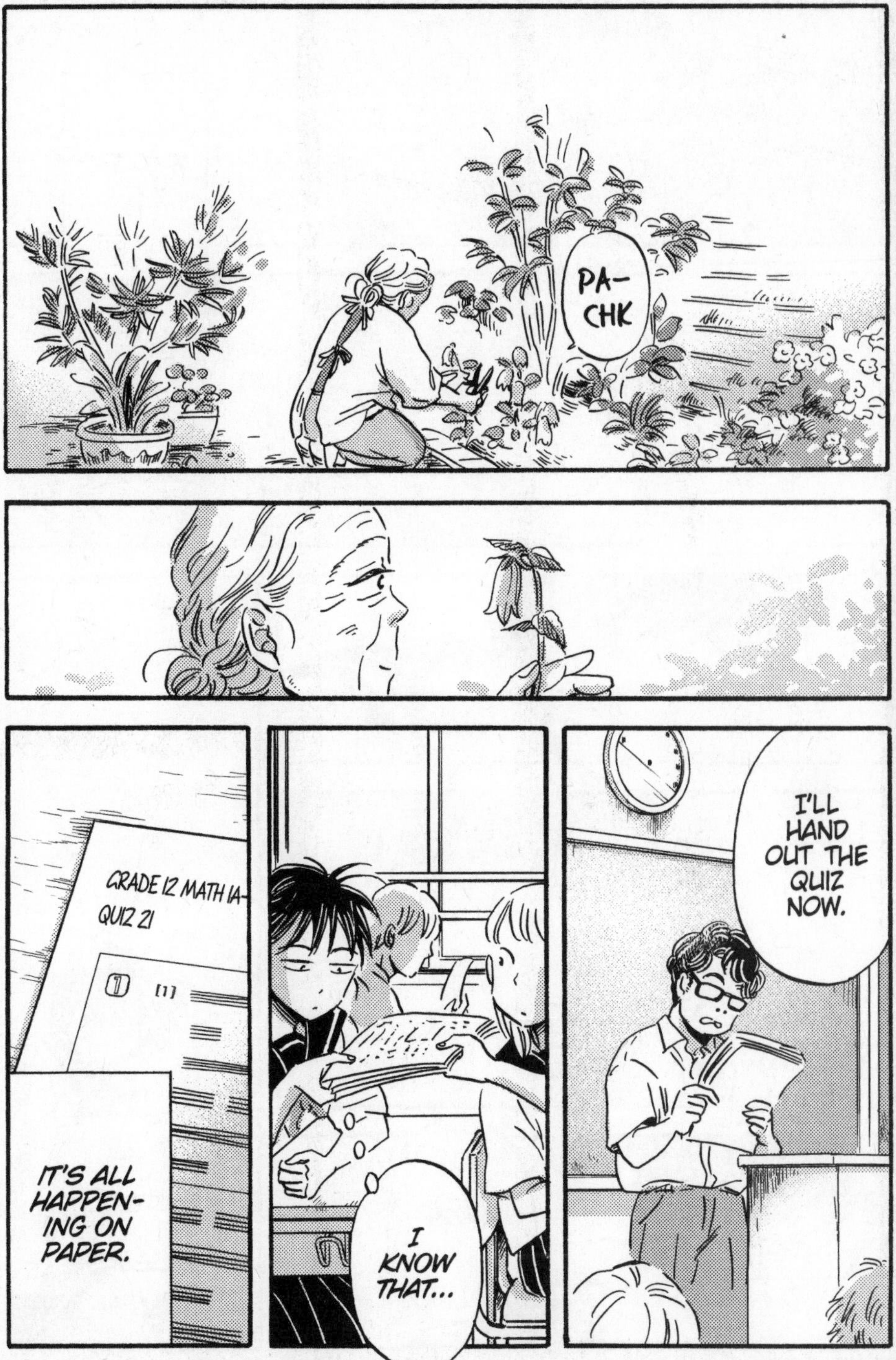
PA-CHK
I'LL HAND OUT THE QUIZ NOW.
I KNOW THAT...
GRADE 12 MATH IA-
QUIZ 21
IT'S ALL HAPPENING ON PAPER.

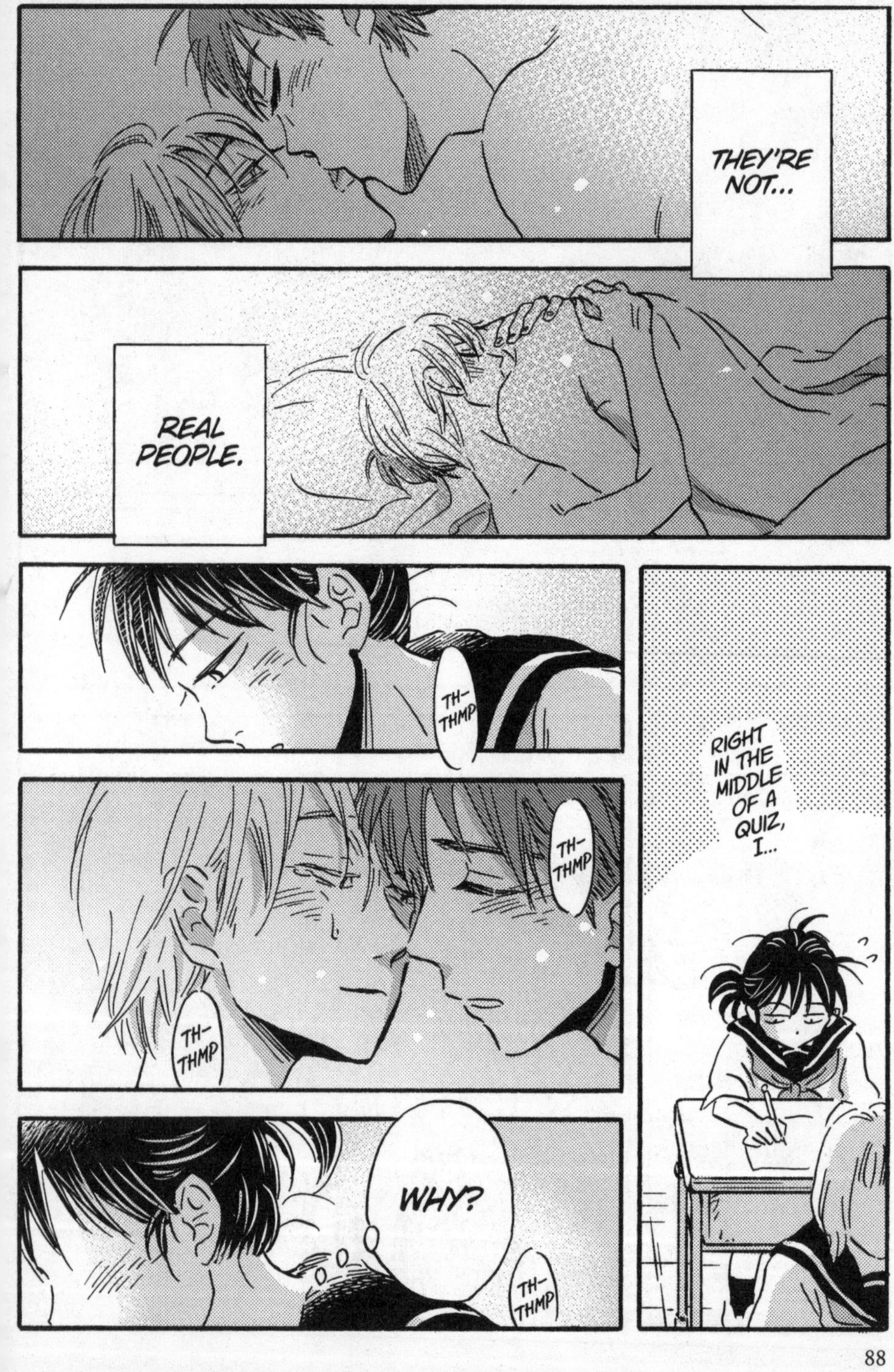
THEY'RE NOT...
REAL PEOPLE.
RIGHT IN THE MIDDLE OF A QUIZ, I...
TH-THMP
TH-THMP
TH-THMP
WHY?
TH-THMP

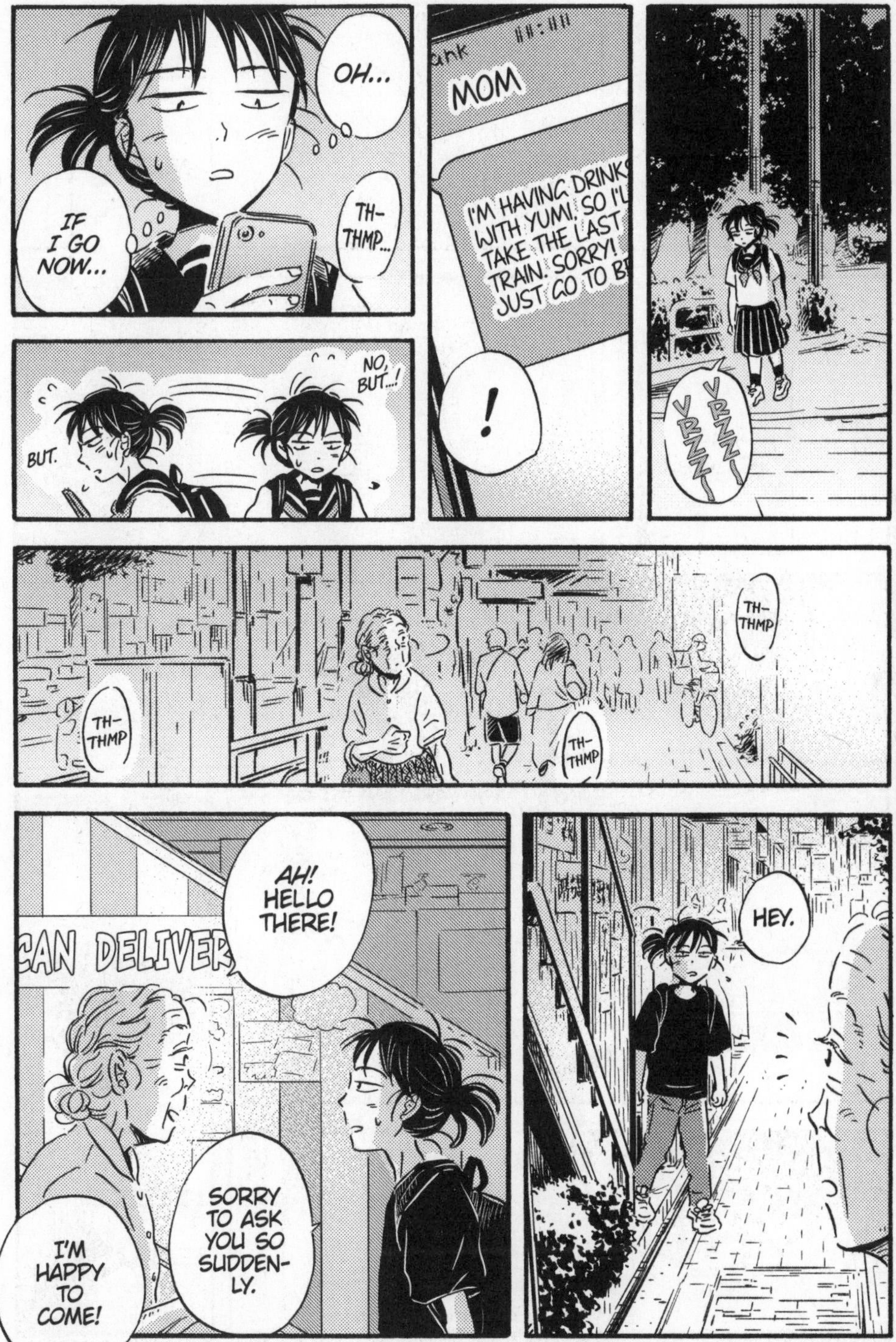
VRZZ VRZZ
MOM
I'M HAVING DRINKS WITH YUMI, SO I'L TAKE THE LAST TRAIN. SORRY! JUST GO TO B
!
OH...
TH-THMP...
IF I GO NOW...
NO, BUT...!
BUT.
TH-THMP
TH-THMP
TH-THMP
HEY.
AH! HELLO THERE!
CAN DELIVER
SORRY TO ASK YOU SO SUDDEN-LY.
I'M HAPPY TO COME!

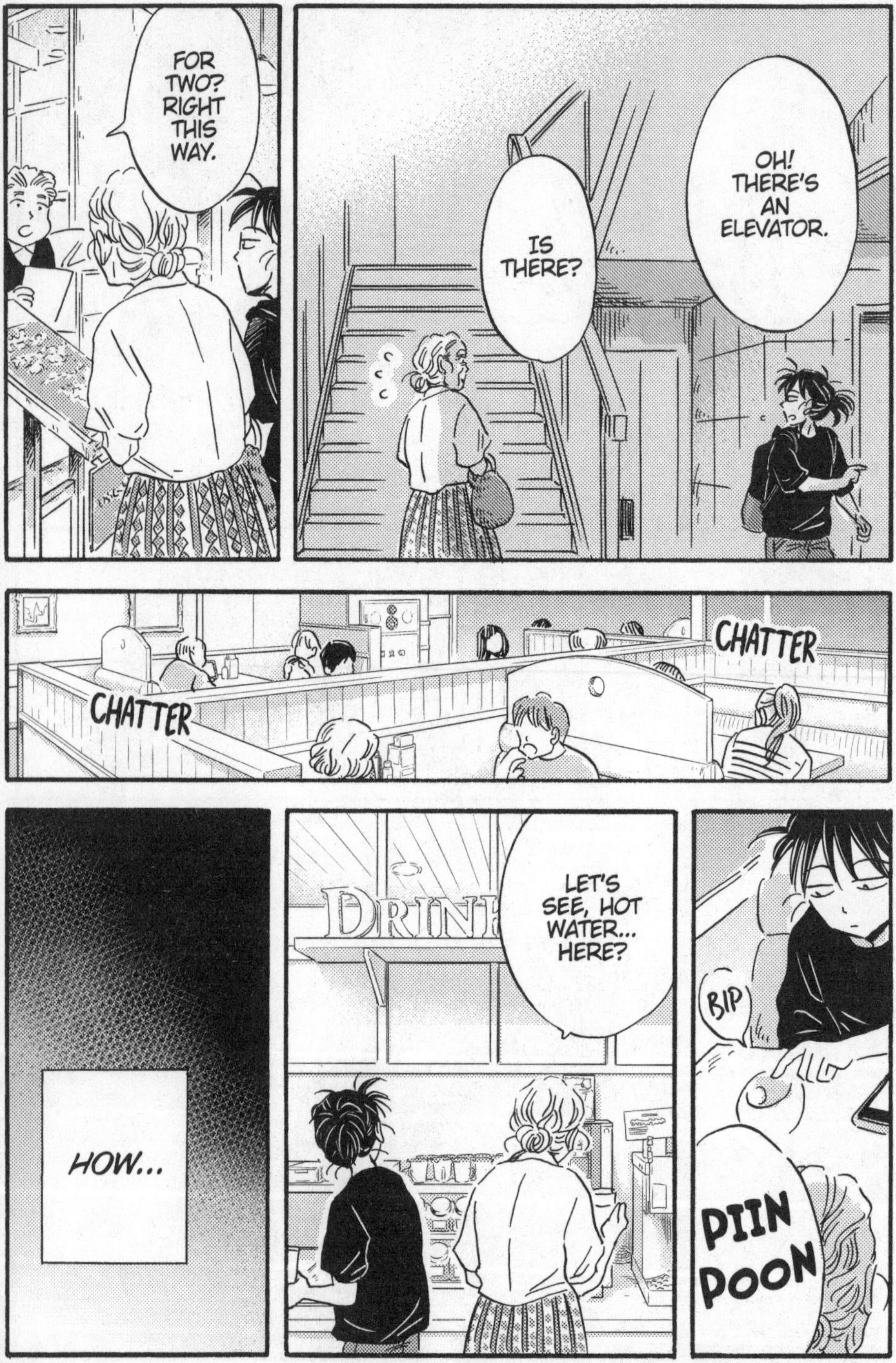
OH! THERE'S AN ELEVATOR.
IS THERE?
FOR TWO? RIGHT THIS WAY.
CHATTER
CHATTER
BIP
PIIN POON
LET'S SEE, HOT WATER... HERE?
HOW...

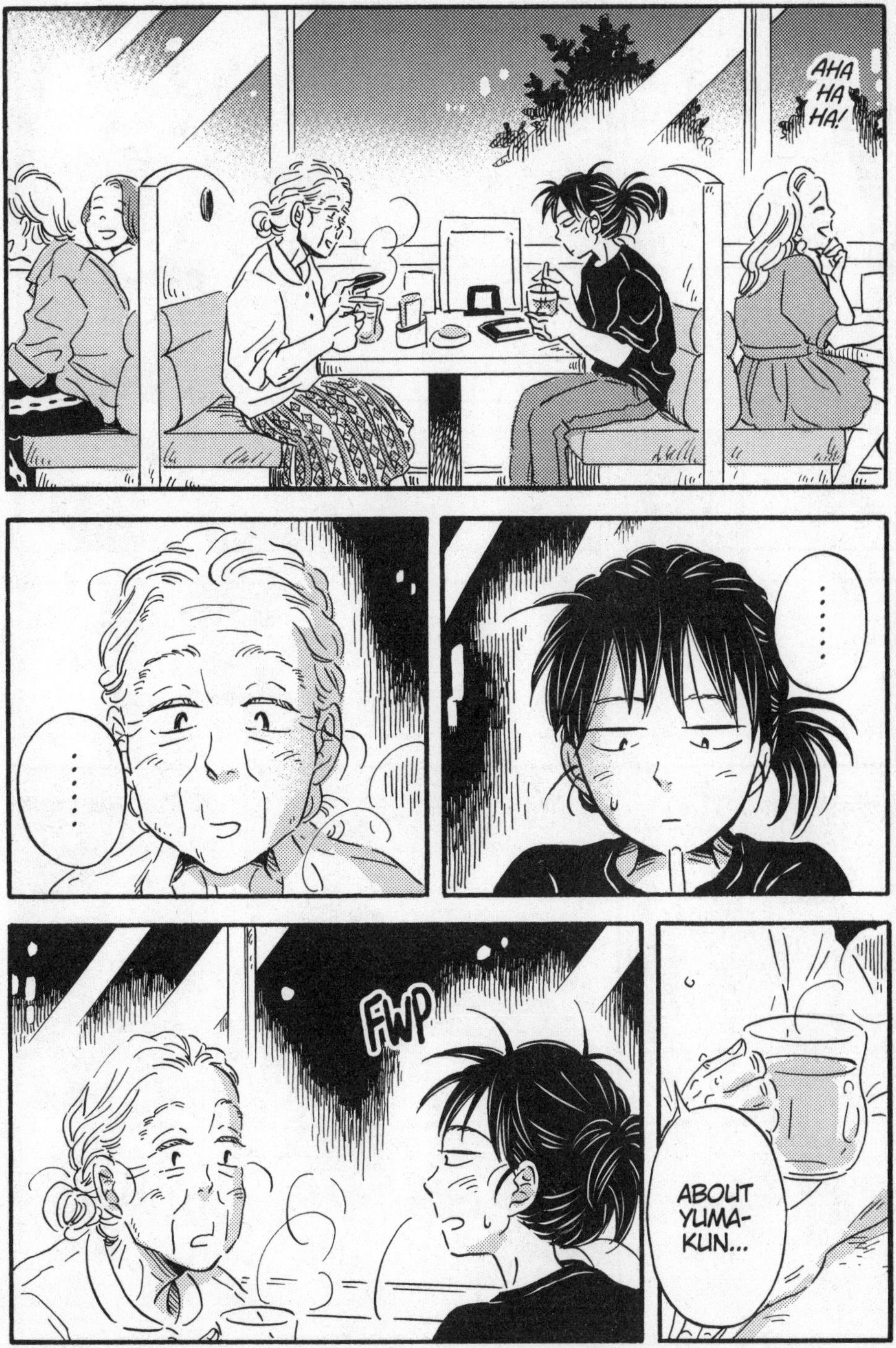
AHA HA HA!
......
......
ABOUT YUMA-KUN...
FWP

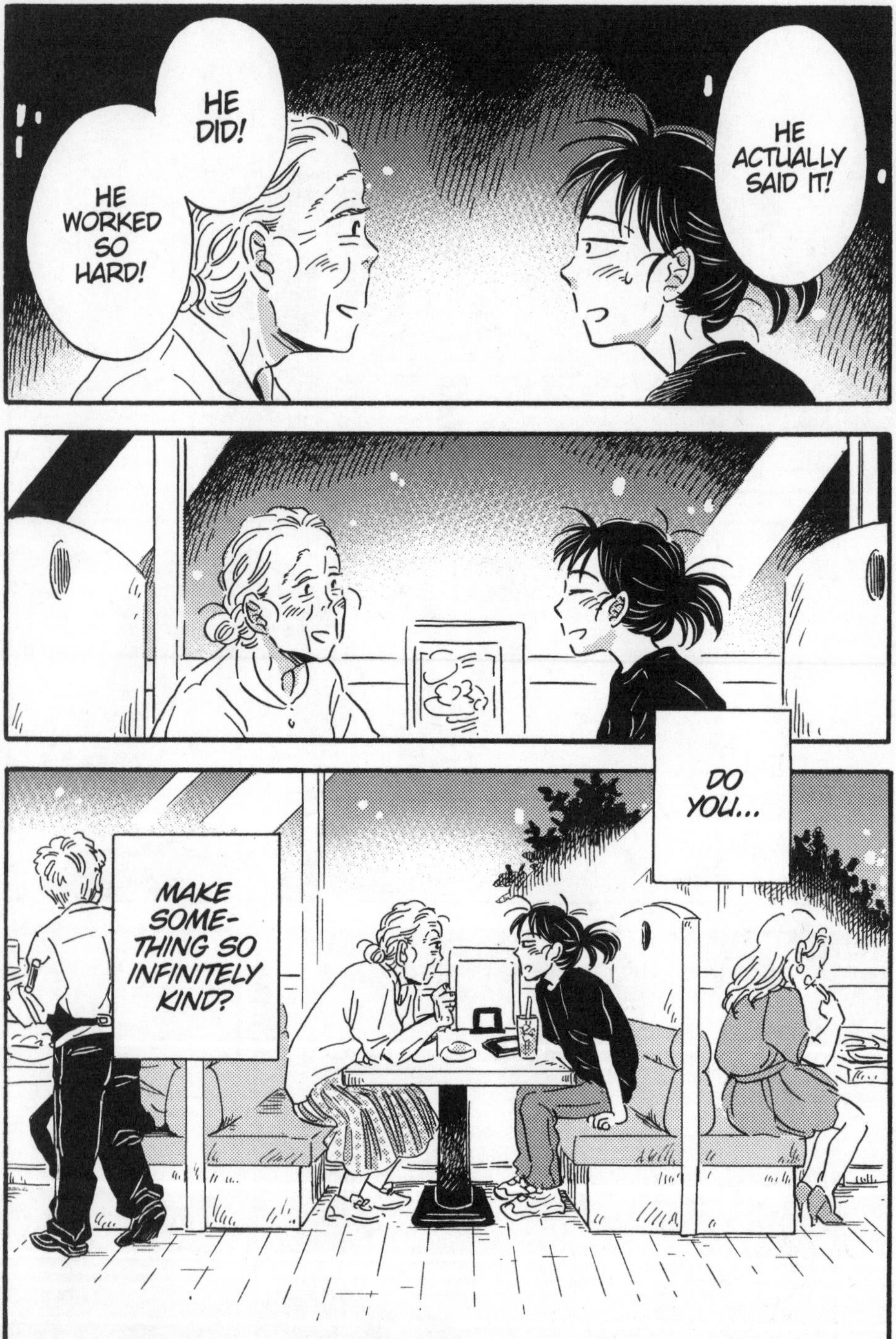
HE ACTUALLY SAID IT!
HE DID!
HE WORKED SO HARD!
DO YOU...
MAKE SOME-THING SO INFINITELY KIND?

Chapter 47/END

Please press
button for service.

metamorphosis

# Chapter 48

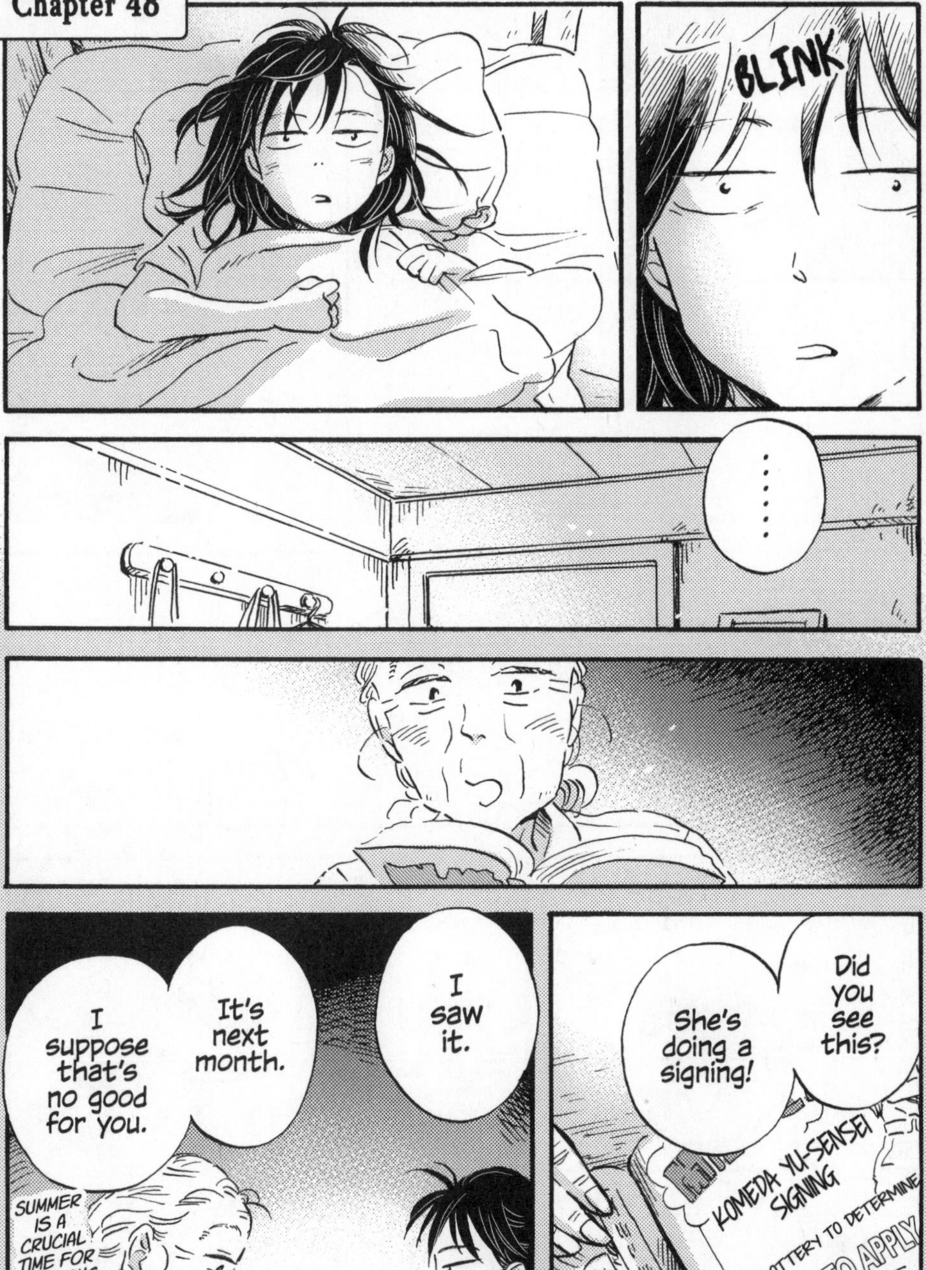

BLINK
......
Did you see this?
She's doing a signing!
KOMEDA YU-SENSEI SIGNING
A LOTTERY TO DETERMINE
HOW TO APPLY
I saw it.
It's next month.
I suppose that's no good for you.
SUMMER IS A CRUCIAL TIME FOR STUDYING FOR ENTRANCE EXAMS.

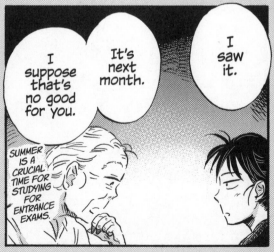

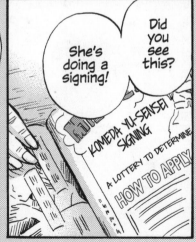

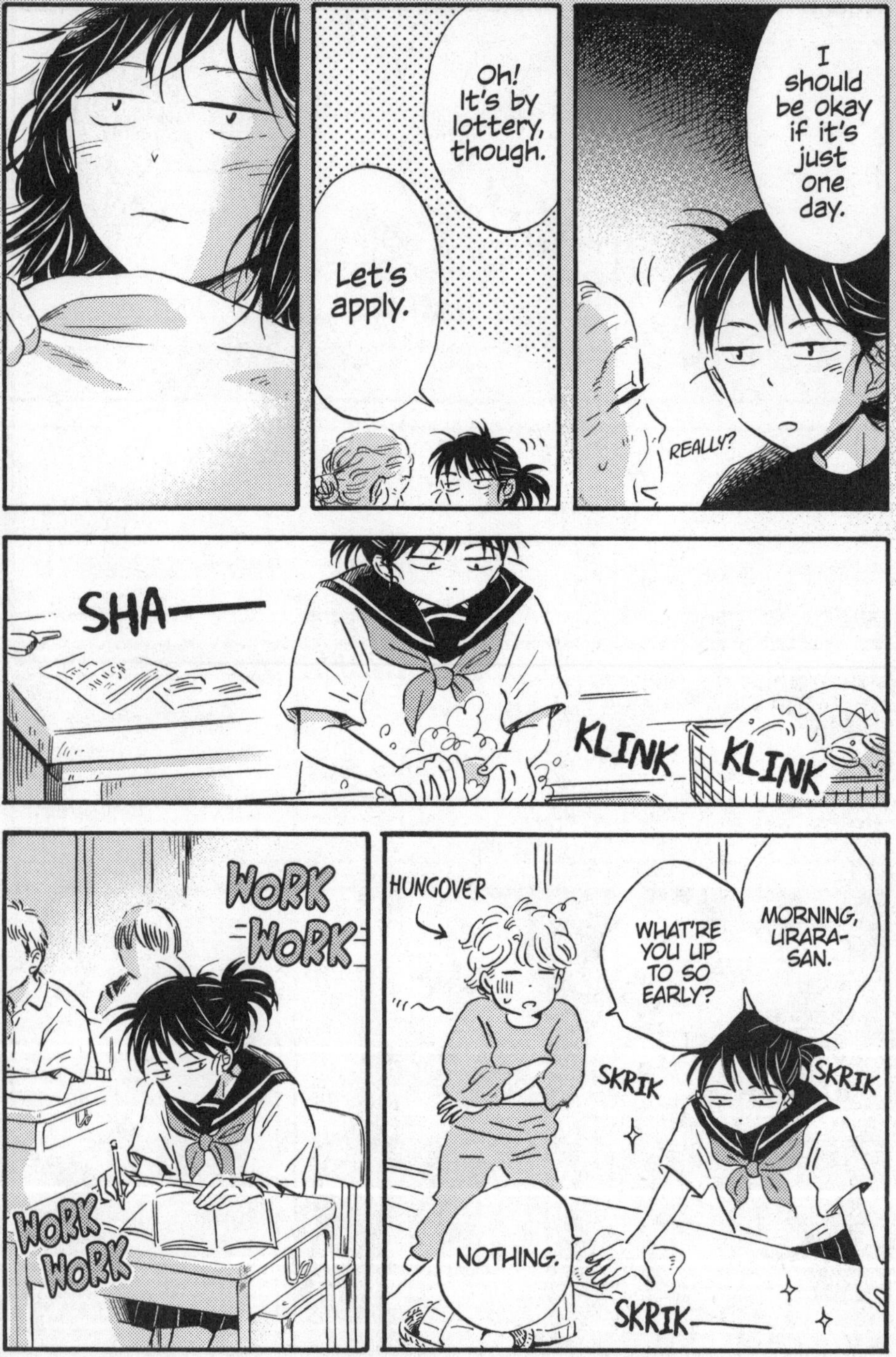
I should be okay if it's just one day.
REALLY?
Oh! It's by lottery, though.
Let's apply.
KLINK
KLINK
SHA——
MORNING, URARA-SAN.
WHAT'RE YOU UP TO SO EARLY?
HUNGOVER
SKRIK
SKRIK
NOTHING.
SKRIK——
WORK WORK
WORK WORK

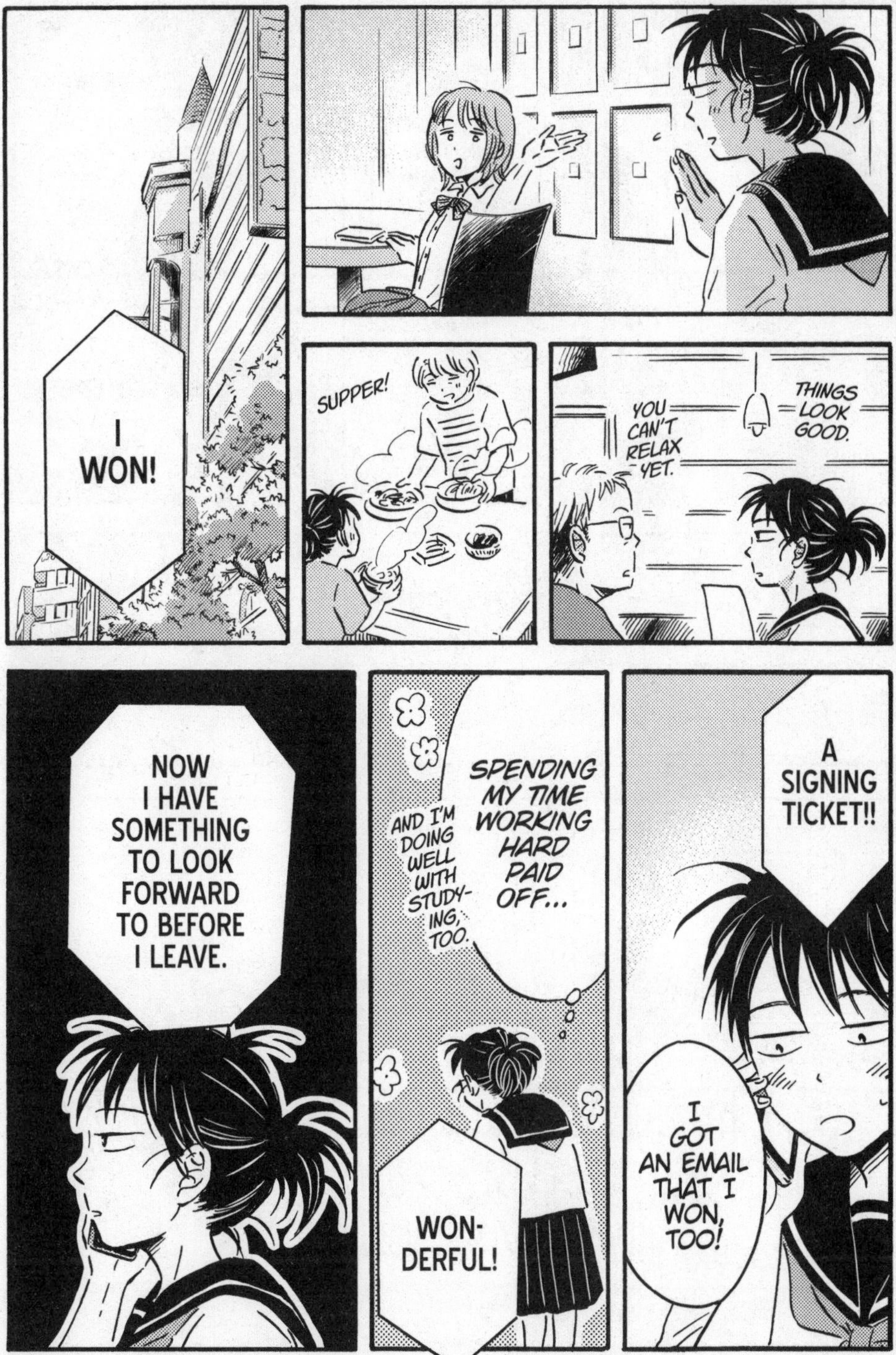
THINGS LOOK GOOD.
YOU CAN'T RELAX YET.
SUPPER!
I WON!
A SIGNING TICKET!!
I GOT AN EMAIL THAT I WON, TOO!
SPENDING MY TIME WORKING HARD PAID OFF...
AND I'M DOING WELL WITH STUDYING, TOO.
WONDERFUL!
NOW I HAVE SOMETHING TO LOOK FORWARD TO BEFORE I LEAVE.

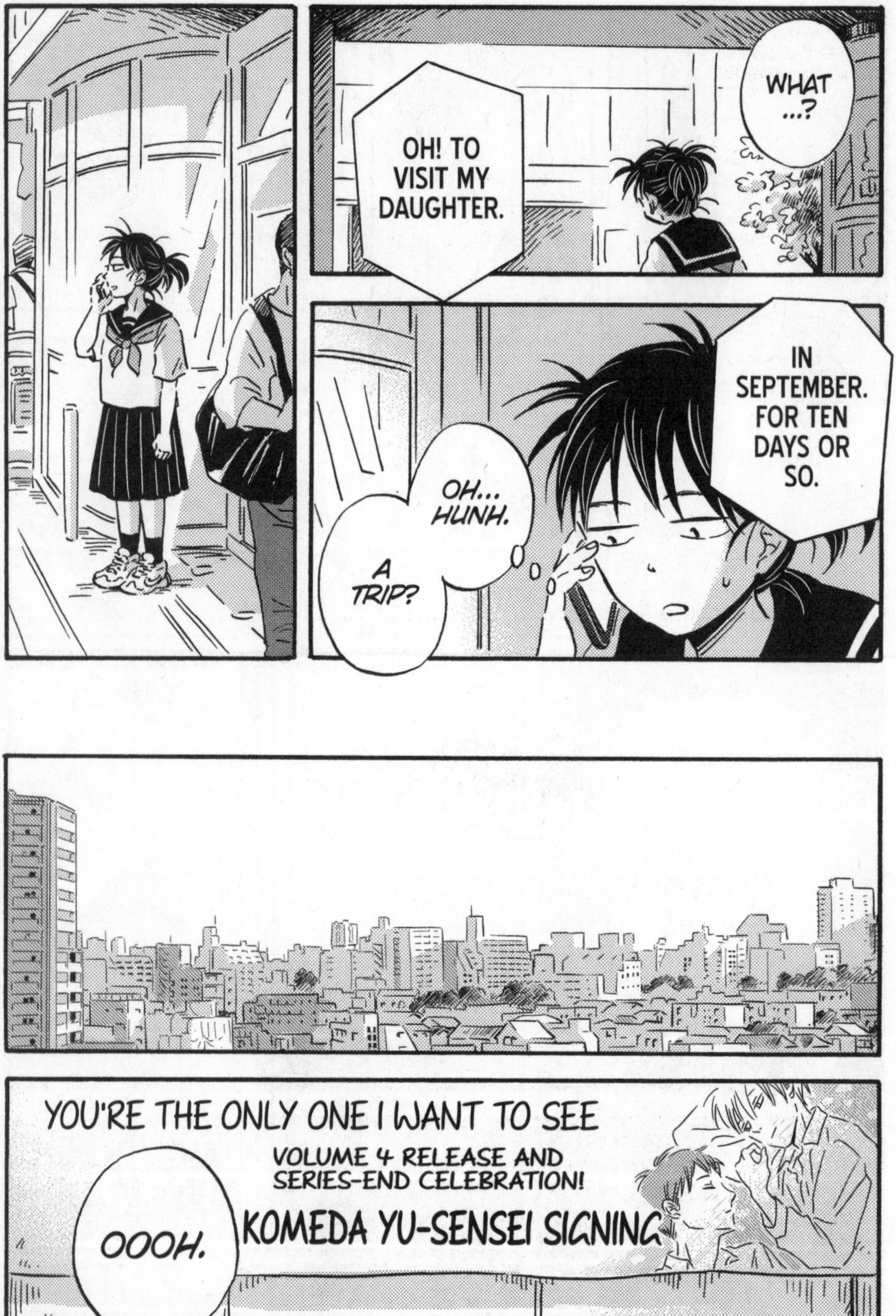
WHAT ...?
OH! TO VISIT MY DAUGHTER.
IN SEPTEMBER. FOR TEN DAYS OR SO.
OH... HUNH.
A TRIP?
YOU'RE THE ONLY ONE I WANT TO SEE
VOLUME 4 RELEASE AND SERIES-END CELEBRATION!
KOMEDA YU-SENSEI SIGNING
OOOH.

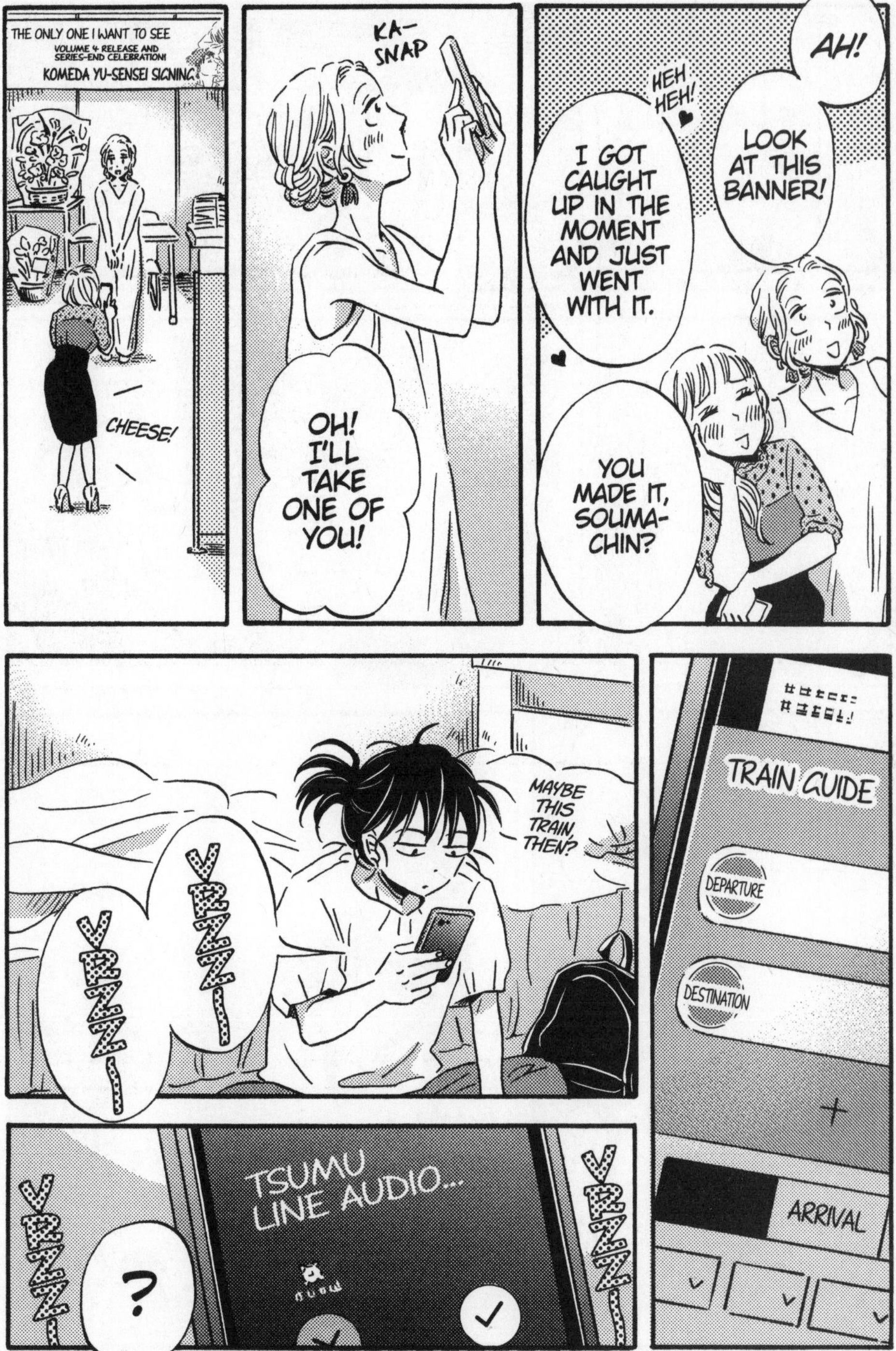
AH!
LOOK AT THIS BANNER!
HEH HEH!
I GOT CAUGHT UP IN THE MOMENT AND JUST WENT WITH IT.
YOU MADE IT, SOUMA-CHIN?
KA-SNAP
OH! I'LL TAKE ONE OF YOU!
THE ONLY ONE I WANT TO SEE
VOLUME 4 RELEASE AND SERIES-END CELEBRATION!
KOMEDA YU-SENSEI SIGNING
CHEESE!
TRAIN GUIDE
DEPARTURE
DESTINATION
ARRIVAL
MAYBE THIS TRAIN, THEN?
VRZZZ
VRZZZ
VRZZZ
TSUMU LINE AUDIO...
?
VRZZZ

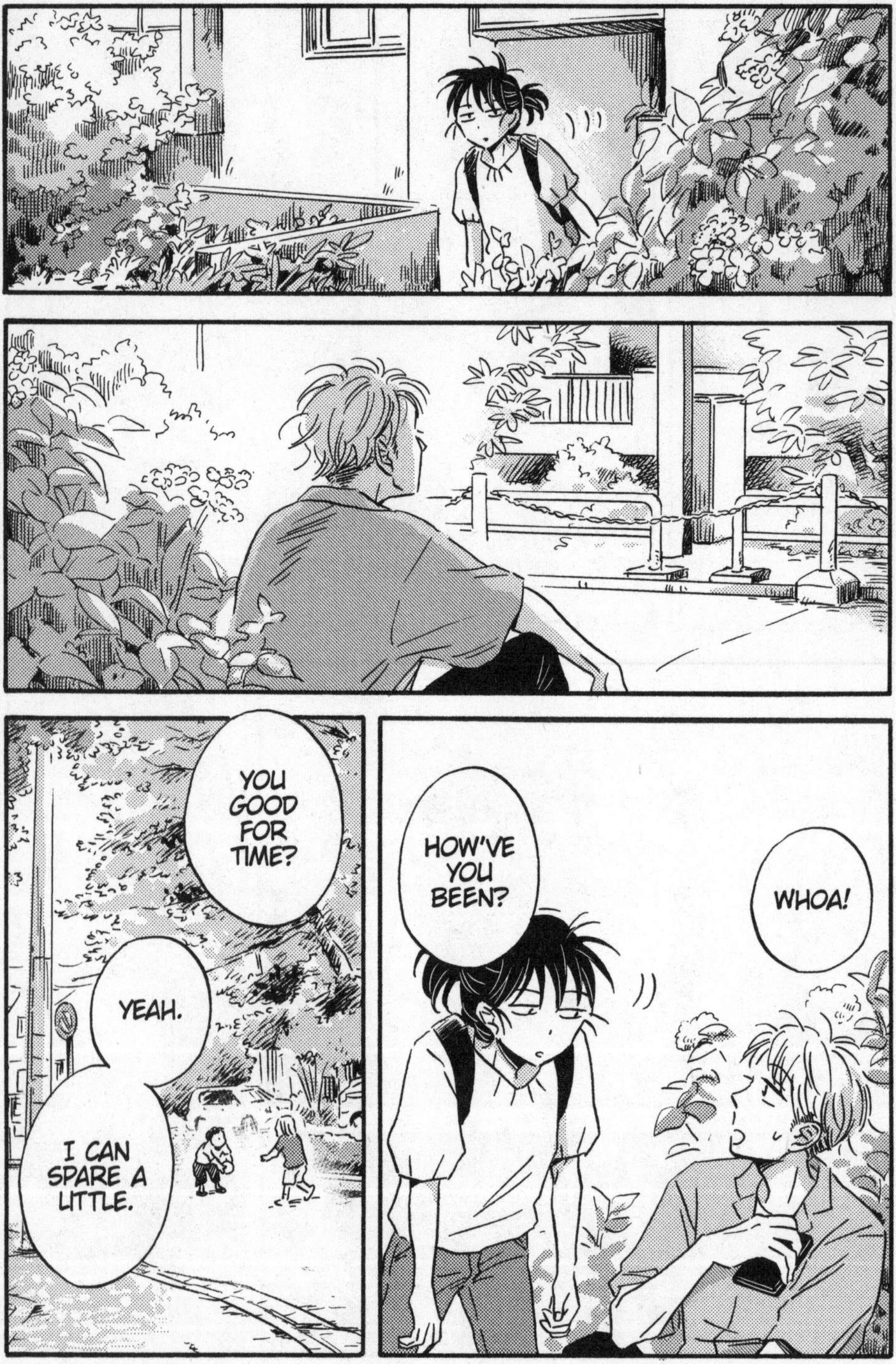
WHOA!
HOW'VE YOU BEEN?
YOU GOOD FOR TIME?
YEAH.
I CAN SPARE A LITTLE.

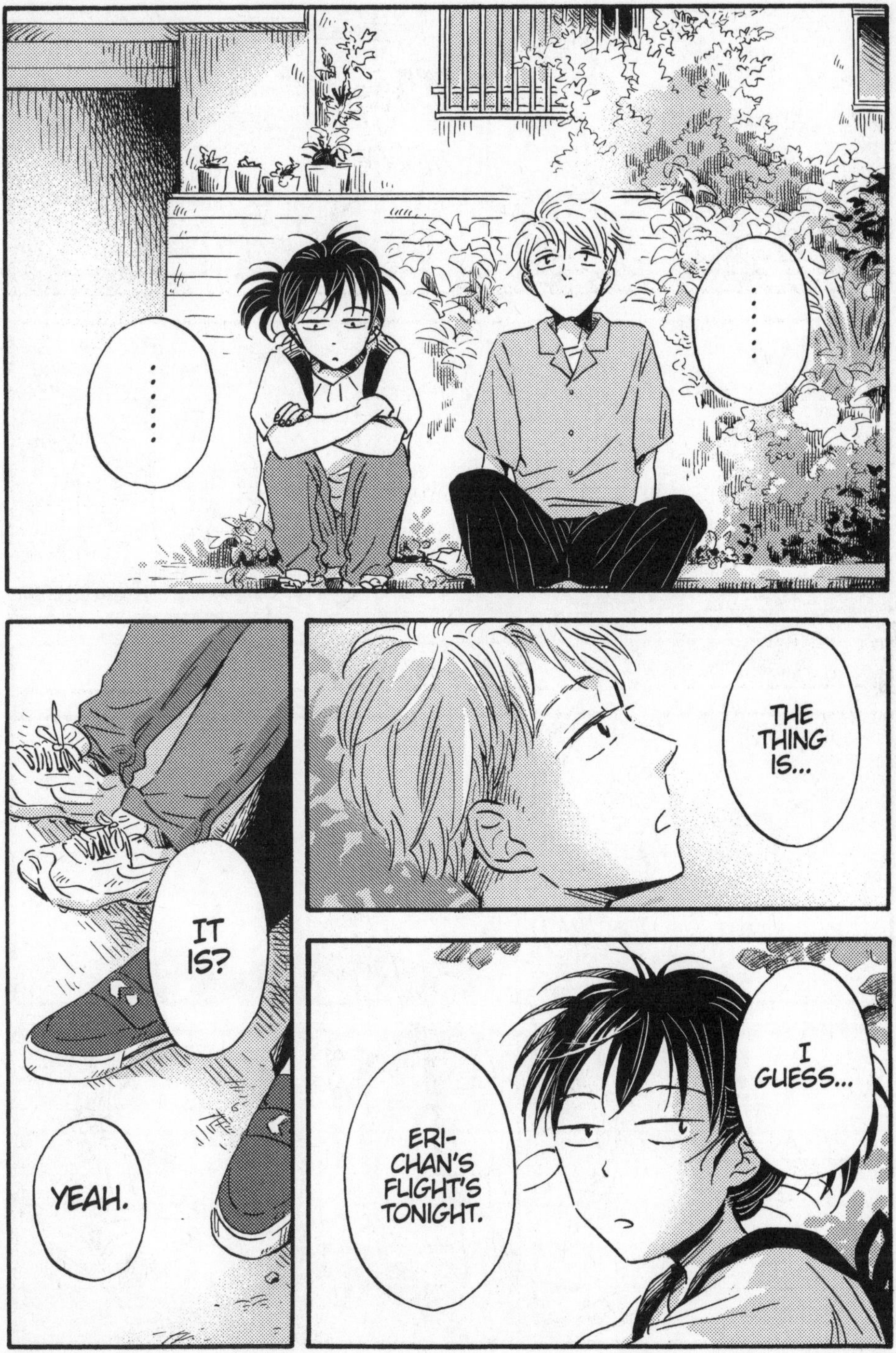
......
......
THE THING IS...
I GUESS...
ERI-CHAN'S FLIGHT'S TONIGHT.
IT IS?
YEAH.

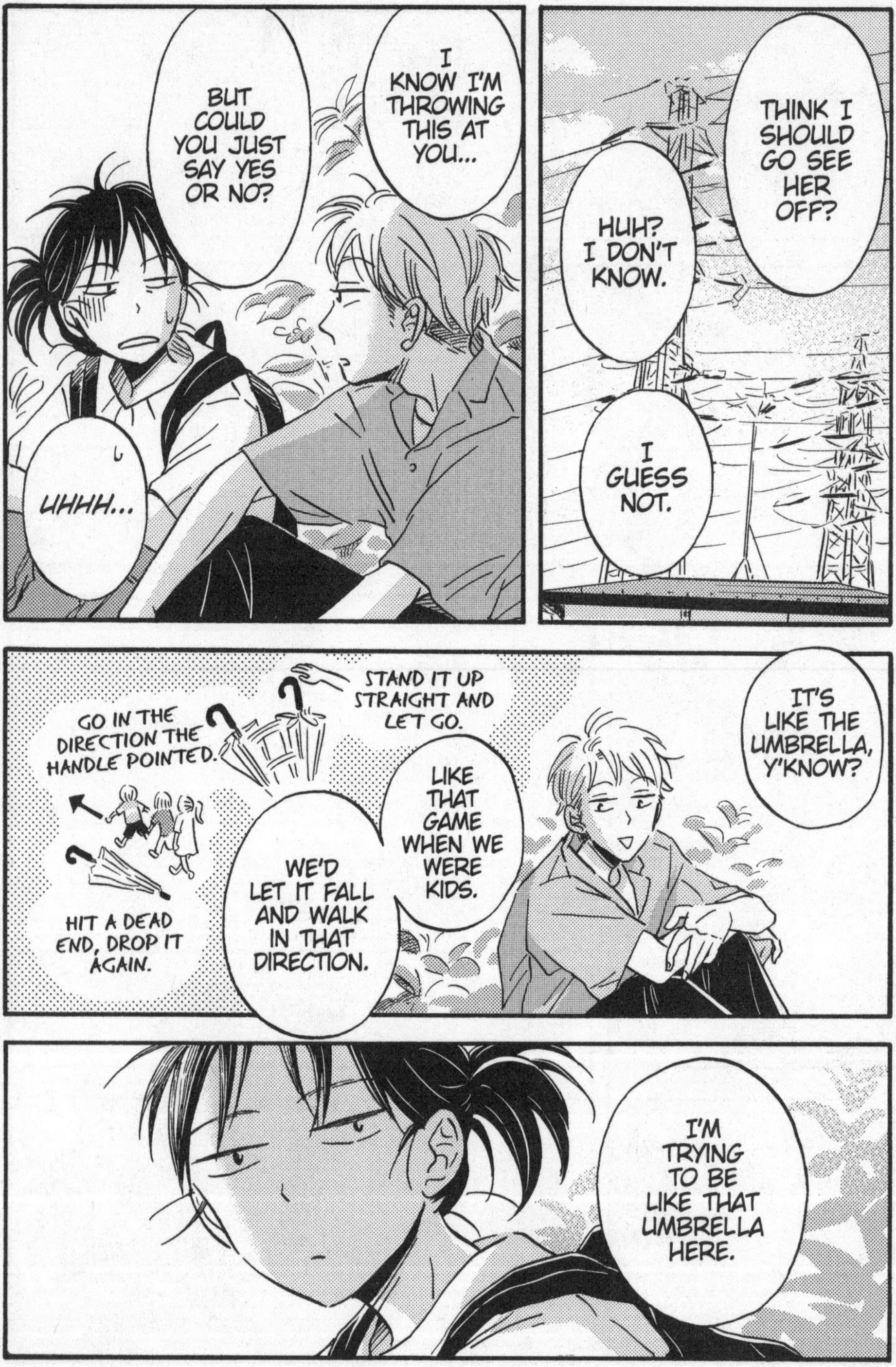
THINK I SHOULD GO SEE HER OFF?
HUH? I DON'T KNOW.
I GUESS NOT.
I KNOW I'M THROWING THIS AT YOU...
BUT COULD YOU JUST SAY YES OR NO?
UHHH...
IT'S LIKE THE UMBRELLA, Y'KNOW?
LIKE THAT GAME WHEN WE WERE KIDS.
STAND IT UP STRAIGHT AND LET GO.
WE'D LET IT FALL AND WALK IN THAT DIRECTION.
GO IN THE DIRECTION THE HANDLE POINTED.
HIT A DEAD END, DROP IT AGAIN.
I'M TRYING TO BE LIKE THAT UMBRELLA HERE.

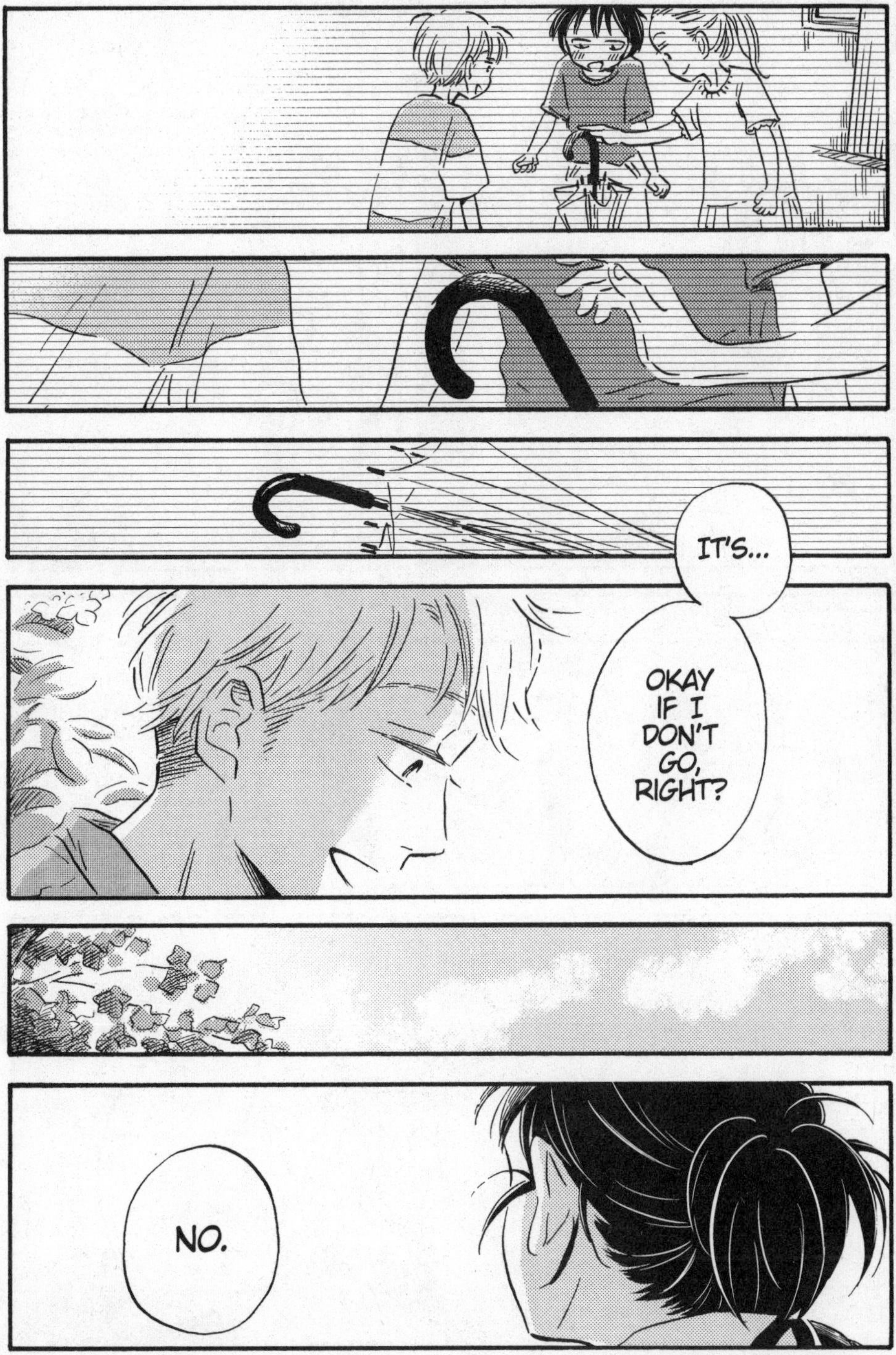
IT'S...
OKAY IF I DON'T GO, RIGHT?
NO.

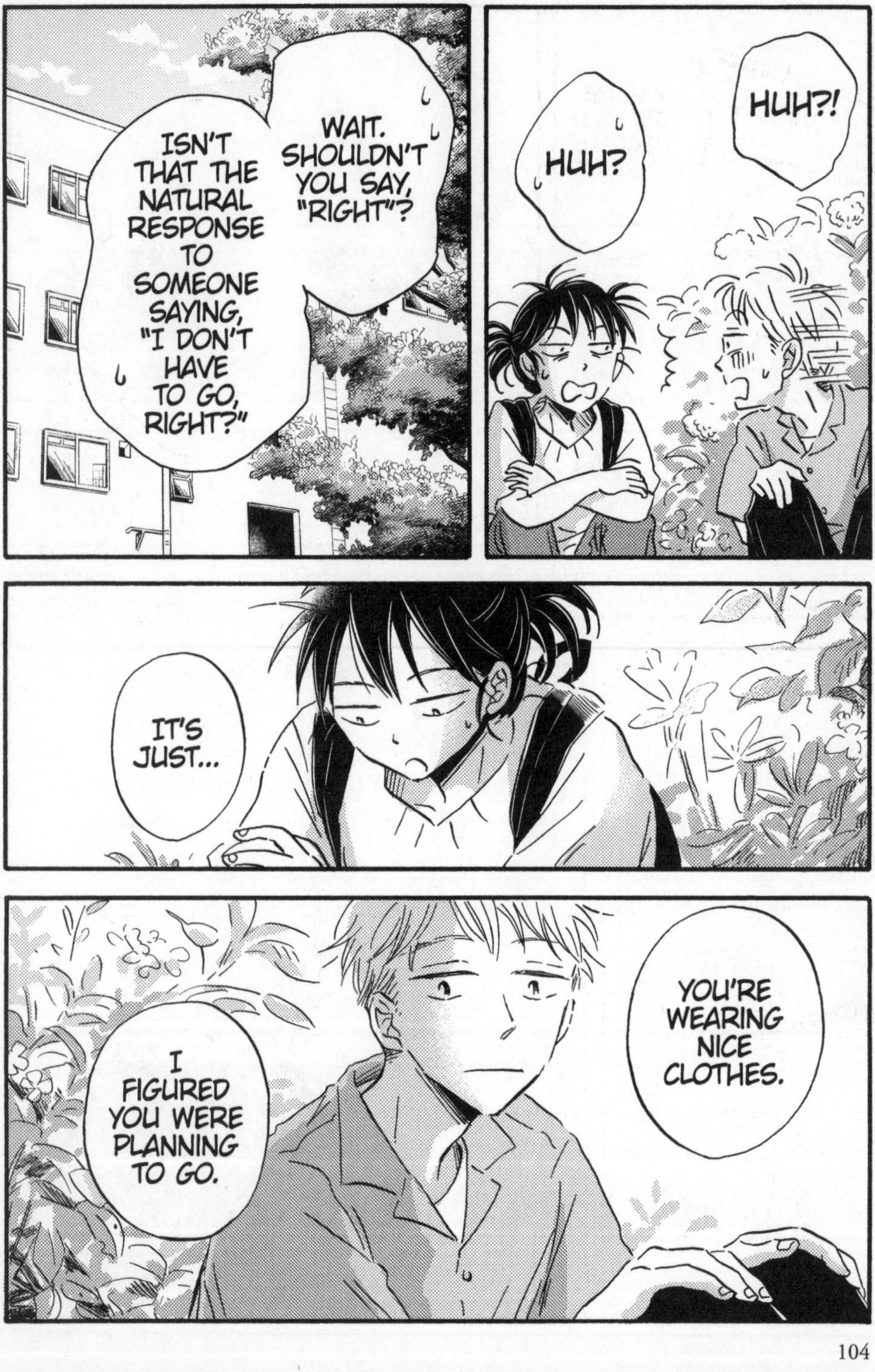
HUH?!
HUH?
WAIT. SHOULDN'T YOU SAY, "RIGHT"?
ISN'T THAT THE NATURAL RESPONSE TO SOMEONE SAYING, "I DON'T HAVE TO GO, RIGHT?"
IT'S JUST...
YOU'RE WEARING NICE CLOTHES.
I FIGURED YOU WERE PLANNING TO GO.

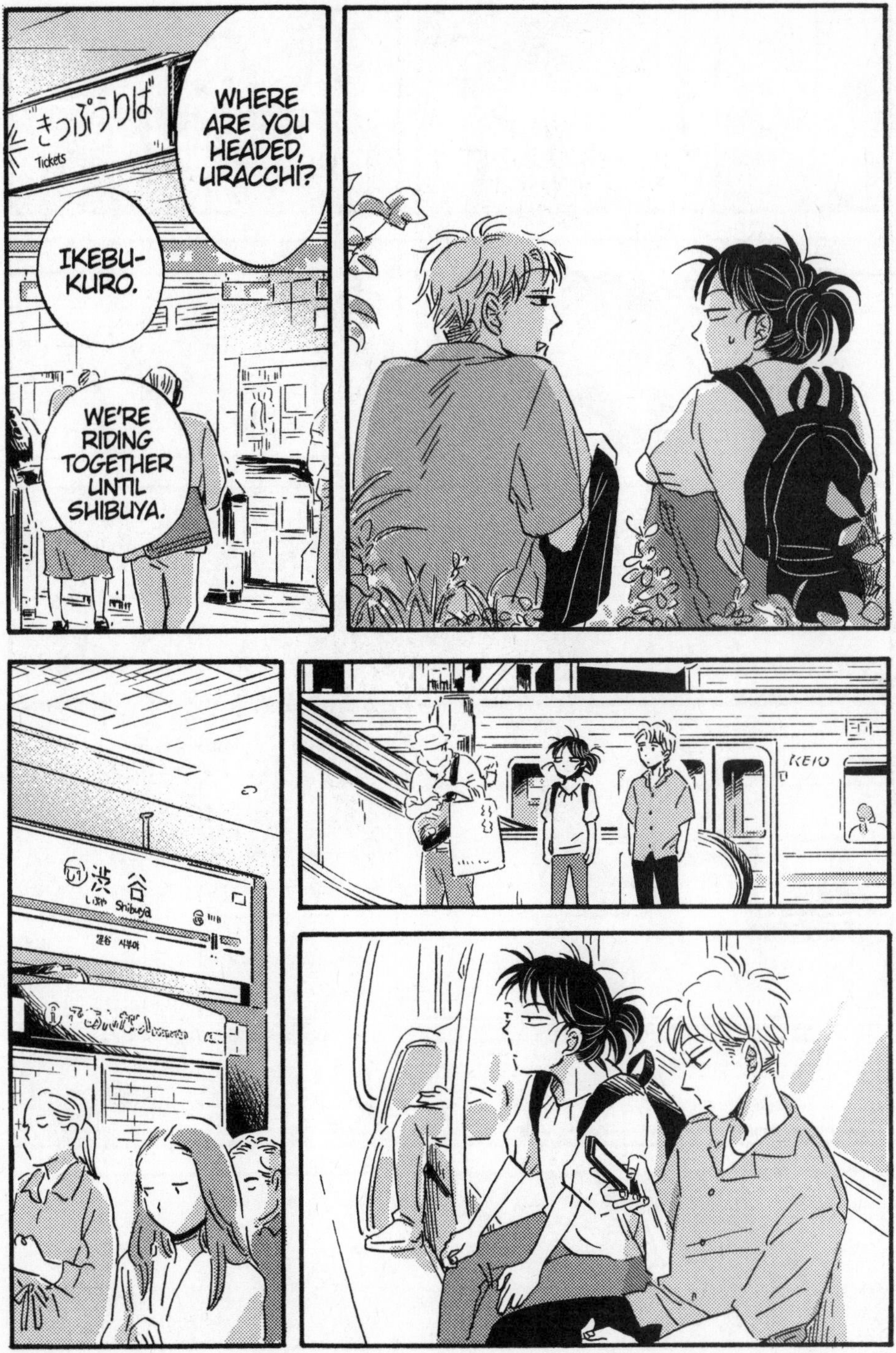

きっぷうりば
Tickets
WHERE ARE YOU HEADED, URACCHI?
IKEBUKURO.
WE'RE RIDING TOGETHER UNTIL SHIBUYA.
KEIO
渋谷
Shibuya

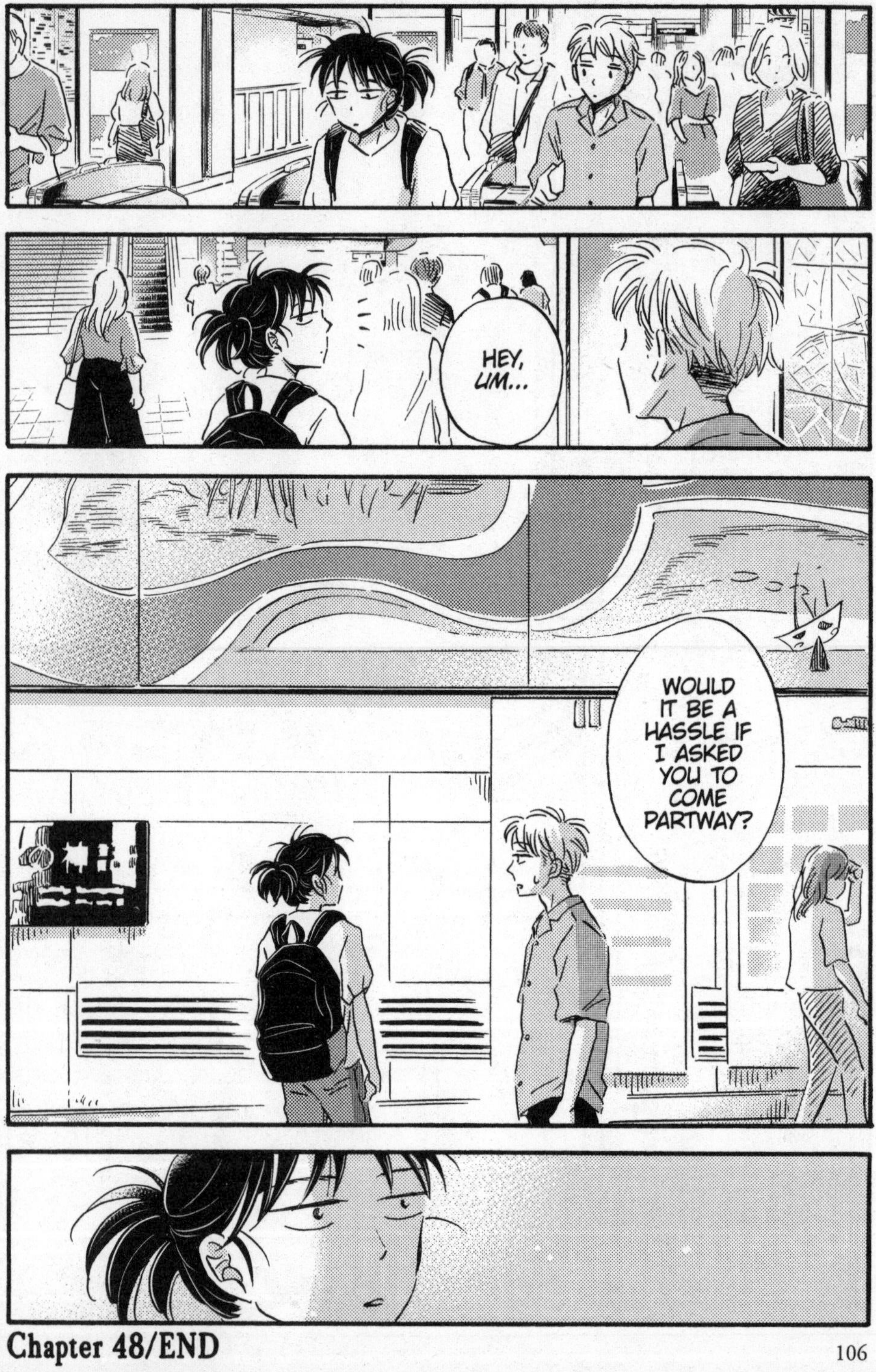
HEY, UM...
WOULD IT BE A HASSLE IF I ASKED YOU TO COME PARTWAY?

Chapter 48/END

metamorphosis

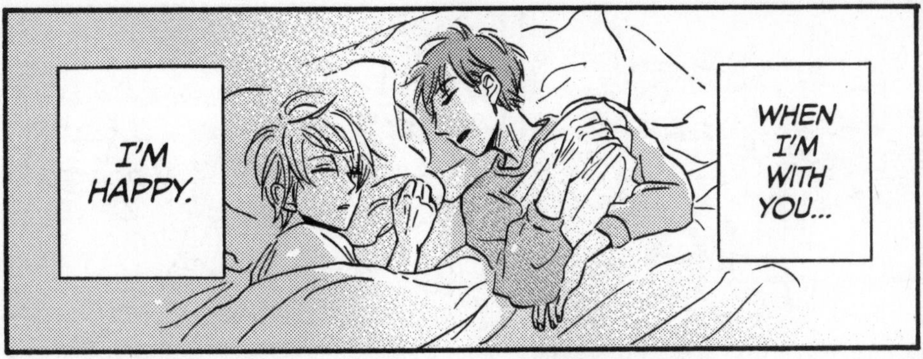
WHEN I'M WITH YOU...
I'M HAPPY.

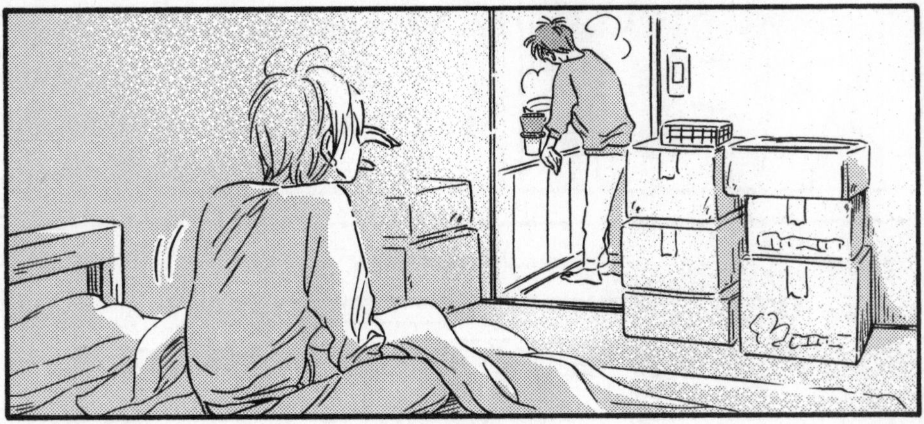

Chapter 49

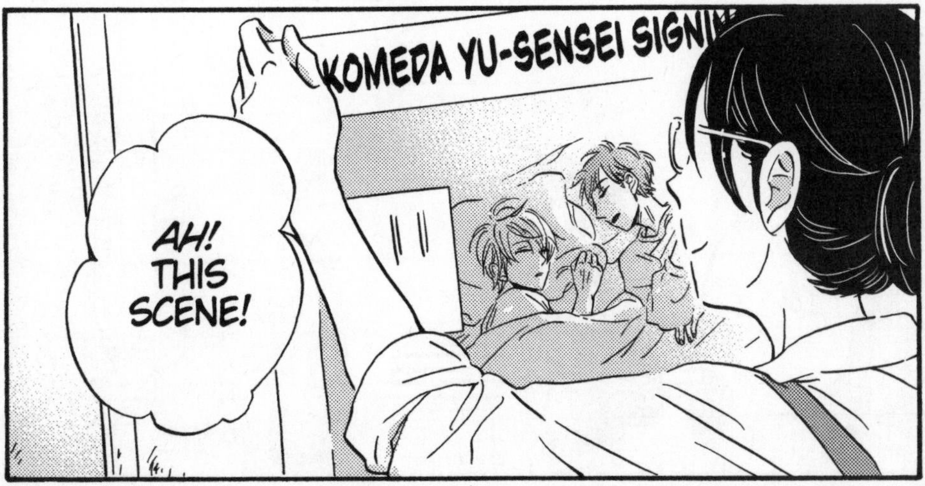
KOMEDA YU-SENSEI SIGN
AH! THIS SCENE!

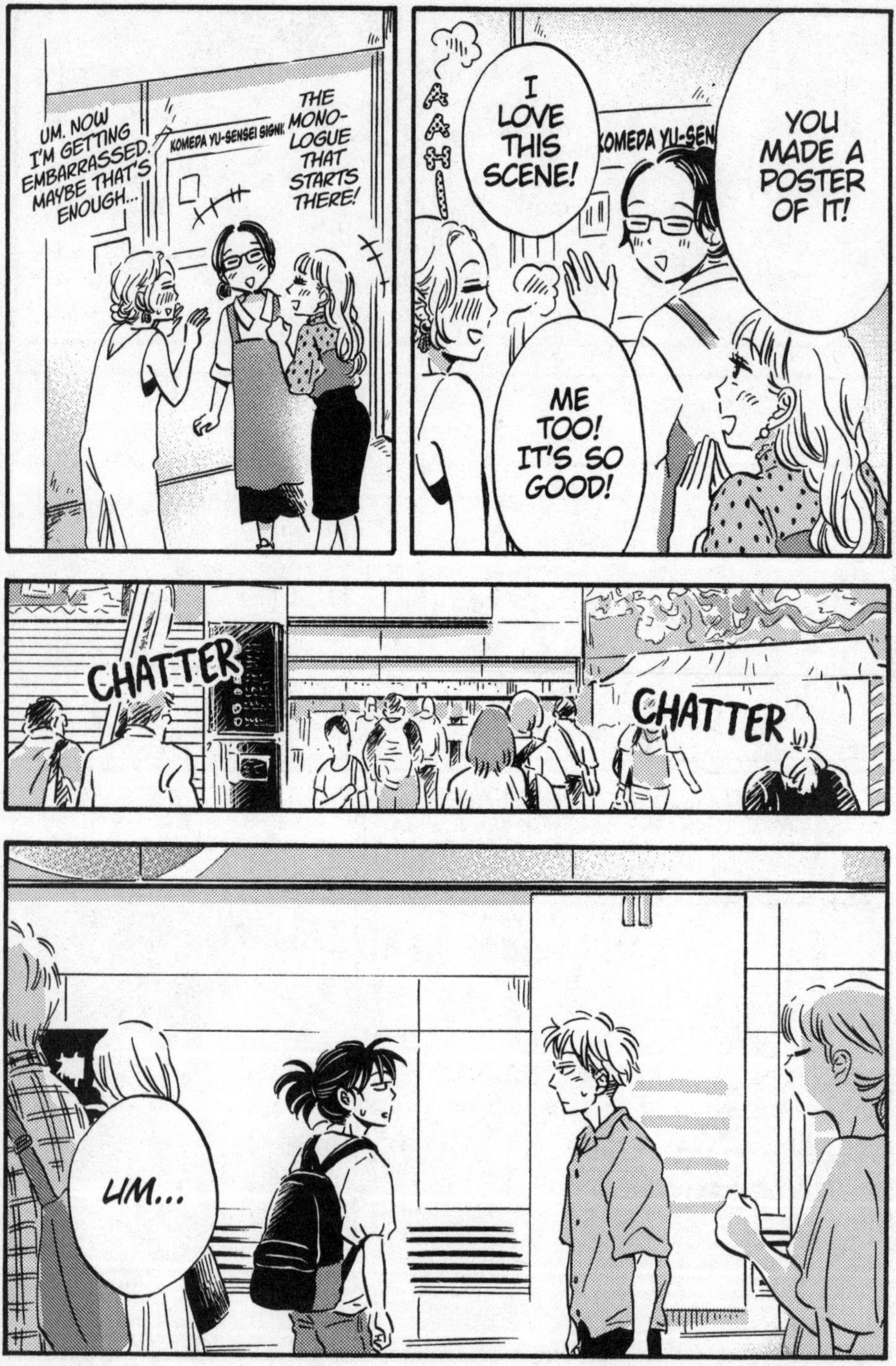
YOU MADE A POSTER OF IT!
KOMEDA YU-SEN
I LOVE THIS SCENE!
AAH—
ME TOO! IT'S SO GOOD!
THE MONOLOGUE THAT STARTS THERE!
KOMEDA YU-SENSEI SIGNI
UM. NOW I'M GETTING EMBARRASSED. MAYBE THAT'S ENOUGH...
CHATTER
CHATTER
UM...

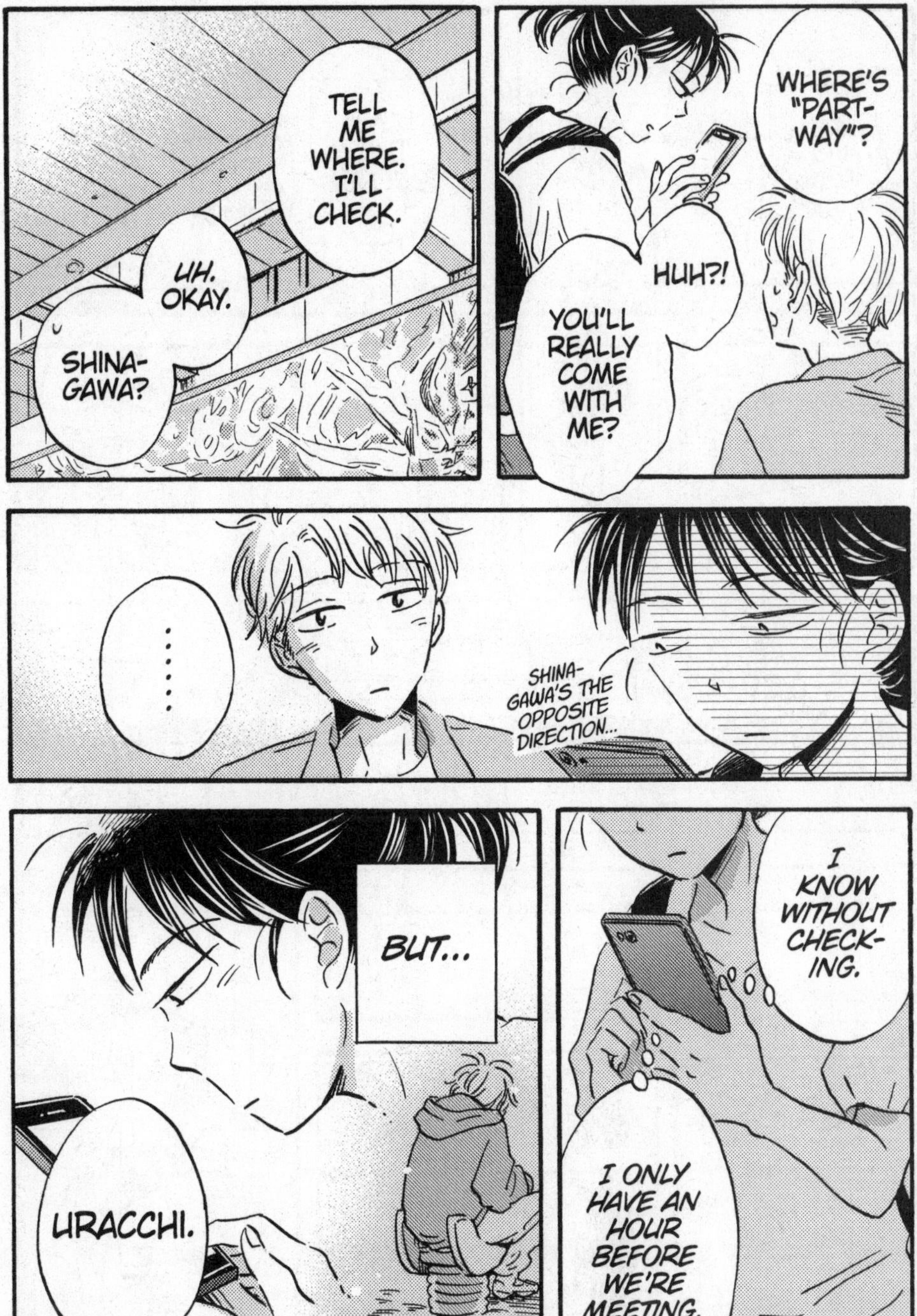
WHERE'S "PART-WAY"?
HUH?!
YOU'LL REALLY COME WITH ME?
TELL ME WHERE. I'LL CHECK.
UH. OKAY.
SHINA-GAWA?
SHINA-GAWA'S THE OPPOSITE DIRECTION...
......
I KNOW WITHOUT CHECK-ING.
I ONLY HAVE AN HOUR BEFORE WE'RE MEETING.
BUT...
URACCHI.

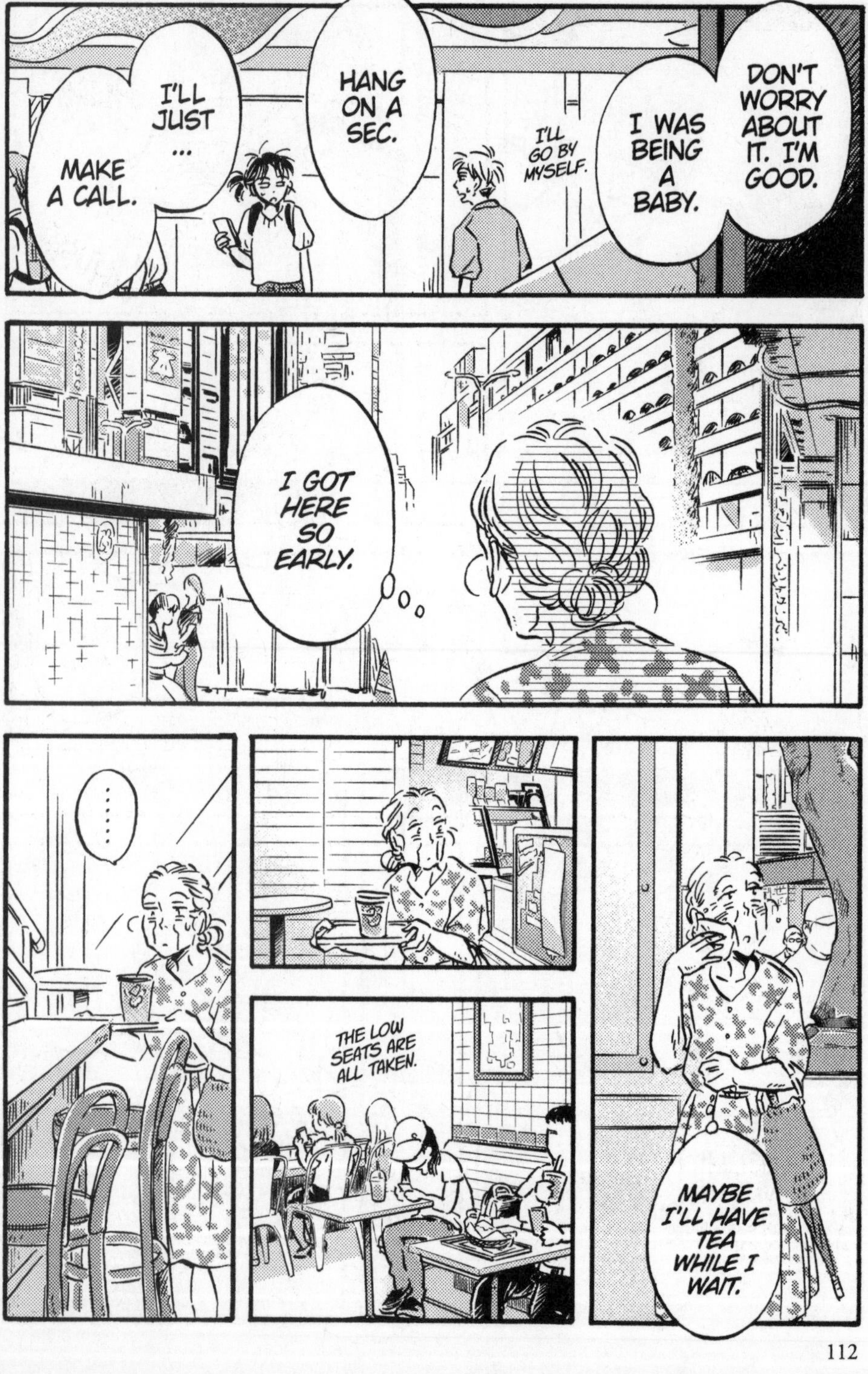
DON'T WORRY ABOUT IT. I'M GOOD.
I WAS BEING A BABY.
I'LL GO BY MYSELF.
HANG ON A SEC.
I'LL JUST ...
MAKE A CALL.
I GOT HERE SO EARLY.
MAYBE I'LL HAVE TEA WHILE I WAIT.
THE LOW SEATS ARE ALL TAKEN.
......

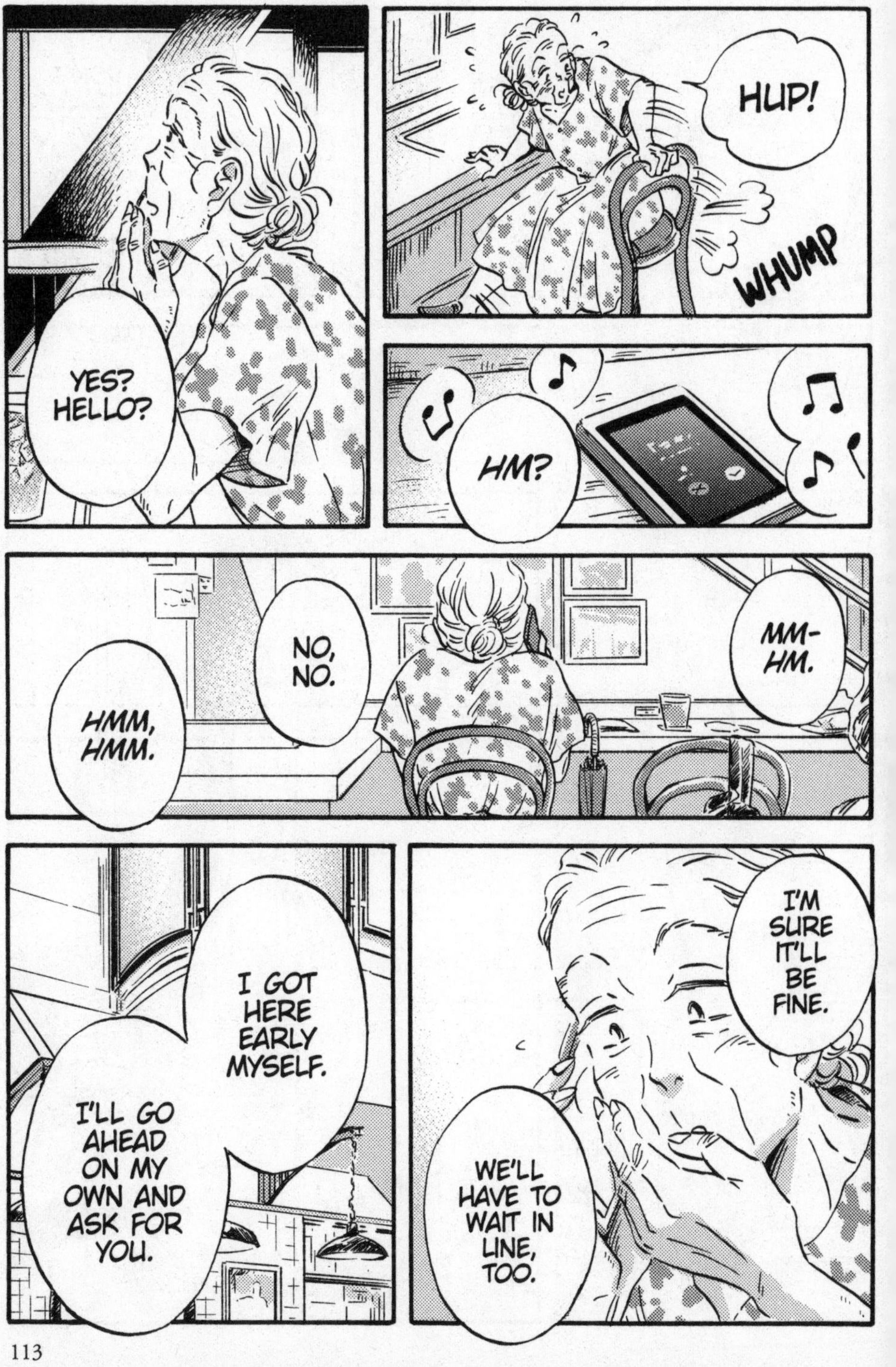
HUP!
WHUMP
HM?
YES? HELLO?
MM-HM.
NO, NO.
HMM, HMM.
I'M SURE IT'LL BE FINE.
WE'LL HAVE TO WAIT IN LINE, TOO.
I GOT HERE EARLY MYSELF.
I'LL GO AHEAD ON MY OWN AND ASK FOR YOU.

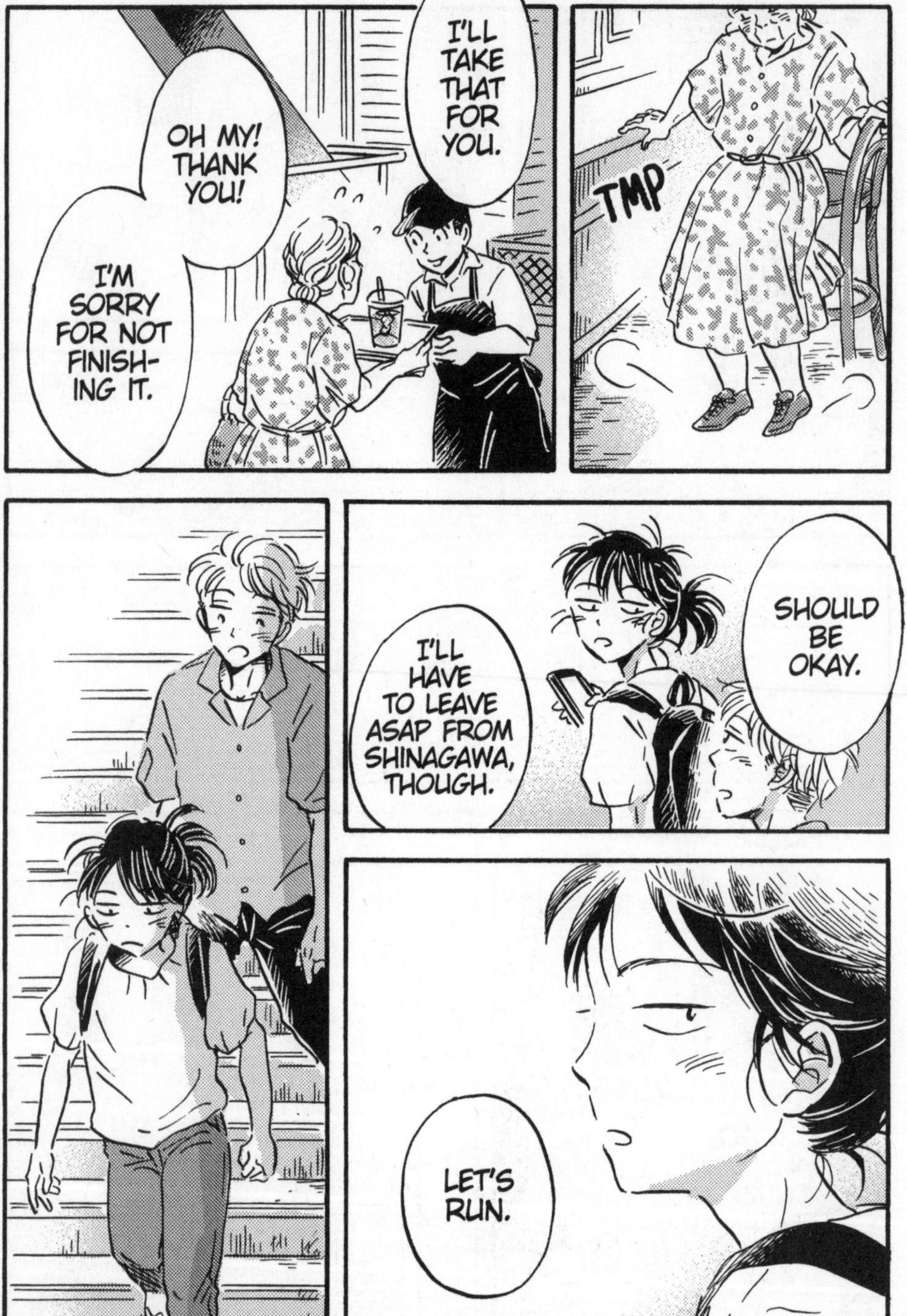
TMP
I'LL TAKE THAT FOR YOU.
OH MY! THANK YOU!
I'M SORRY FOR NOT FINISHING IT.
SHOULD BE OKAY.
I'LL HAVE TO LEAVE ASAP FROM SHINAGAWA, THOUGH.
LET'S RUN.

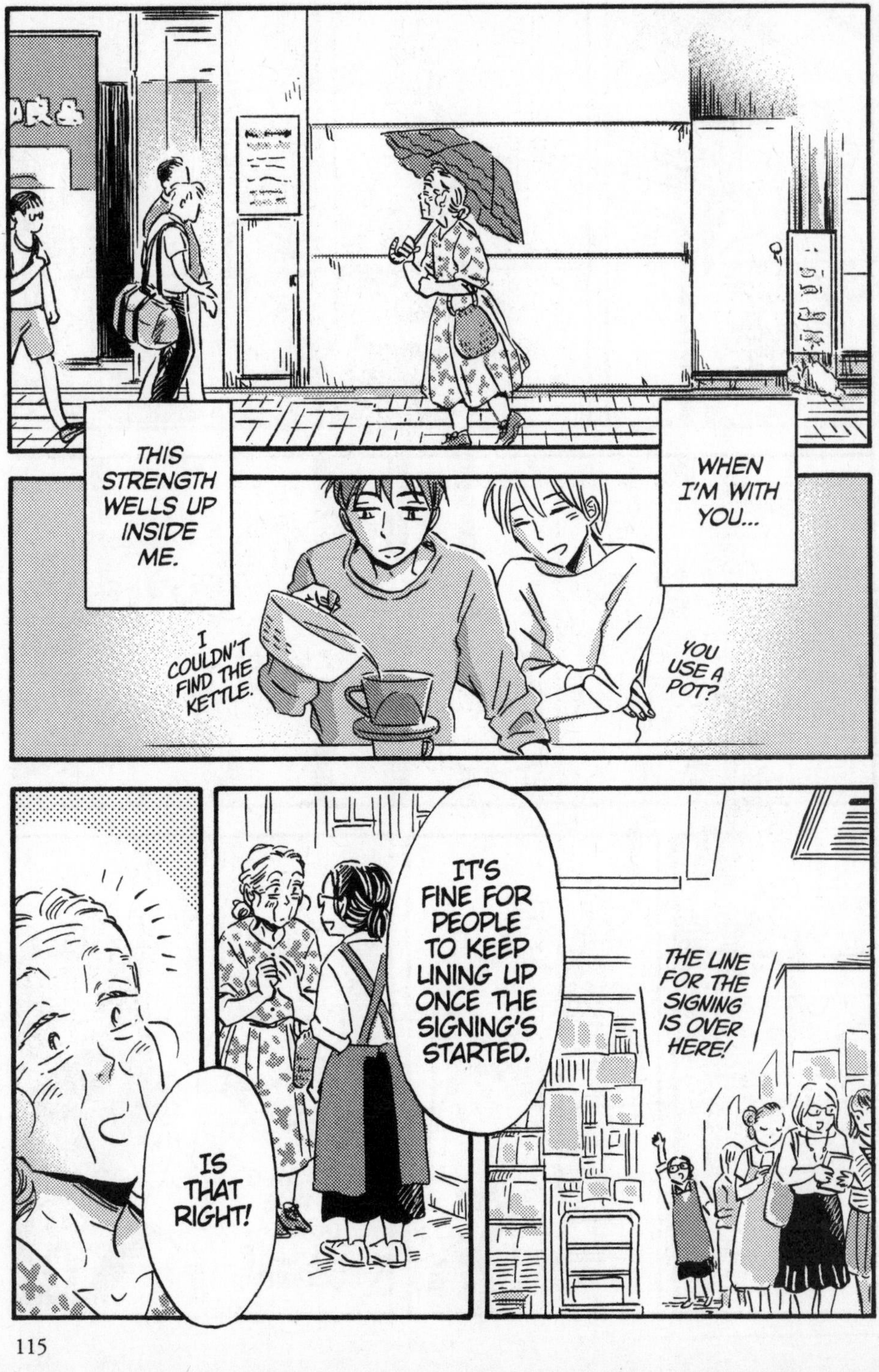
WHEN I'M WITH YOU...
THIS STRENGTH WELLS UP INSIDE ME.
YOU USE A POT?
I COULDN'T FIND THE KETTLE.
THE LINE FOR THE SIGNING IS OVER HERE!
IT'S FINE FOR PEOPLE TO KEEP LINING UP ONCE THE SIGNING'S STARTED.
IS THAT RIGHT!

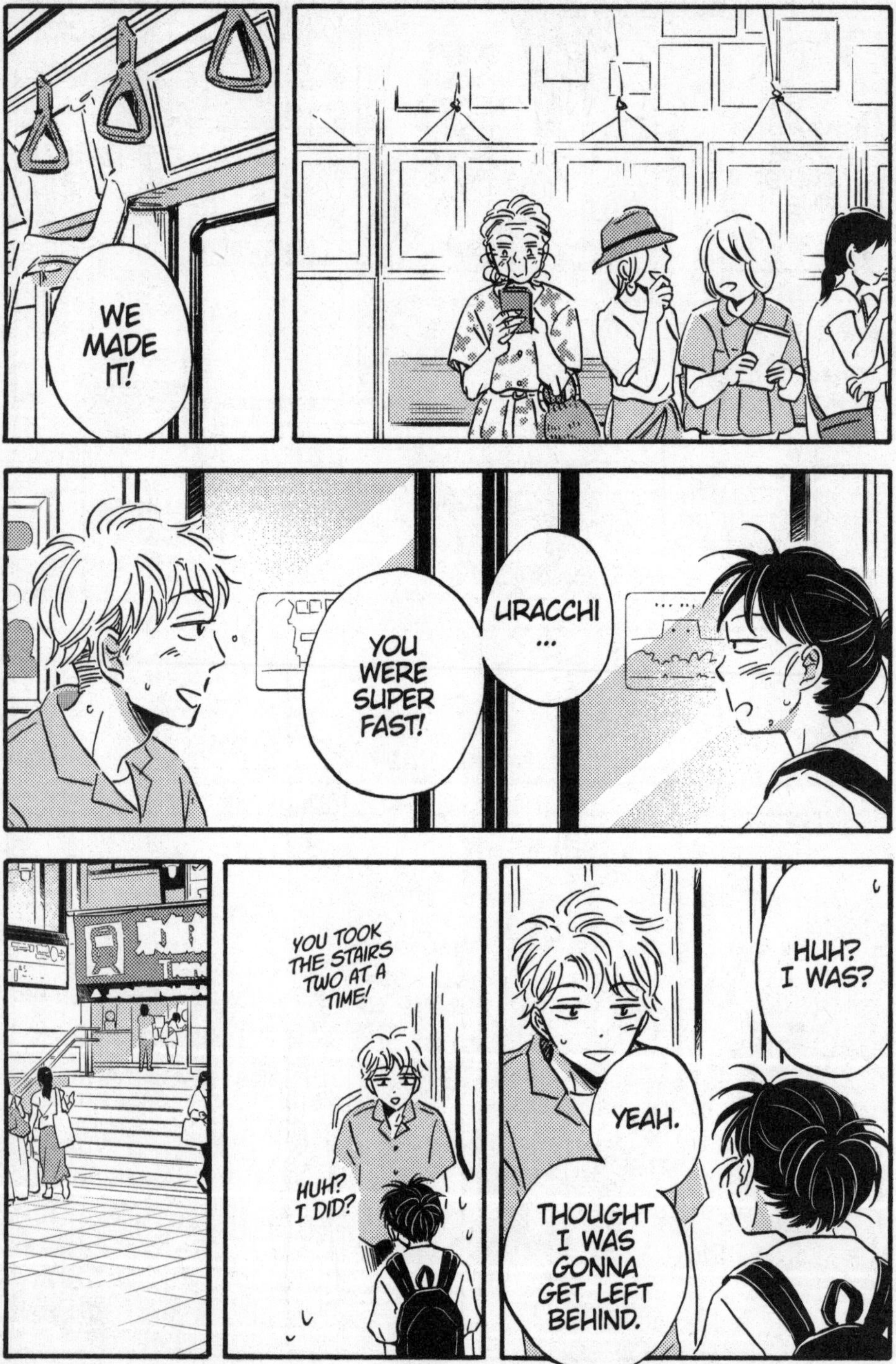
WE MADE IT!
URACCHI ...
YOU WERE SUPER FAST!
HUH? I WAS?
YEAH.
THOUGHT I WAS GONNA GET LEFT BEHIND.
YOU TOOK THE STAIRS TWO AT A TIME!
HUH? I DID?

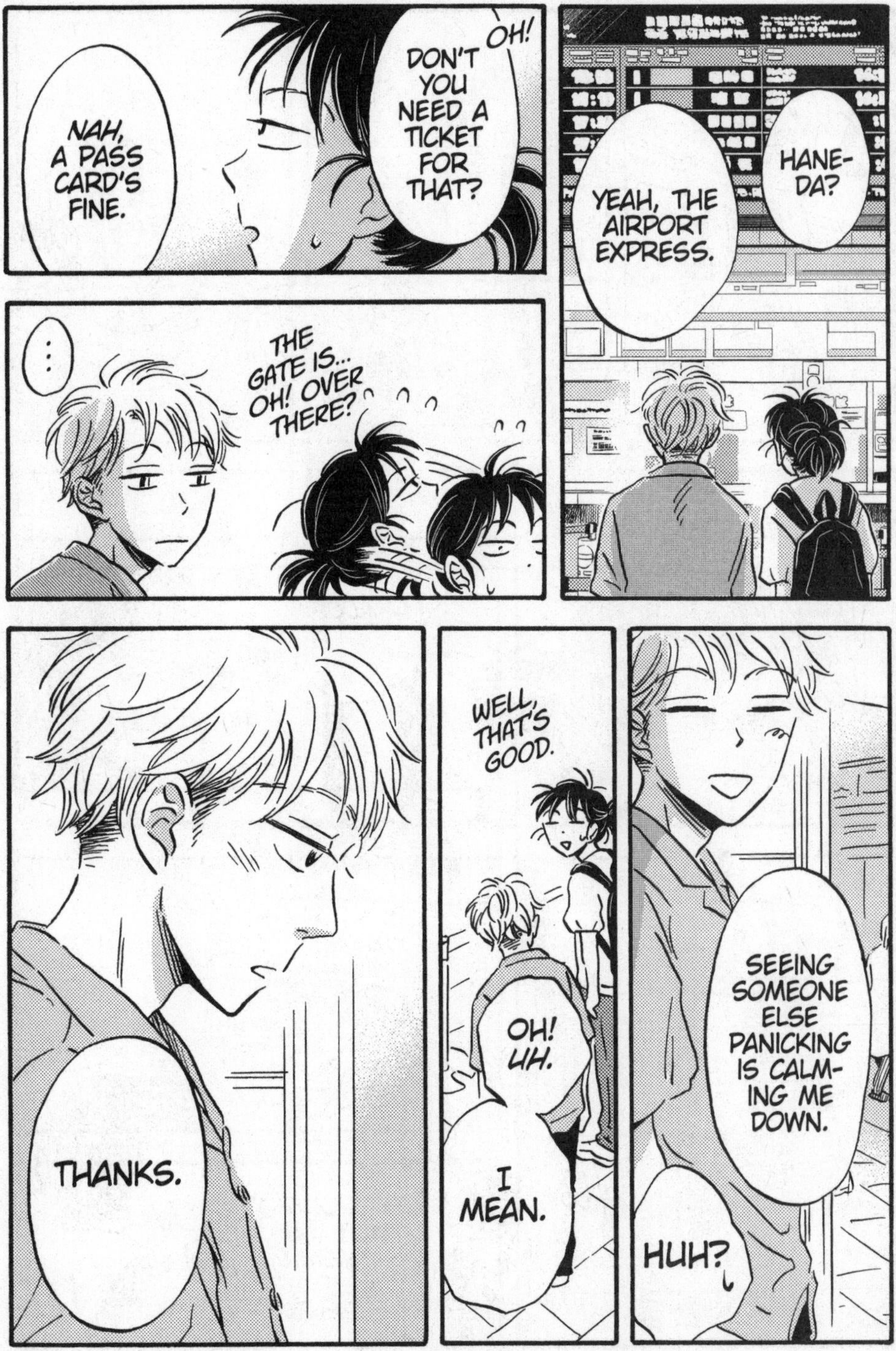
HANE-DA?
YEAH, THE AIRPORT EXPRESS.
OH!
DON'T YOU NEED A TICKET FOR THAT?
NAH, A PASS CARD'S FINE.
THE GATE IS... OH! OVER THERE?
...
SEEING SOMEONE ELSE PANICKING IS CALMING ME DOWN.
HUH?
WELL, THAT'S GOOD.
OH! UH.
I MEAN.
THANKS.

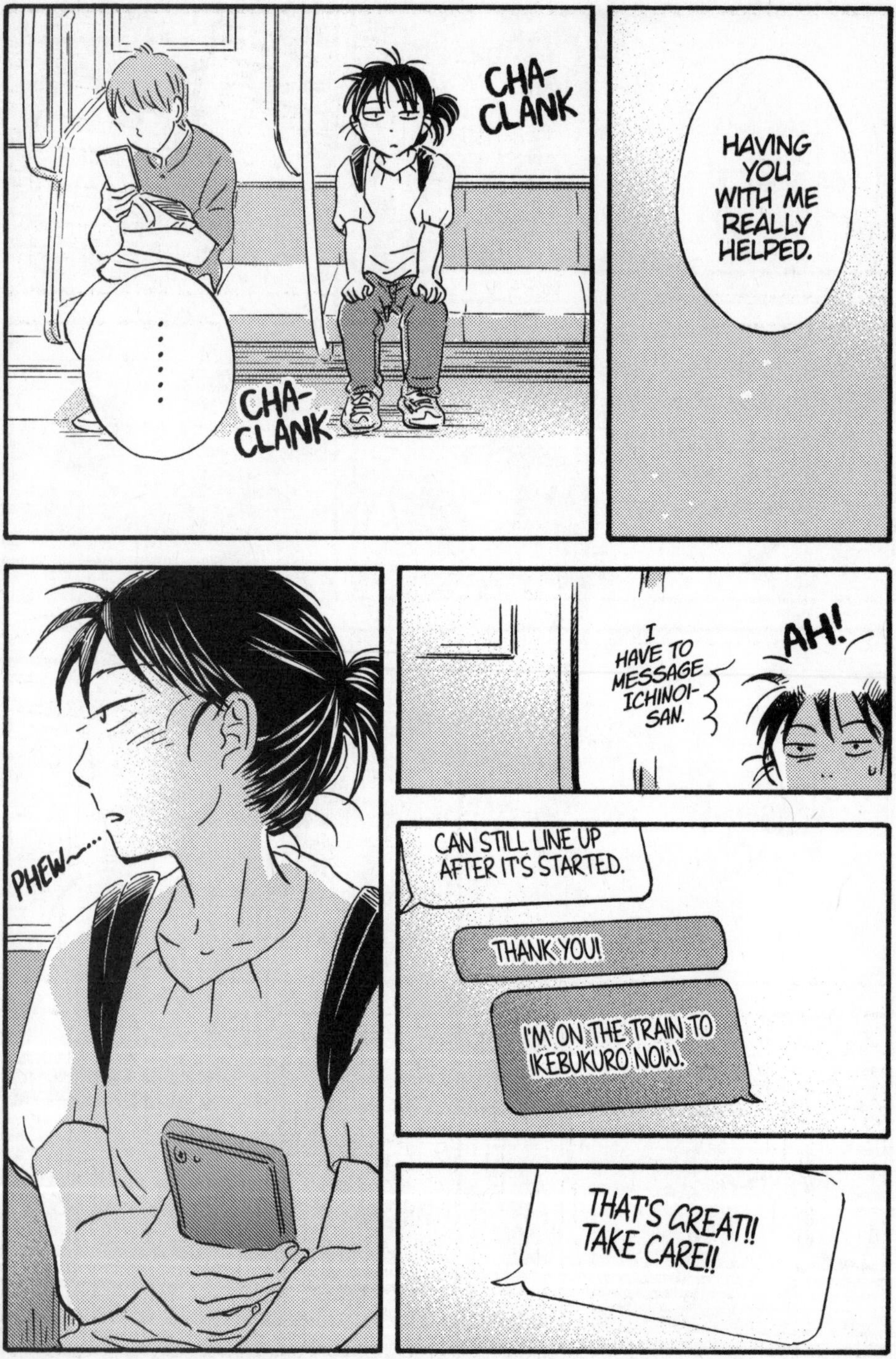
HAVING YOU WITH ME REALLY HELPED.
CHA-CLANK
......
CHA-CLANK
AH!
I HAVE TO MESSAGE ICHINOI-SAN.
CAN STILL LINE UP AFTER IT'S STARTED.
THANK YOU!
I'M ON THE TRAIN TO IKEBUKURO NOW.
THAT'S GREAT!! TAKE CARE!!
PHEW~.....

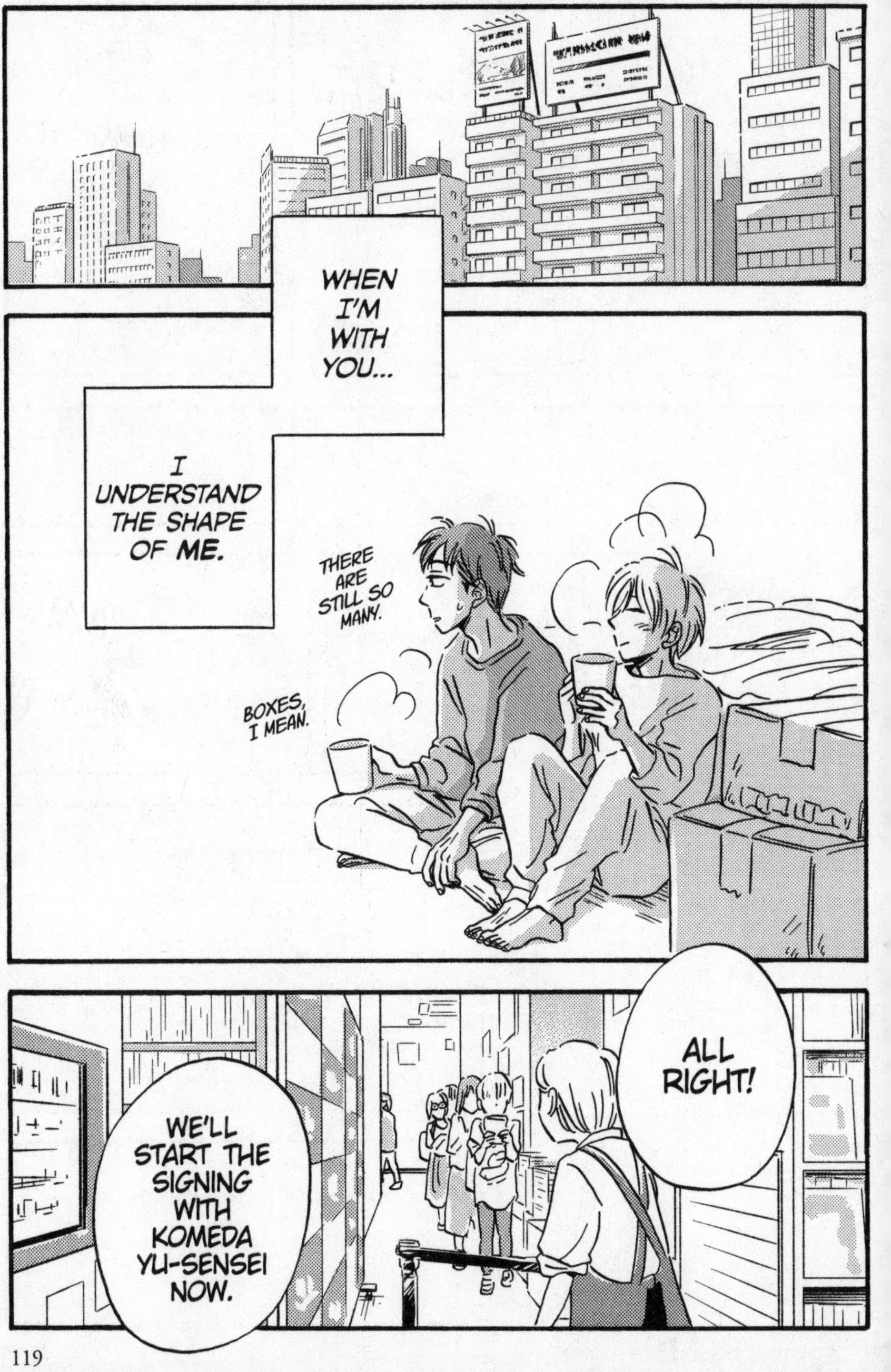
WHEN I'M WITH YOU...
I UNDERSTAND THE SHAPE OF ME.
THERE ARE STILL SO MANY.
BOXES, I MEAN.
ALL RIGHT!
WE'LL START THE SIGNING WITH KOMEDA YU-SENSEI NOW.

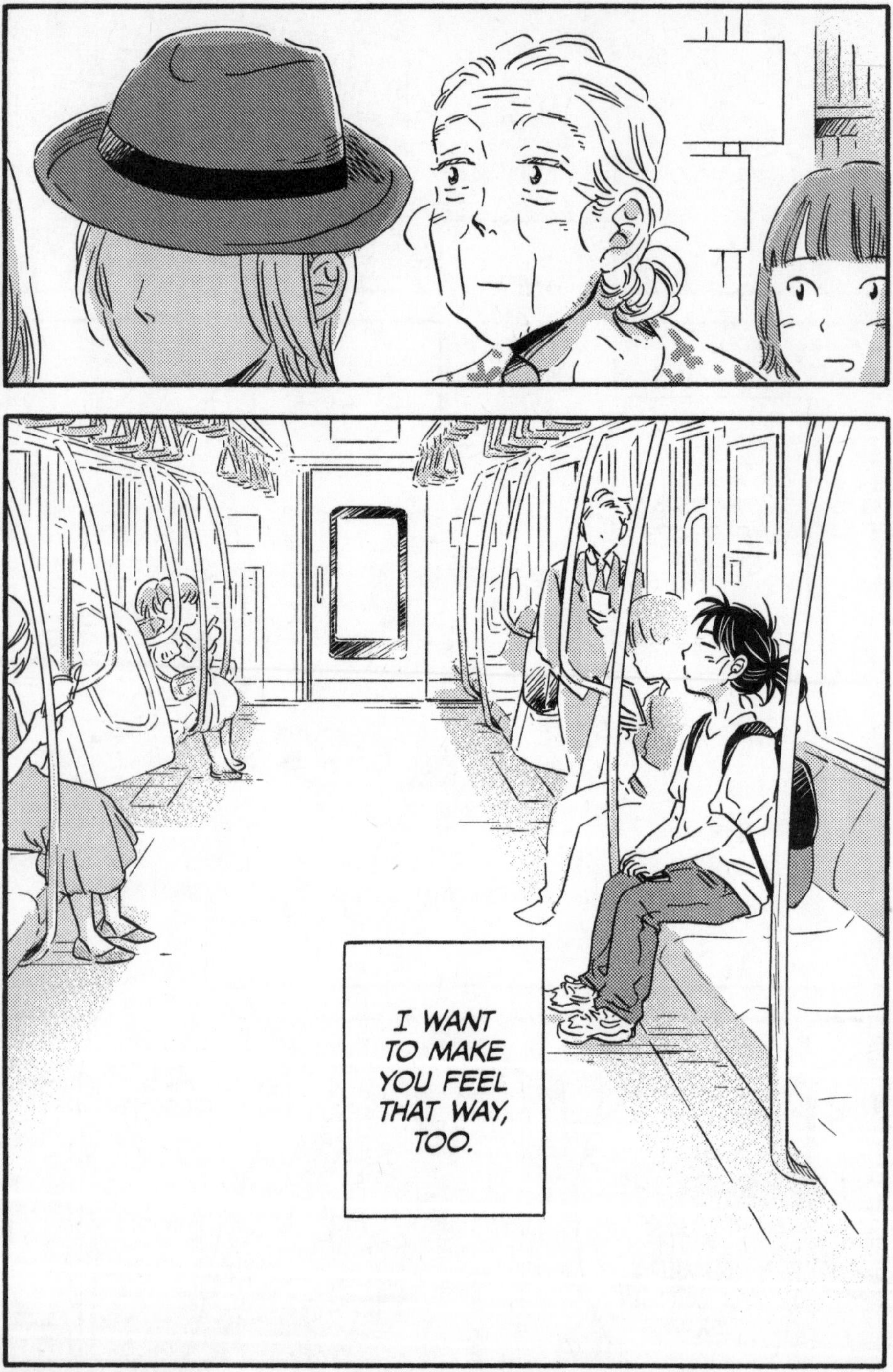
I WANT TO MAKE YOU FEEL THAT WAY, TOO.

Chapter 49/END

metamorphosis

## Chapter 50

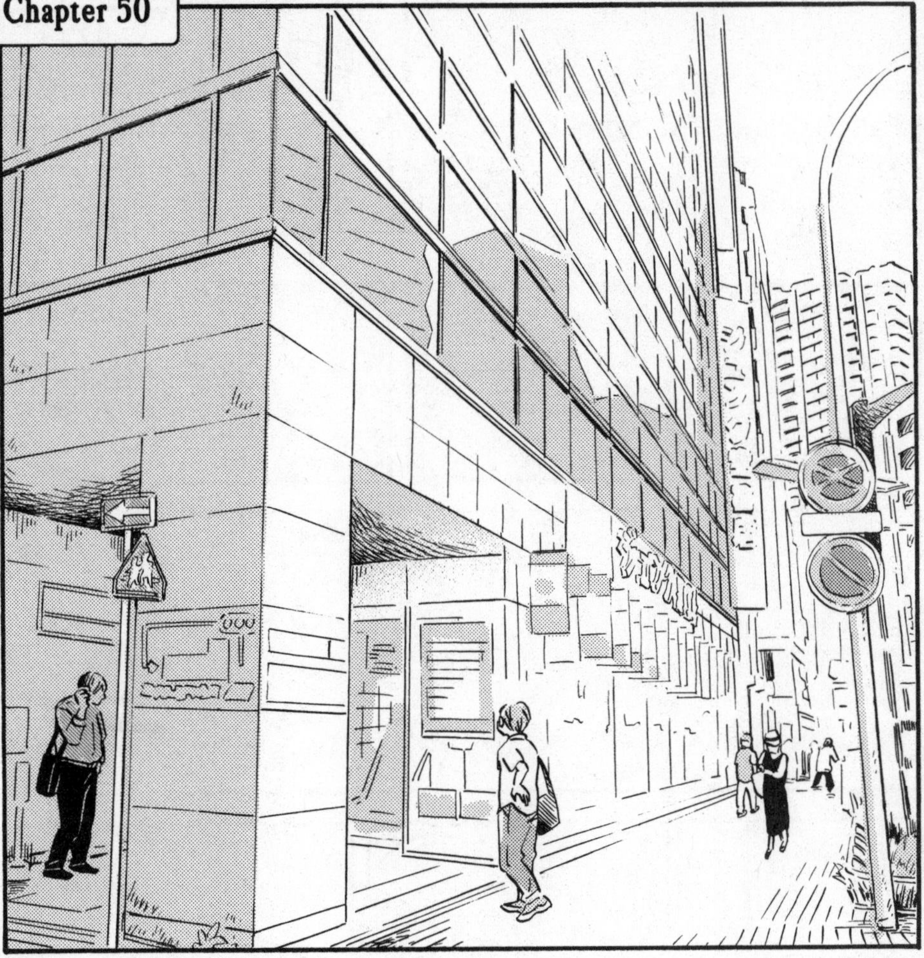

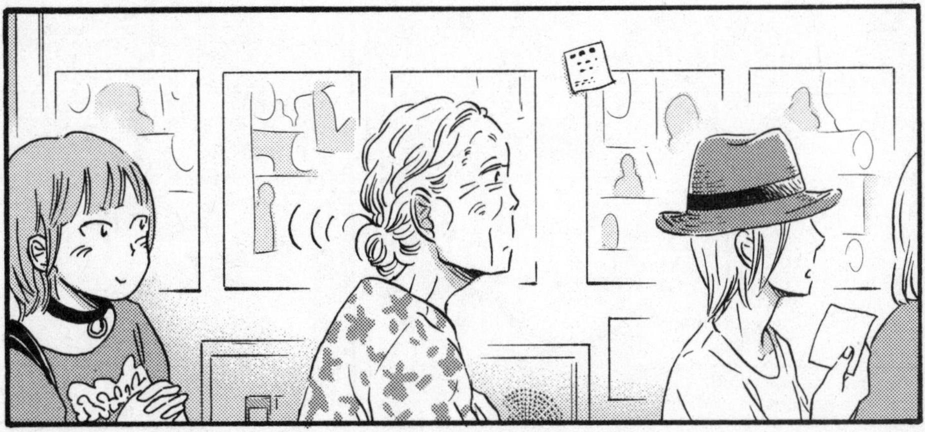

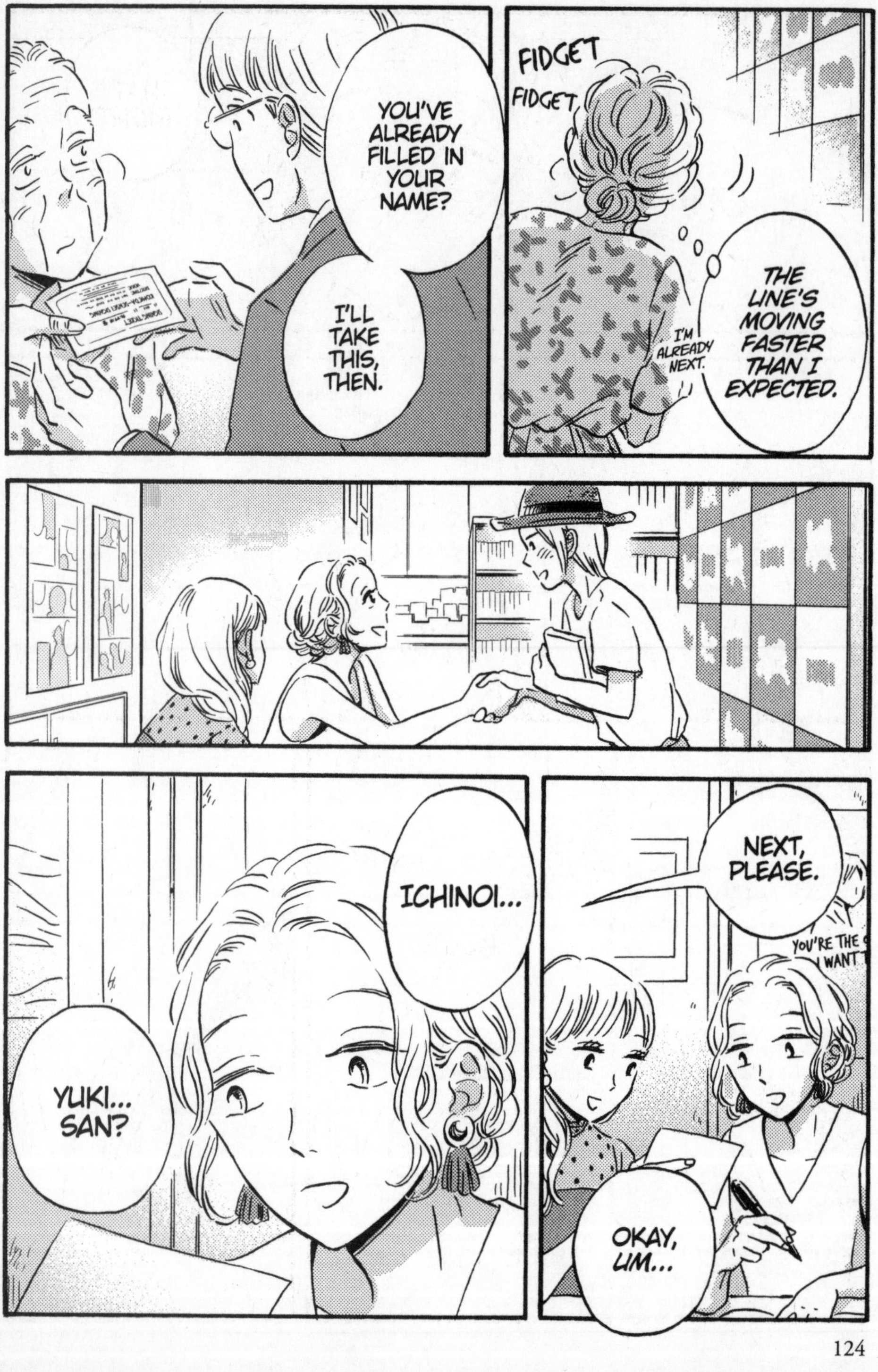
FIDGET FIDGET
I'M ALREADY NEXT.
THE LINE'S MOVING FASTER THAN I EXPECTED.
YOU'VE ALREADY FILLED IN YOUR NAME?
I'LL TAKE THIS, THEN.
NEXT, PLEASE.
YOU'RE THE I WANT
OKAY, UM...
ICHINOI...
YUKI... SAN?

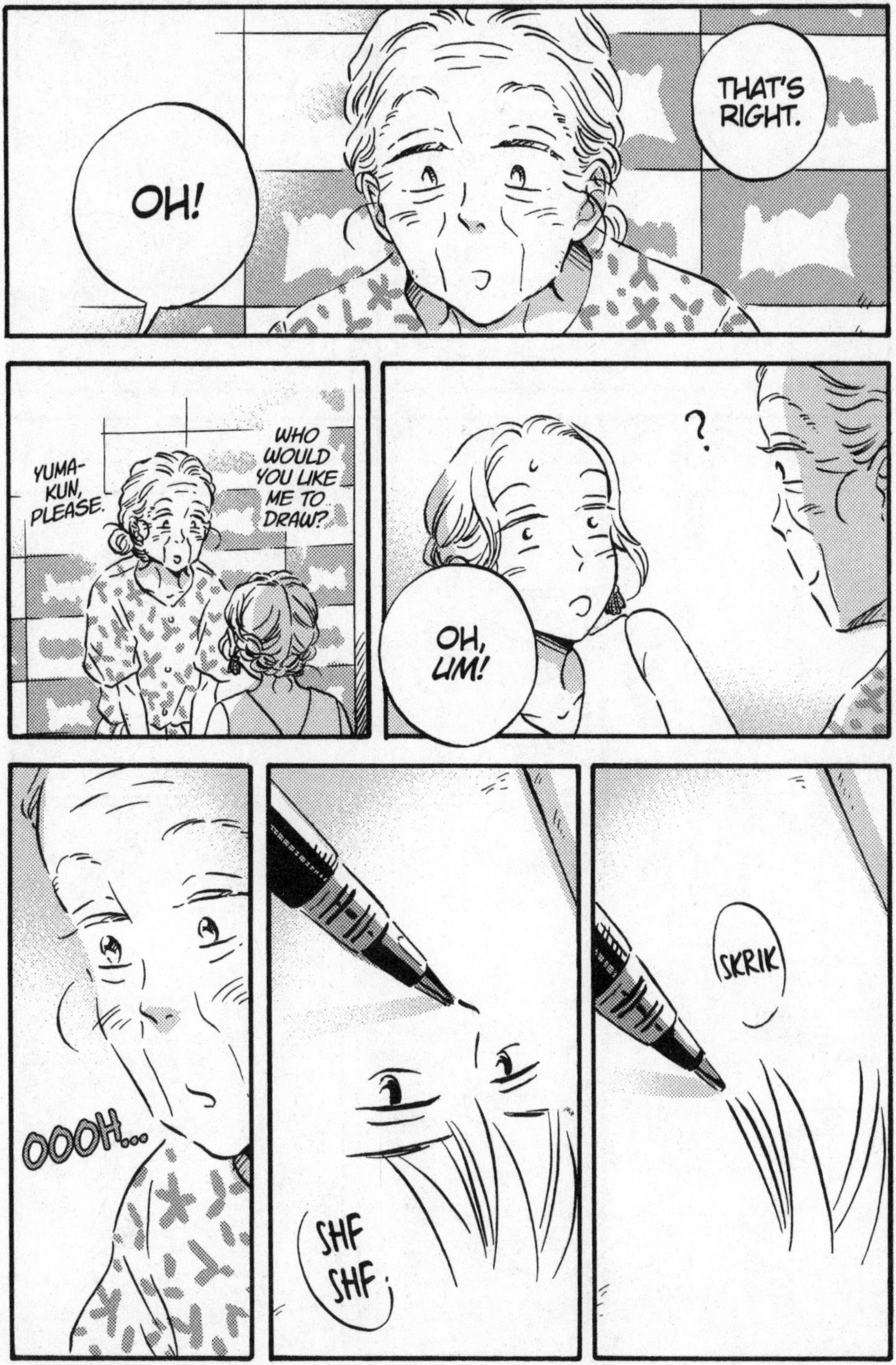
THAT'S RIGHT.
OH!
?
OH, UM!
WHO WOULD YOU LIKE ME TO DRAW?
YUMA-KUN, PLEASE.
SKRIK
SHF SHF
OOOH...

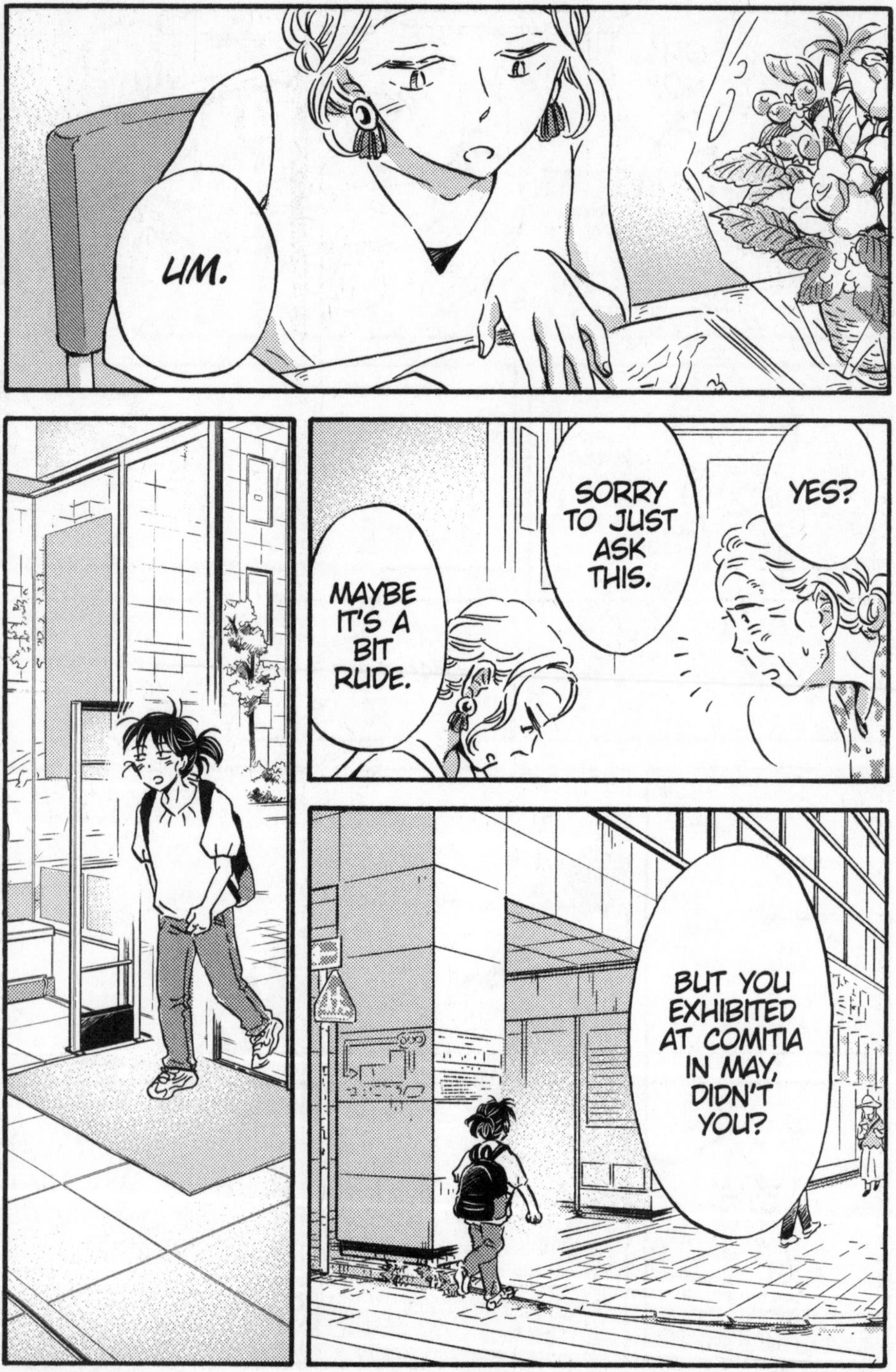
UM.
YES?
SORRY TO JUST ASK THIS.
MAYBE IT'S A BIT RUDE.
BUT YOU EXHIBITED AT COMITIA IN MAY, DIDN'T YOU?

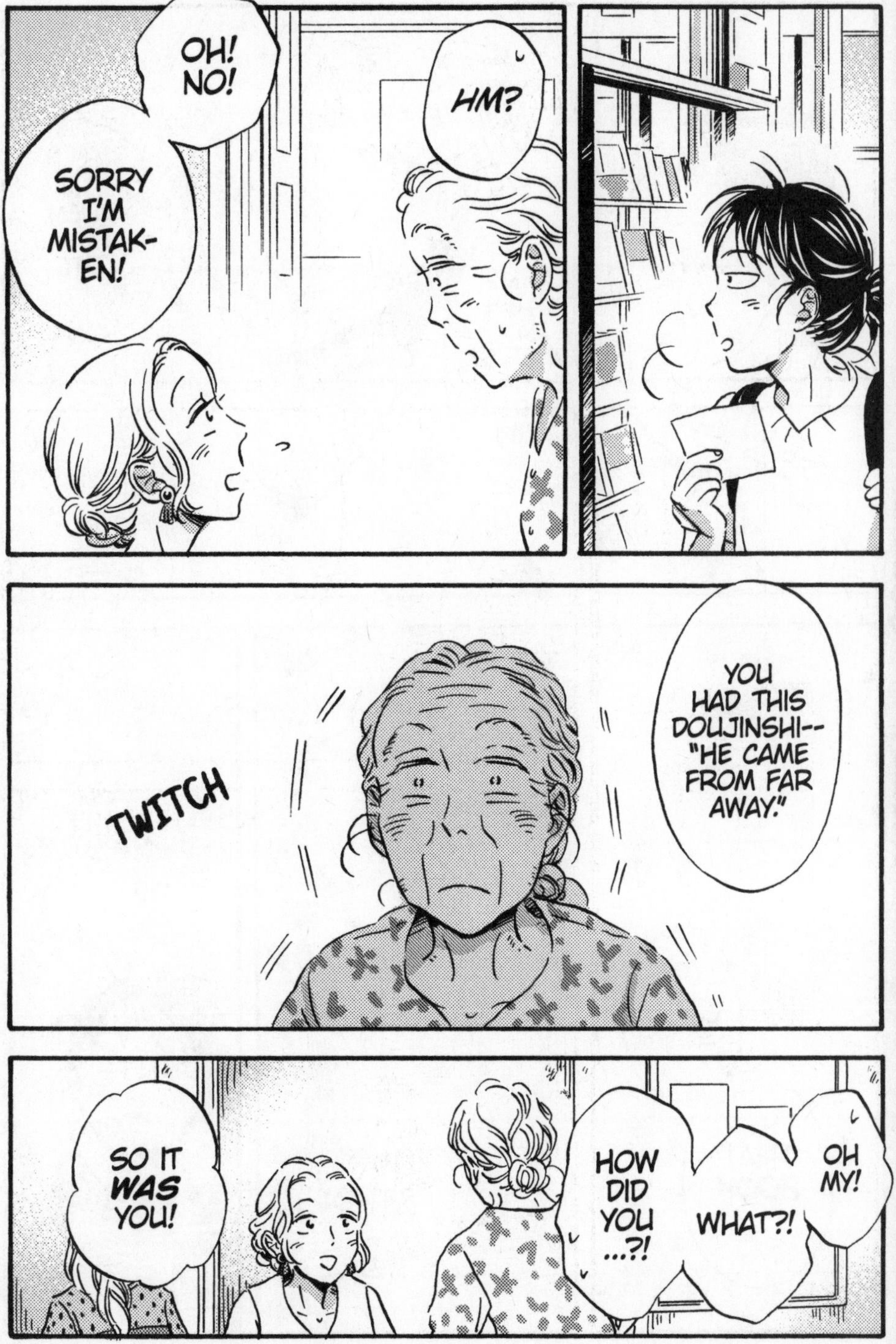
HM?
OH! NO!
SORRY I'M MISTAK-EN!
YOU HAD THIS DOUJINSHI-- "HE CAME FROM FAR AWAY."
TWITCH
OH MY!
WHAT?!
HOW DID YOU ...?!
SO IT WAS YOU!

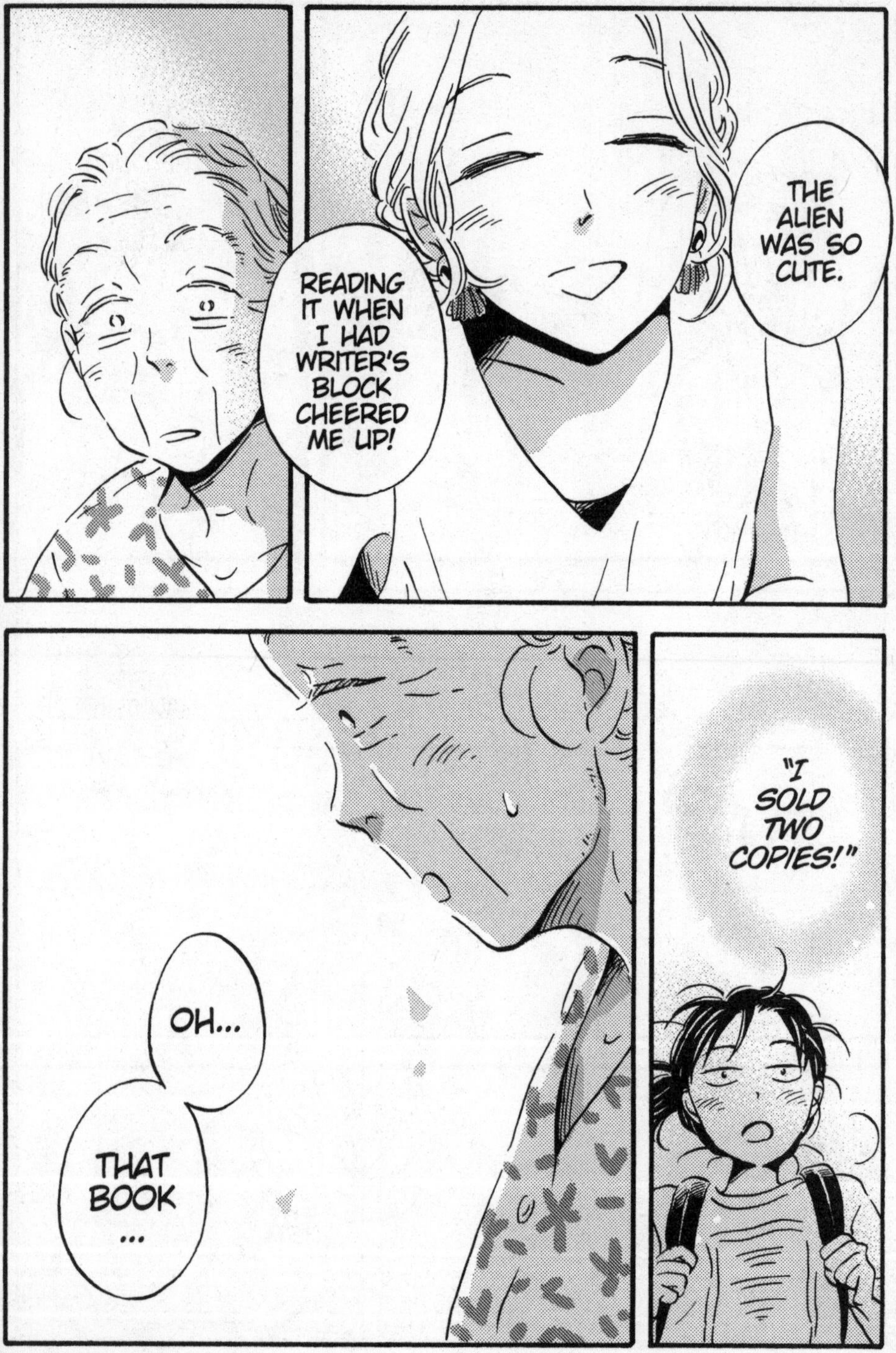
THE ALIEN WAS SO CUTE.
READING IT WHEN I HAD WRITER'S BLOCK CHEERED ME UP!
"I SOLD TWO COPIES!"
OH...
THAT BOOK ...

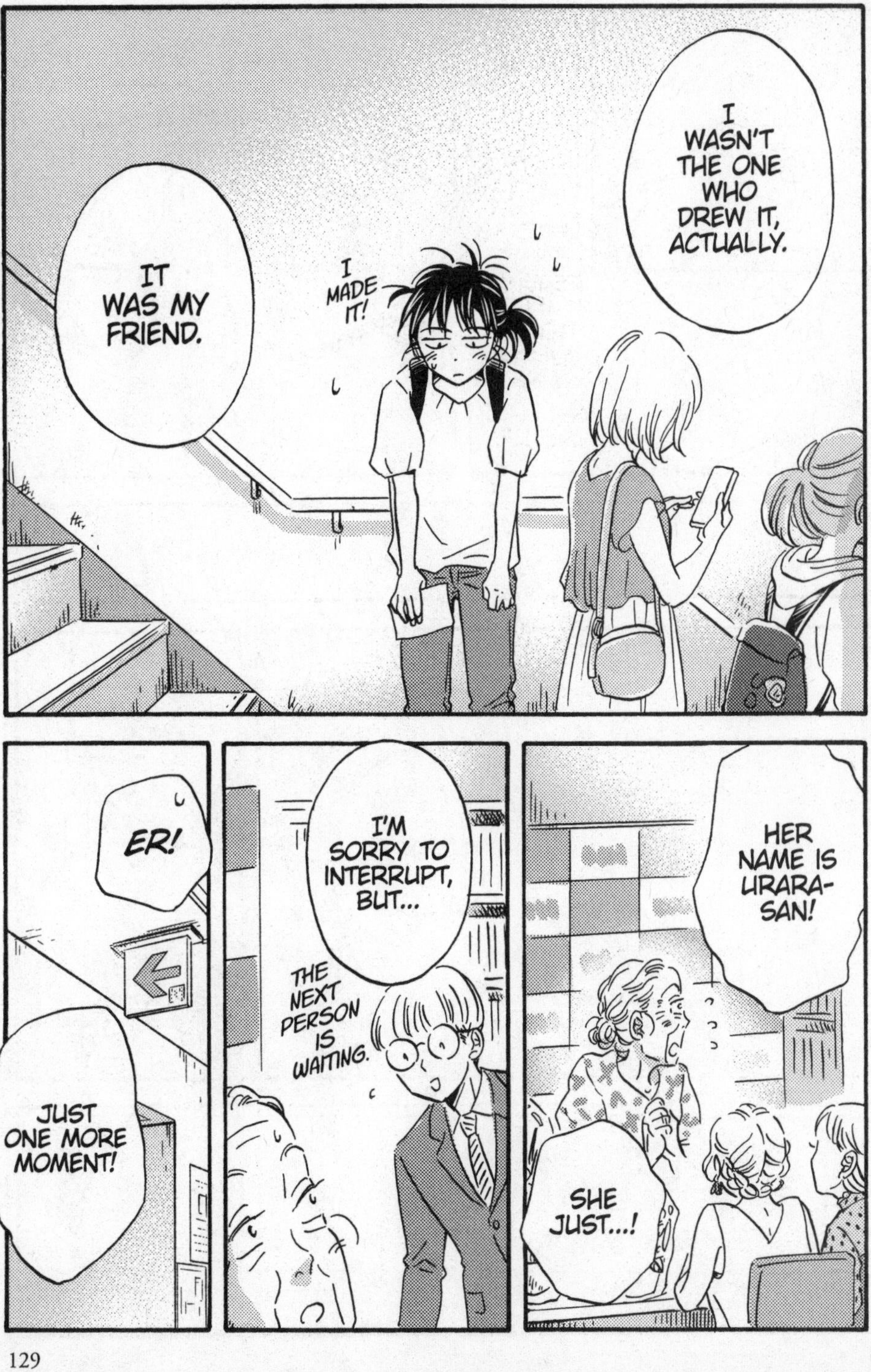
I WASN'T THE ONE WHO DREW IT, ACTUALLY.
I MADE IT!
IT WAS MY FRIEND.
HER NAME IS URARA-SAN!
SHE JUST...!
I'M SORRY TO INTERRUPT, BUT...
THE NEXT PERSON IS WAITING.
ER!
JUST ONE MORE MOMENT!

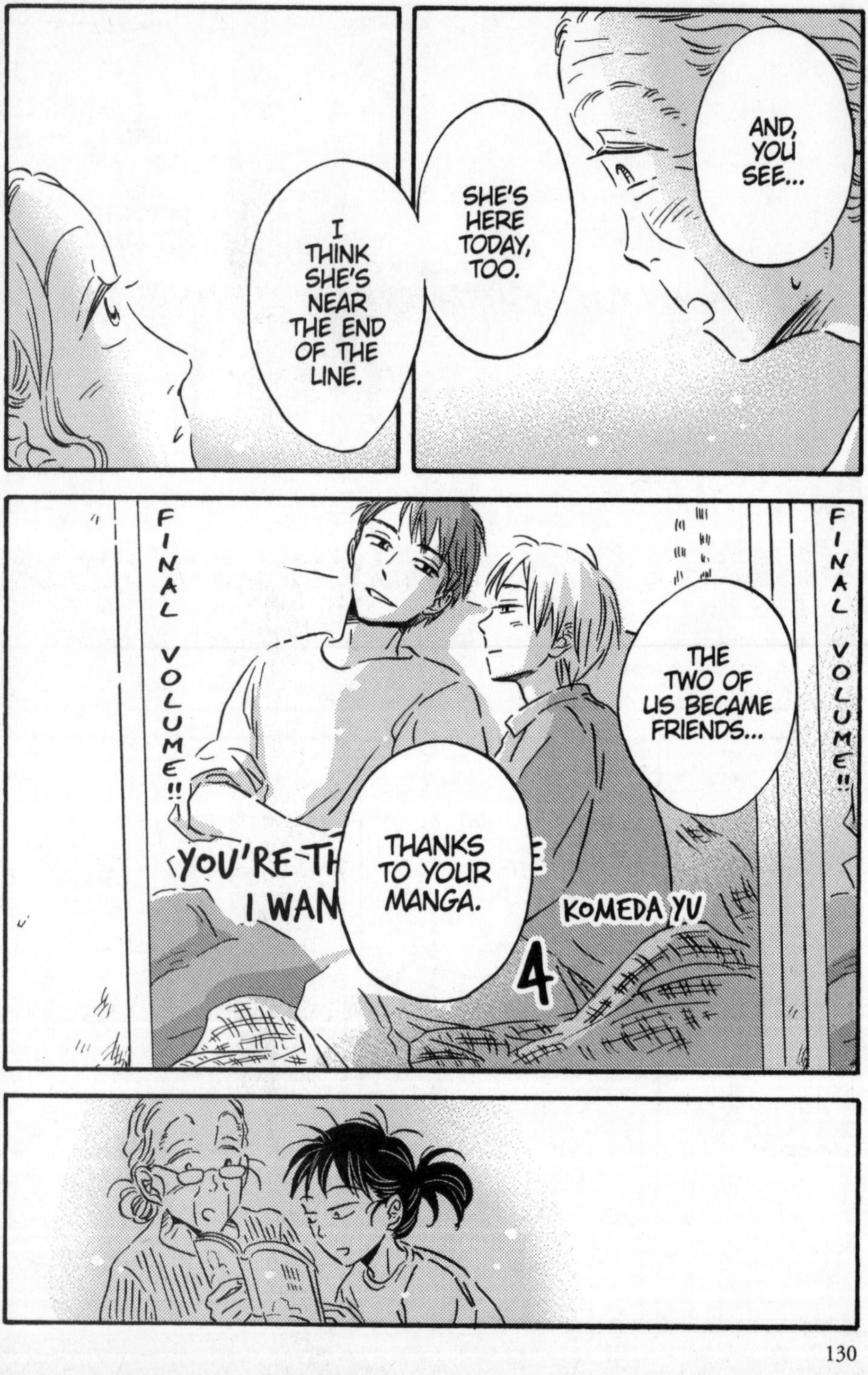

AND, YOU SEE...
SHE'S HERE TODAY, TOO.
I THINK SHE'S NEAR THE END OF THE LINE.
FINAL VOLUME!!
THE TWO OF US BECAME FRIENDS...
THANKS TO YOUR MANGA.
KOMEDA YU
4
FINAL VOLUME!!

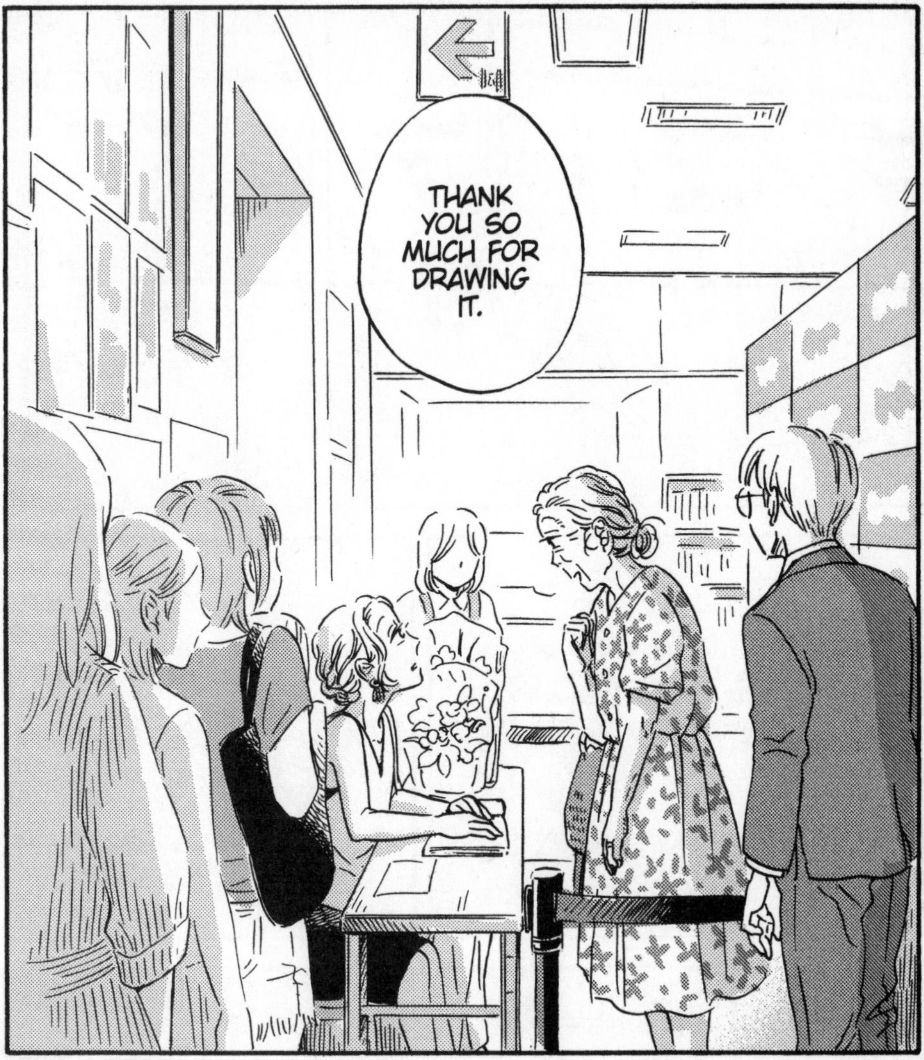
THANK YOU SO MUCH FOR DRAWING IT.

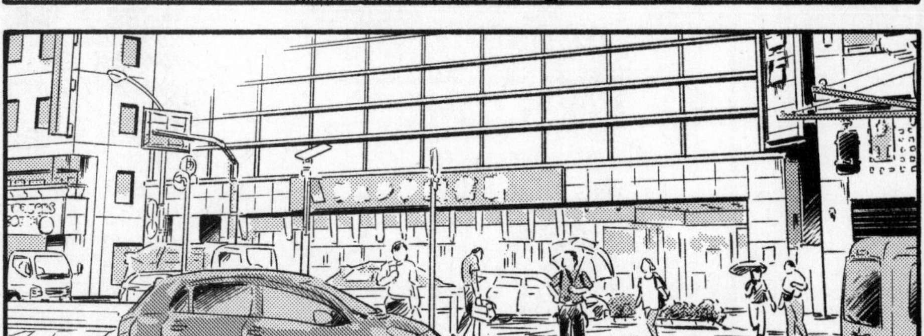

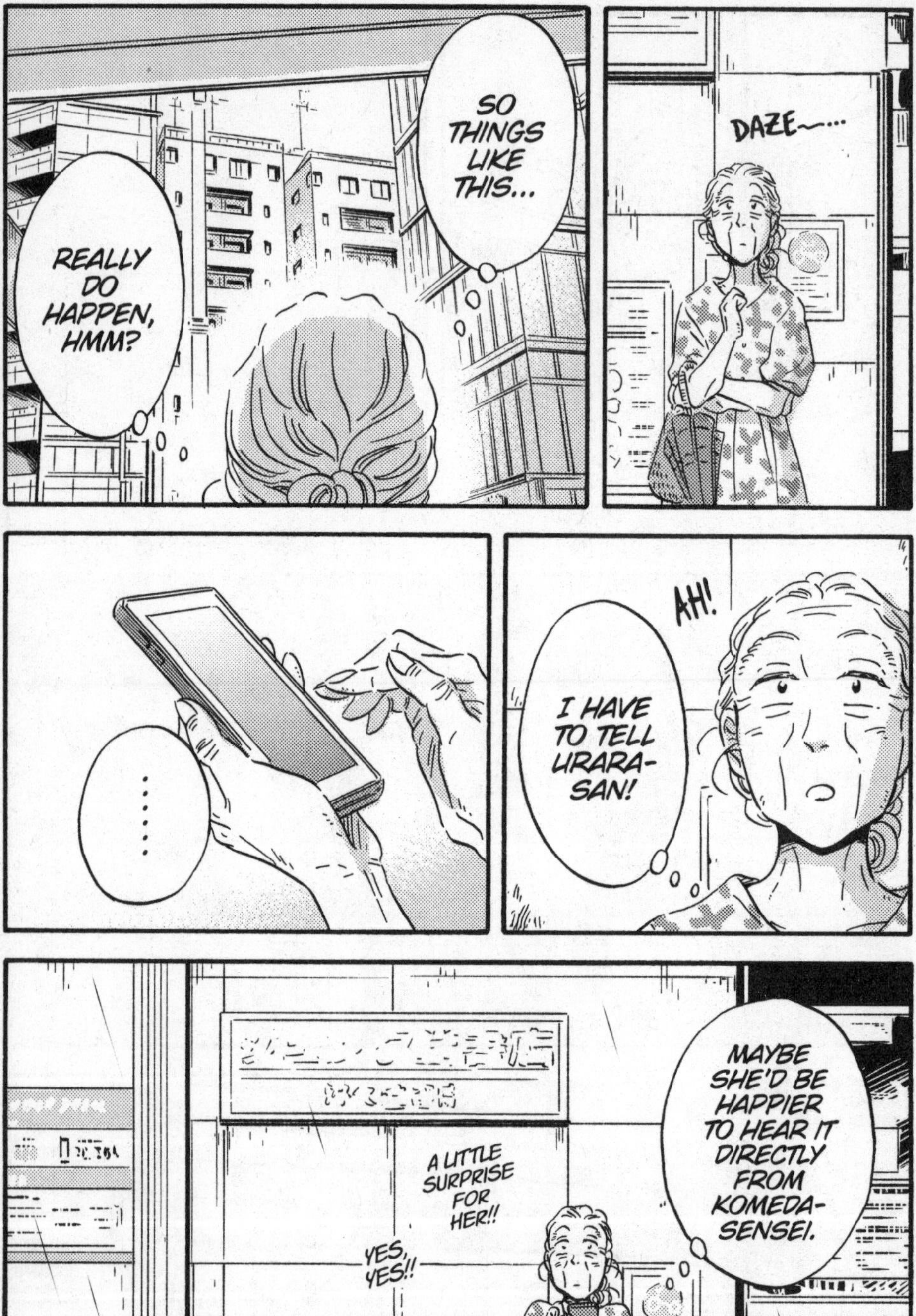
DAZE~...
SO THINGS LIKE THIS...
REALLY DO HAPPEN, HMM?
AH!
I HAVE TO TELL URARA-SAN!
......
MAYBE SHE'D BE HAPPIER TO HEAR IT DIRECTLY FROM KOMEDA-SENSEI.
A LITTLE SURPRISE FOR HER!!
YES, YES!!

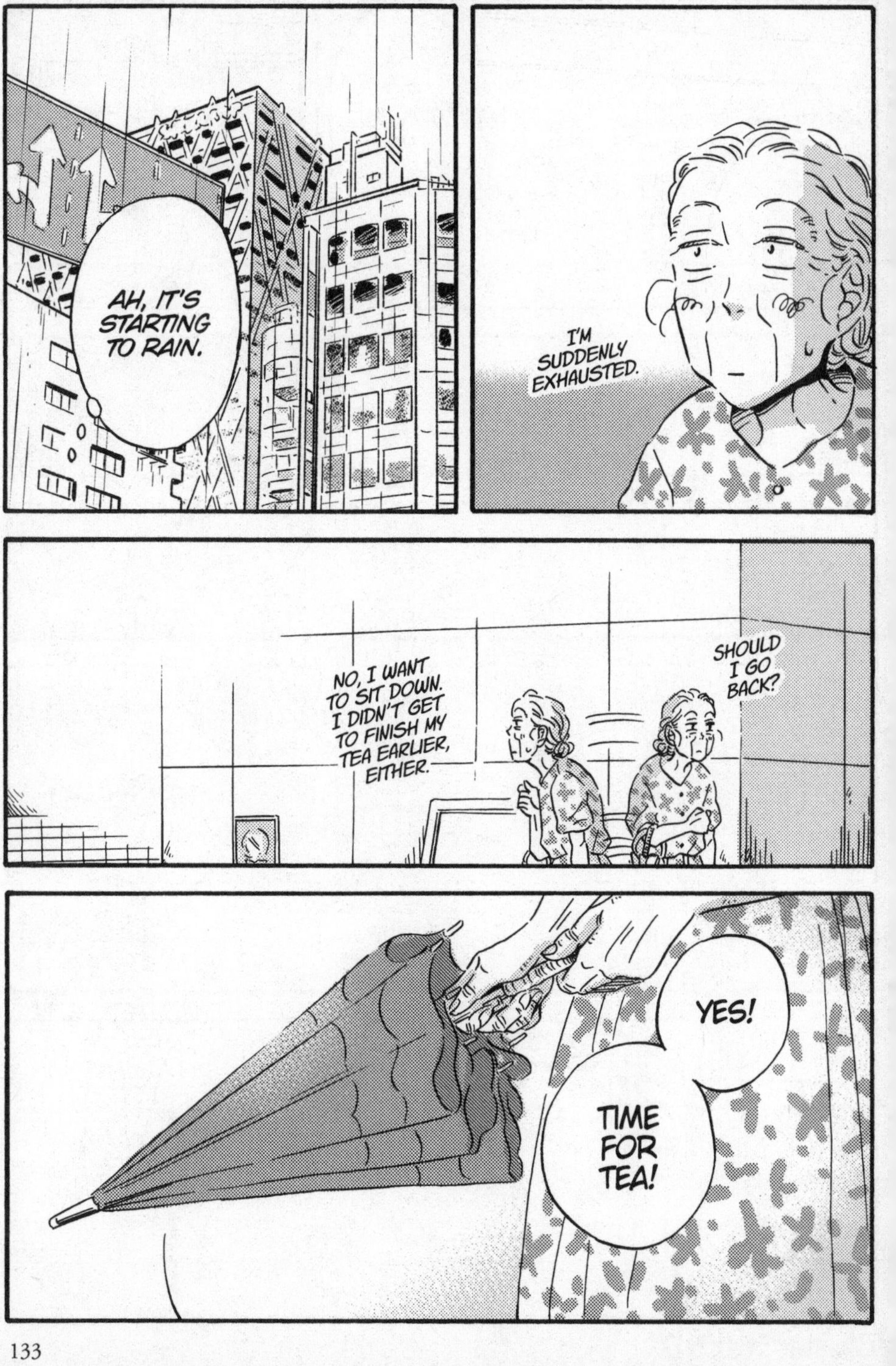
I'M SUDDENLY EXHAUSTED.
AH, IT'S STARTING TO RAIN.
SHOULD I GO BACK?
NO, I WANT TO SIT DOWN. I DIDN'T GET TO FINISH MY TEA EARLIER, EITHER.
YES!
TIME FOR TEA!

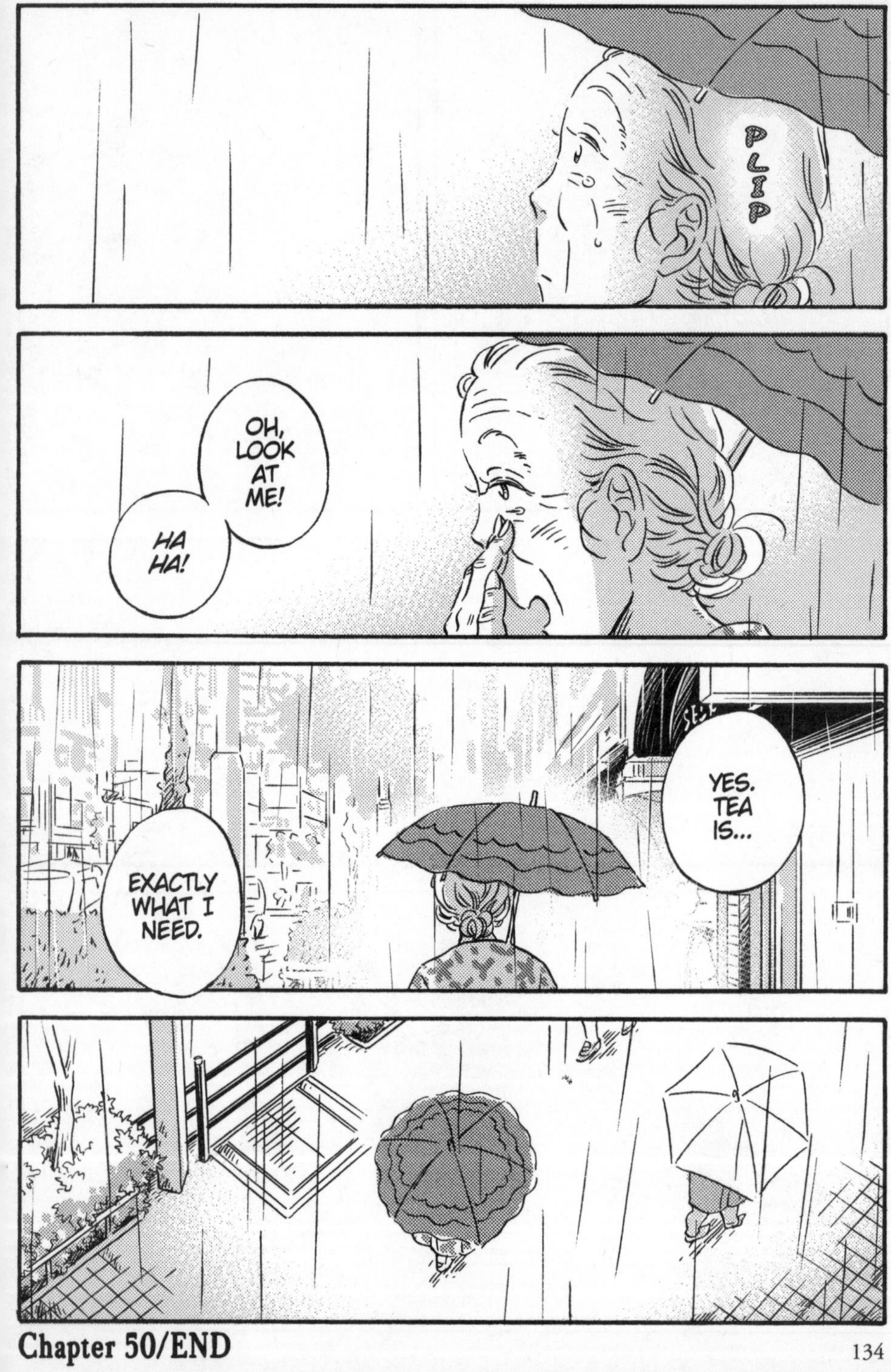
PLIP
OH, LOOK AT ME!
HA HA!
YES. TEA IS...
EXACTLY WHAT I NEED.

Chapter 50/END

SIGNING TICKET

" ___ "

KOMEDA-SENSEI SIGNING

DATE/TIME:

VENUE:

# Chapter 51

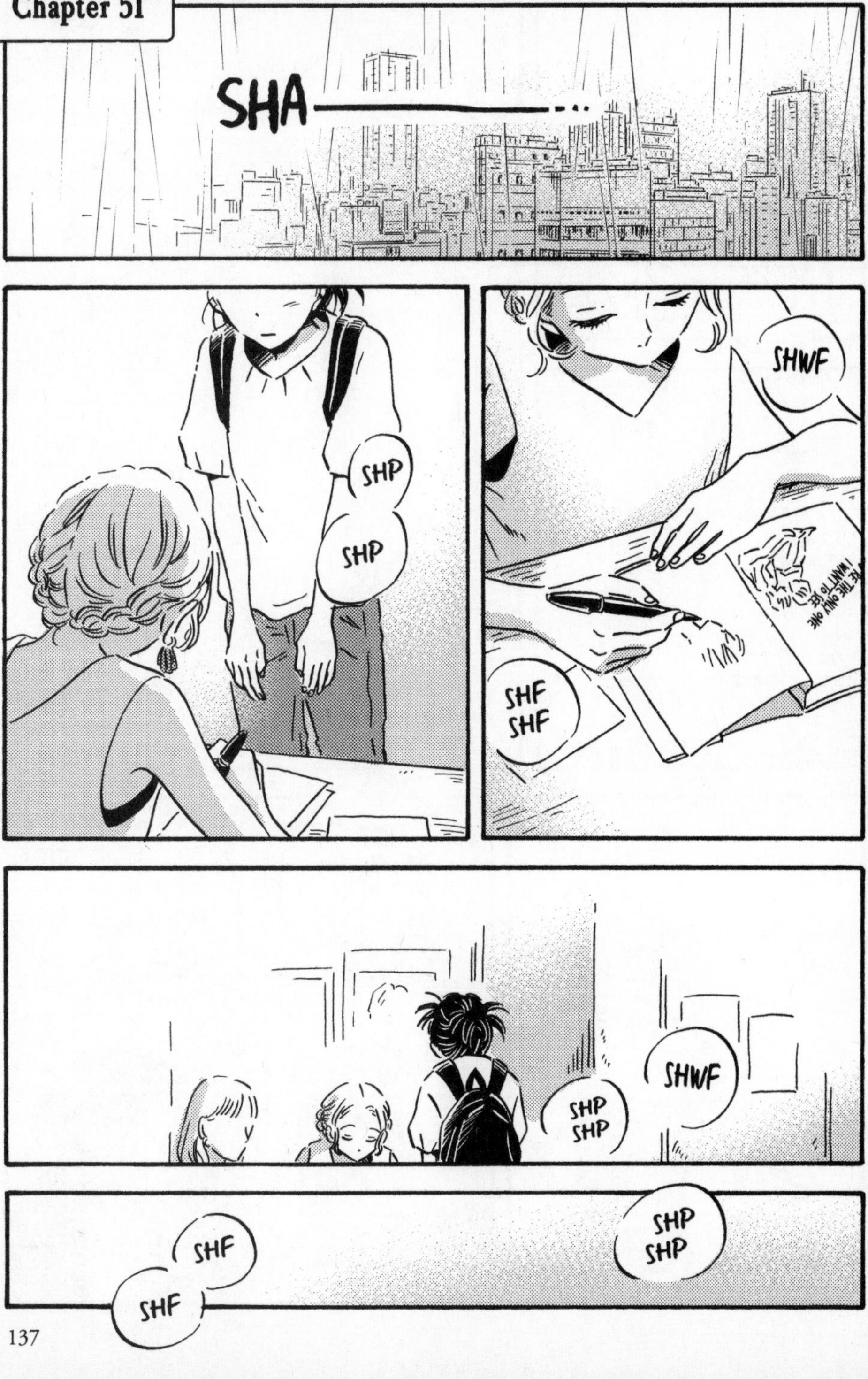
SHA——...
SHWF
SHF SHF
SHP
SHP
SHWF
SHP SHP
SHP SHP
SHF
SHF

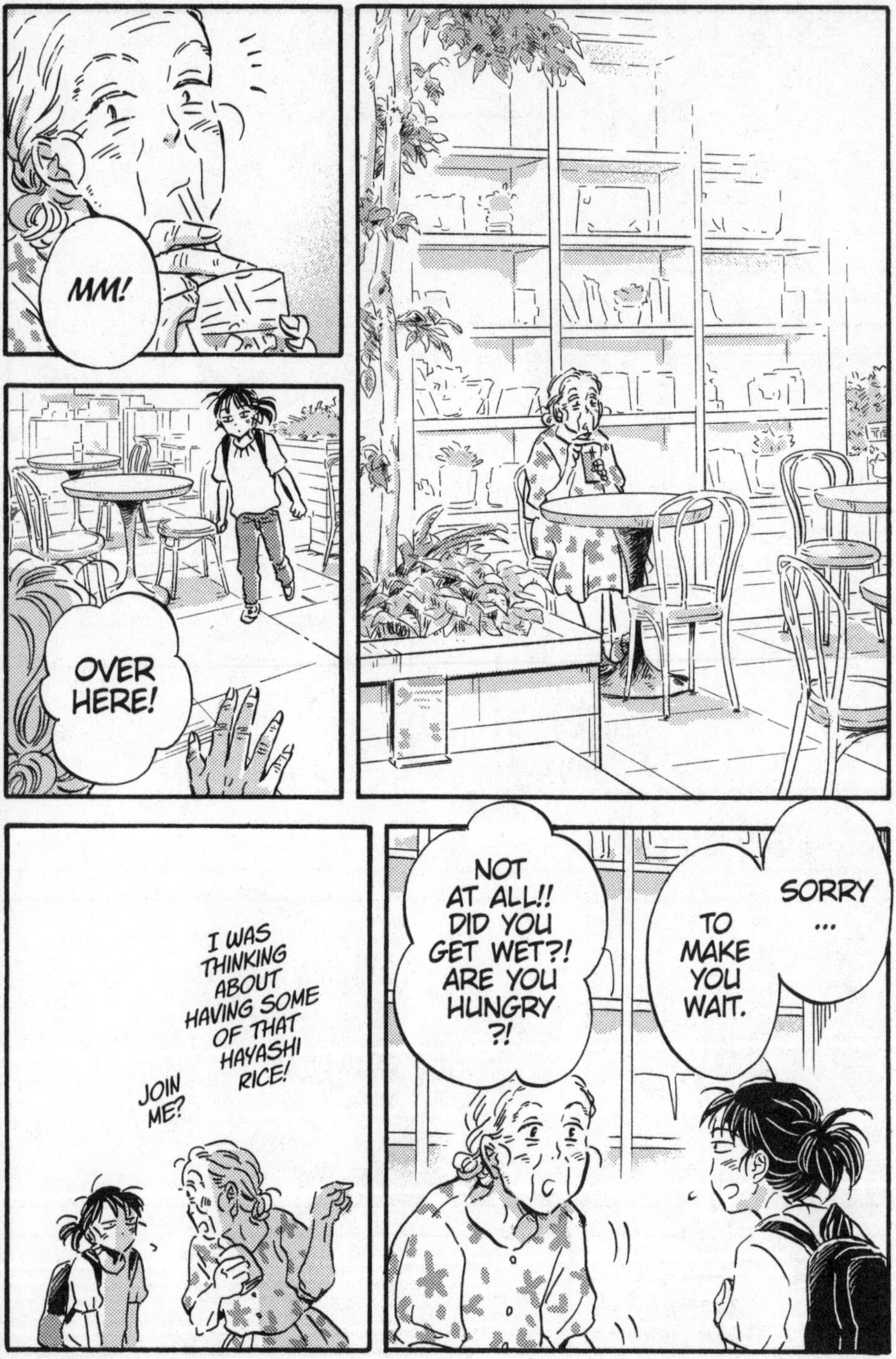
MM!
OVER HERE!
SORRY ... TO MAKE YOU WAIT.
NOT AT ALL!! DID YOU GET WET?! ARE YOU HUNGRY ?!
I WAS THINKING ABOUT HAVING SOME OF THAT HAYASHI RICE!
JOIN ME?

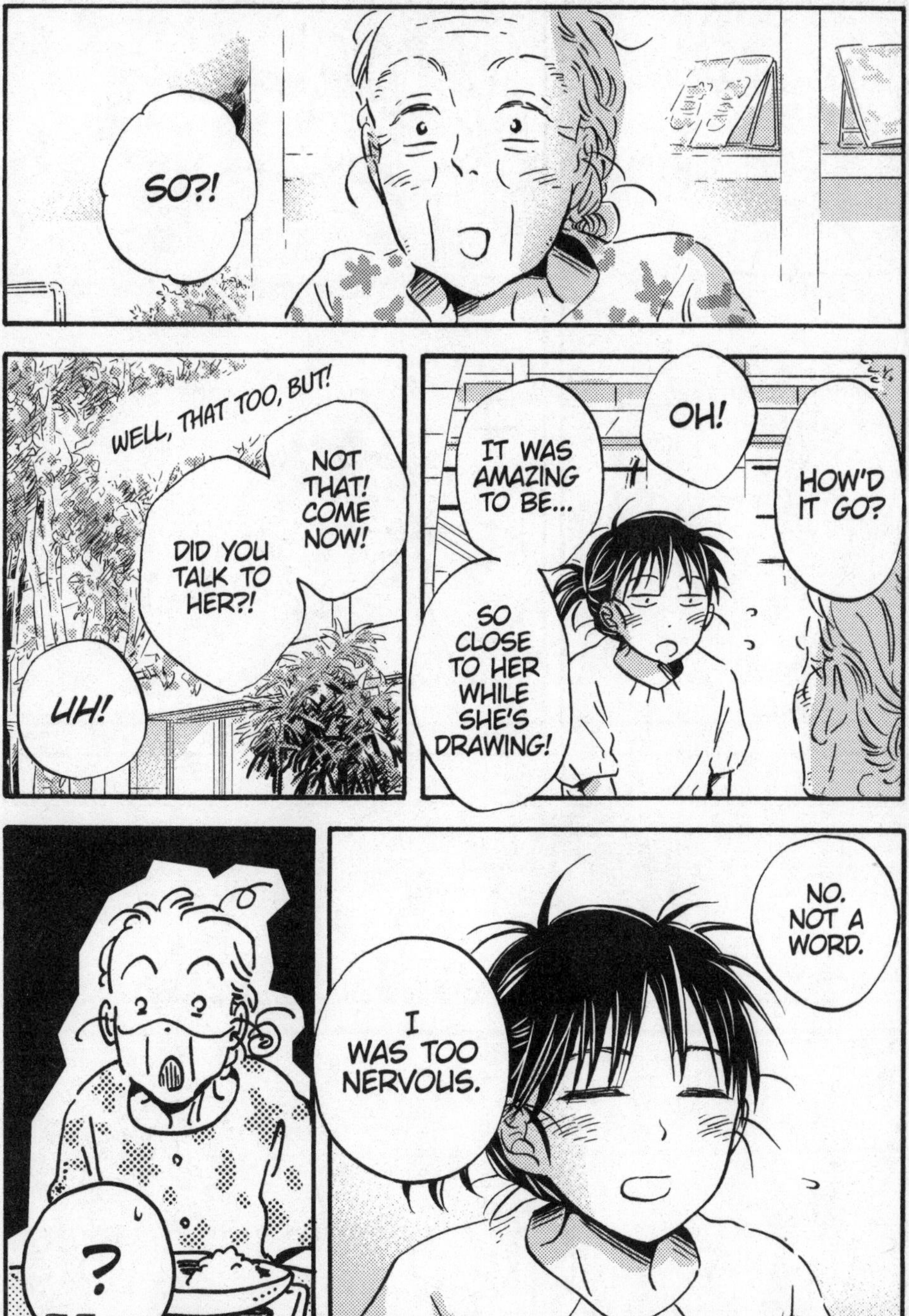
SO?!
HOW'D IT GO?
OH!
IT WAS AMAZING TO BE...
SO CLOSE TO HER WHILE SHE'S DRAWING!
WELL, THAT TOO, BUT!
NOT THAT! COME NOW!
DID YOU TALK TO HER?!
UH!
NO. NOT A WORD.
I WAS TOO NERVOUS.
?

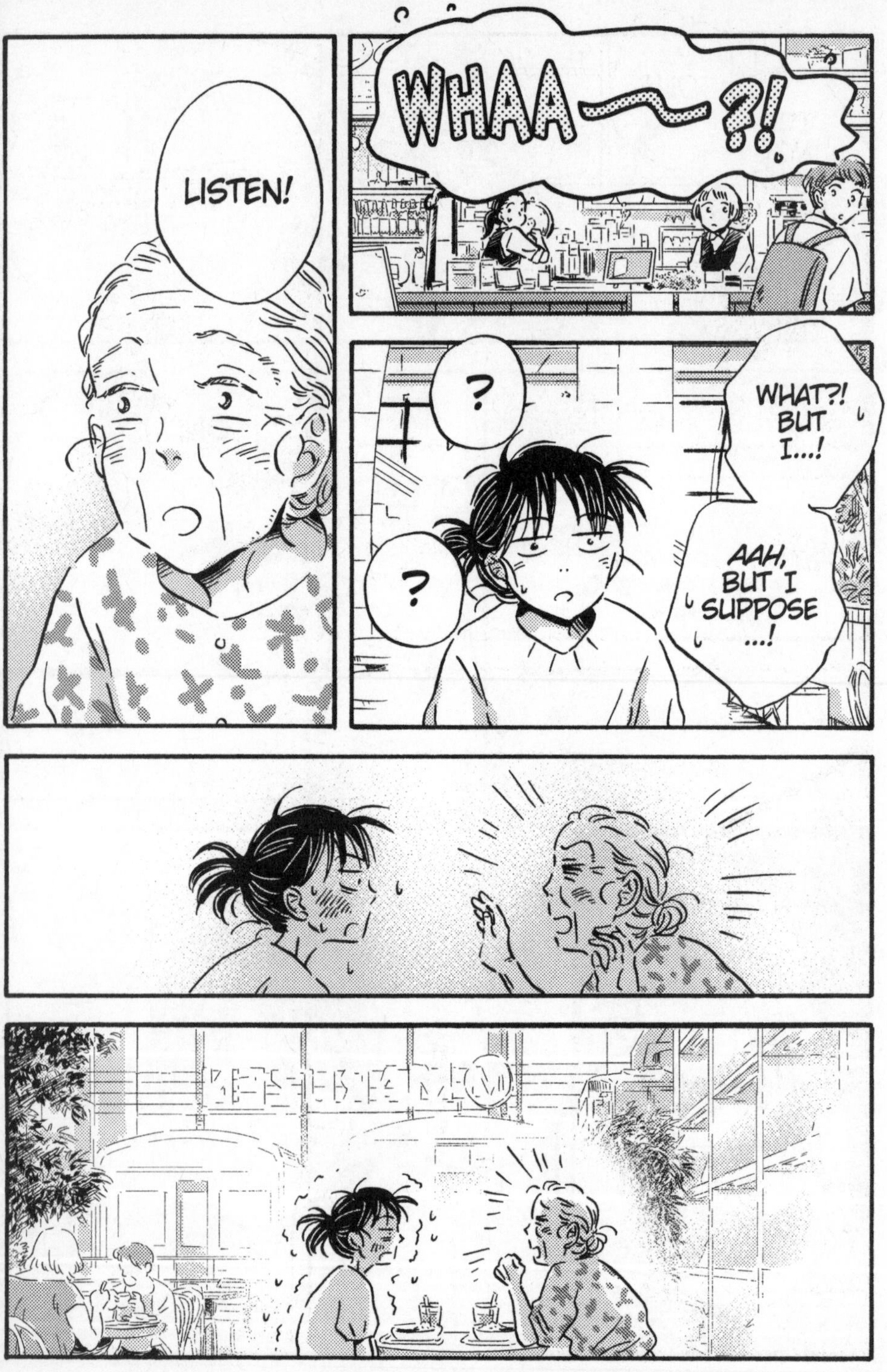
WHAA~~?!
WHAT?! BUT I...!
?
AAH, BUT I SUPPOSE ...!
?
LISTEN!

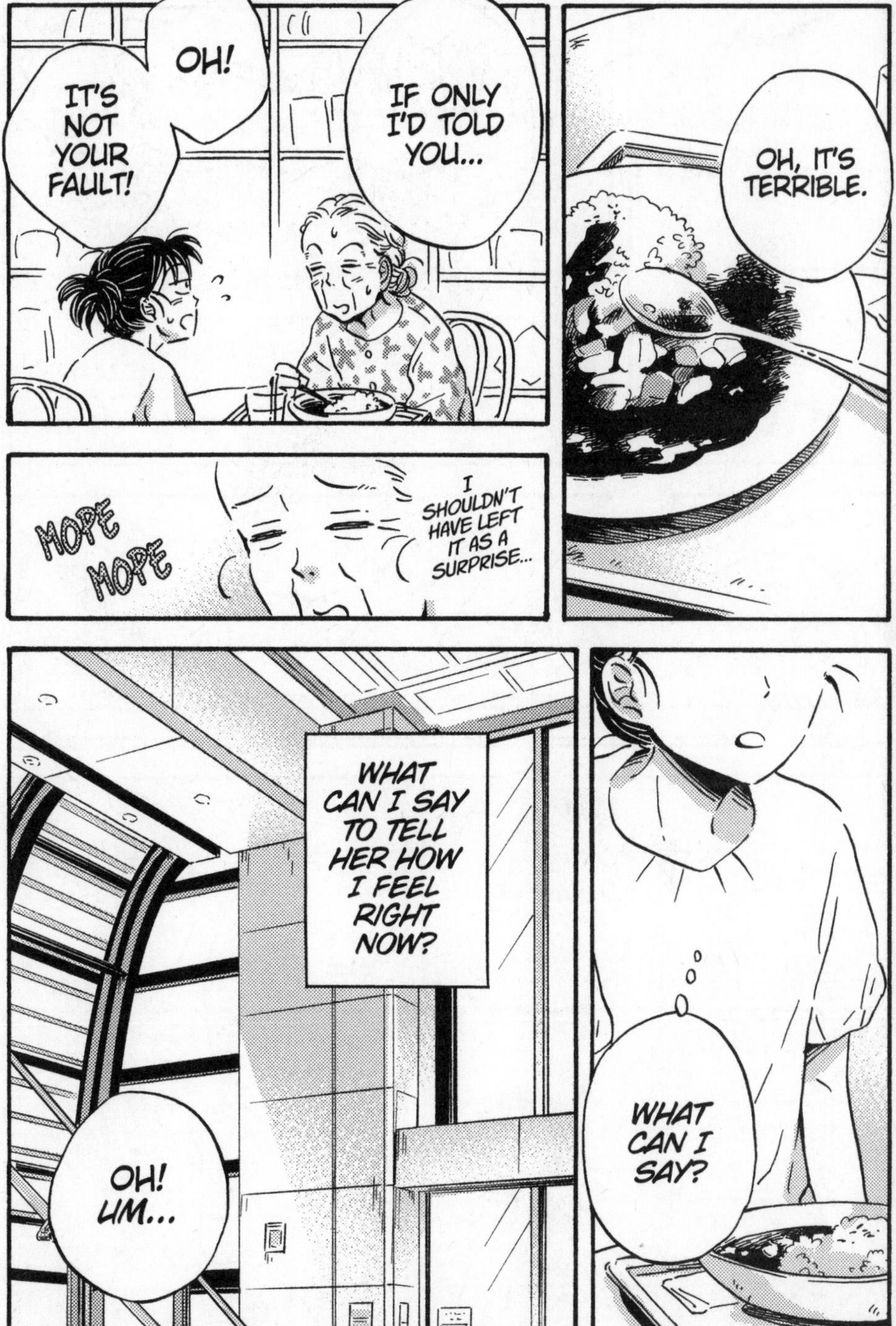
OH, IT'S TERRIBLE.
IF ONLY I'D TOLD YOU...
OH!
IT'S NOT YOUR FAULT!
I SHOULDN'T HAVE LEFT IT AS A SURPRISE...
MOPE MOPE
WHAT CAN I SAY?
WHAT CAN I SAY TO TELL HER HOW I FEEL RIGHT NOW?
OH! UM...

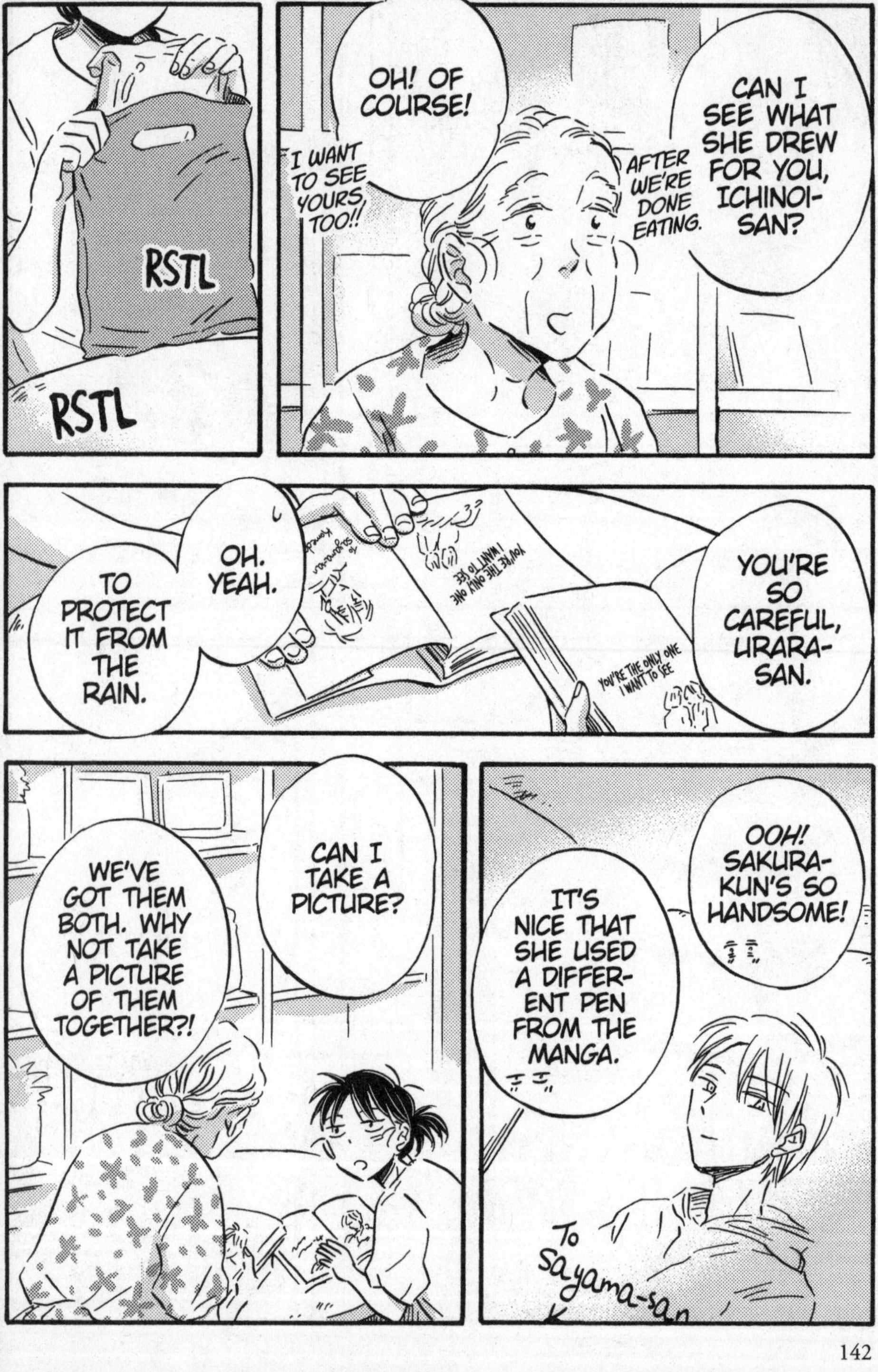
CAN I SEE WHAT SHE DREW FOR YOU, ICHINOI-SAN?
AFTER WE'RE DONE EATING.
OH! OF COURSE!
I WANT TO SEE YOURS, TOO!!
RSTL
RSTL
YOU'RE SO CAREFUL, URARA-SAN.
YOU'RE THE ONLY ONE I WANT TO SEE
YOU'RE THE ONLY ONE I WANT TO SEE
OH. YEAH.
TO PROTECT IT FROM THE RAIN.
OOH! SAKURA-KUN'S SO HANDSOME!
IT'S NICE THAT SHE USED A DIFFERENT PEN FROM THE MANGA.
To Sayama-san
CAN I TAKE A PICTURE?
WE'VE GOT THEM BOTH. WHY NOT TAKE A PICTURE OF THEM TOGETHER?!

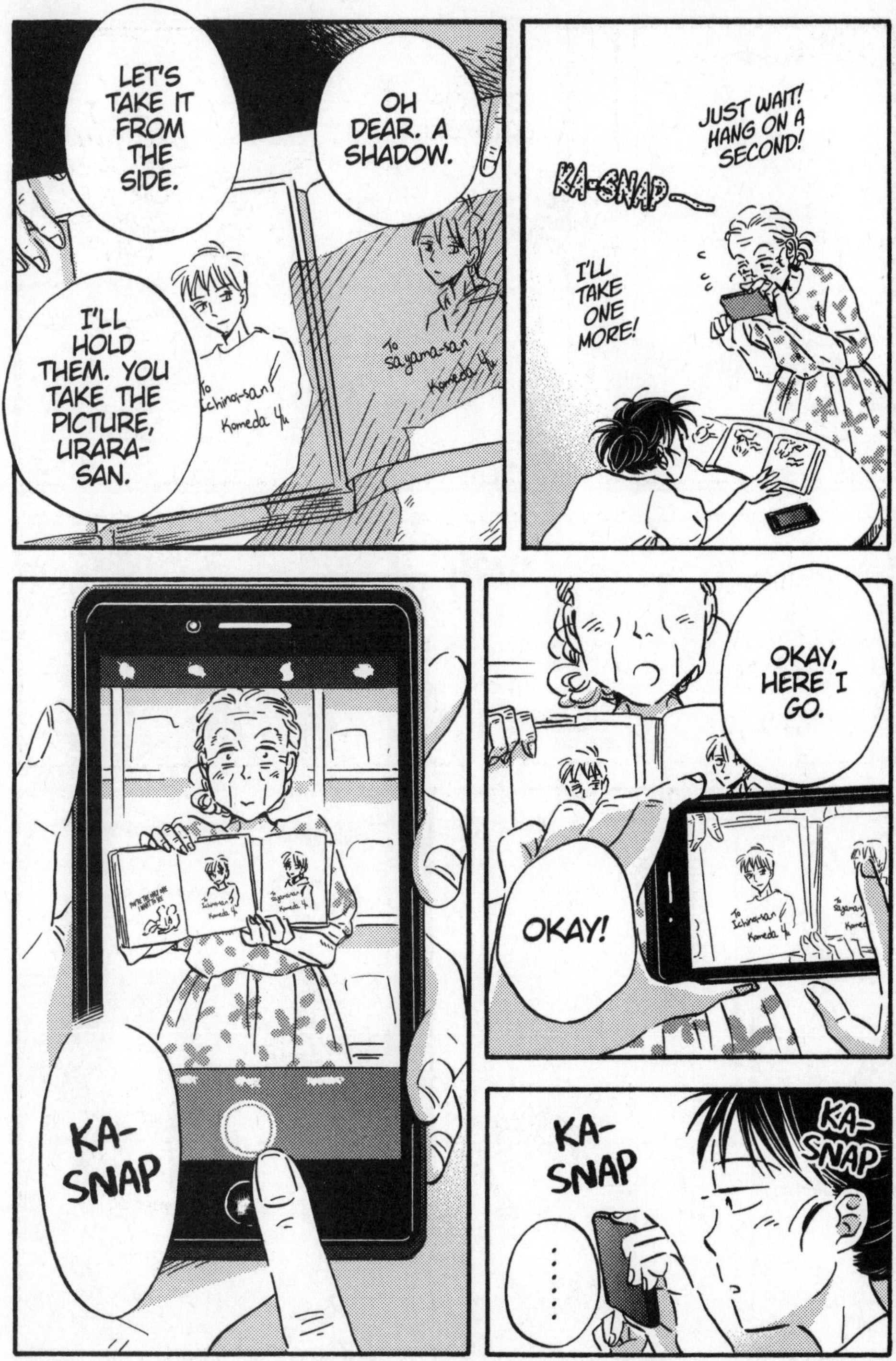
JUST WAIT! HANG ON A SECOND!
KA-SNAP—
I'LL TAKE ONE MORE!
OH DEAR. A SHADOW.
LET'S TAKE IT FROM THE SIDE.
To Sayama-san Komeda Yu
To Ichinai-san Komeda Yu
I'LL HOLD THEM. YOU TAKE THE PICTURE, URARA-SAN.
OKAY, HERE I GO.
OKAY!
KA-SNAP
KA-SNAP
......
KA-SNAP

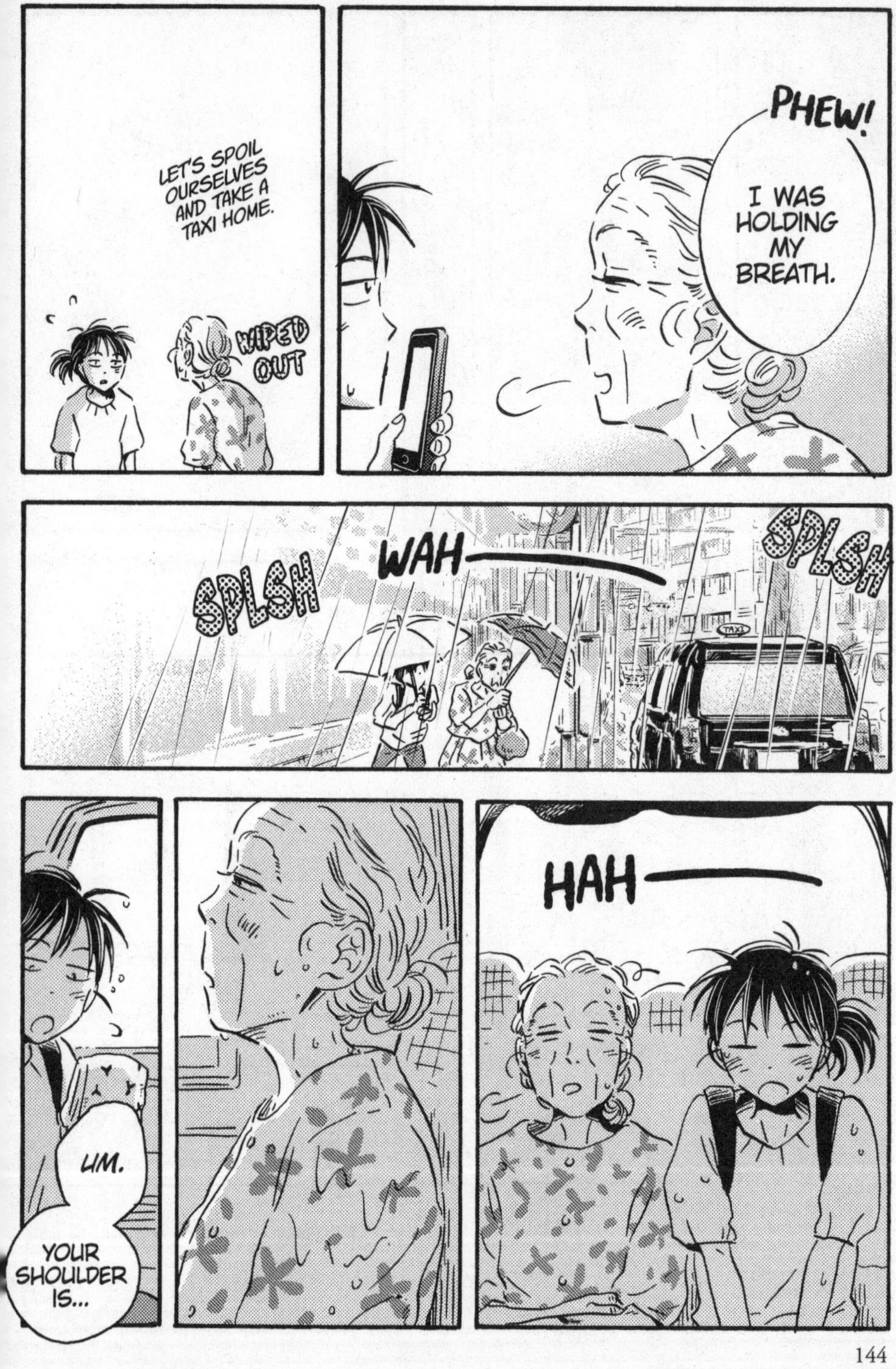
PHEW!
I WAS HOLDING MY BREATH.
LET'S SPOIL OURSELVES AND TAKE A TAXI HOME.
WIPED OUT
SPLSH
WAH——
SPLSH
HAH——
UM.
YOUR SHOULDER IS...

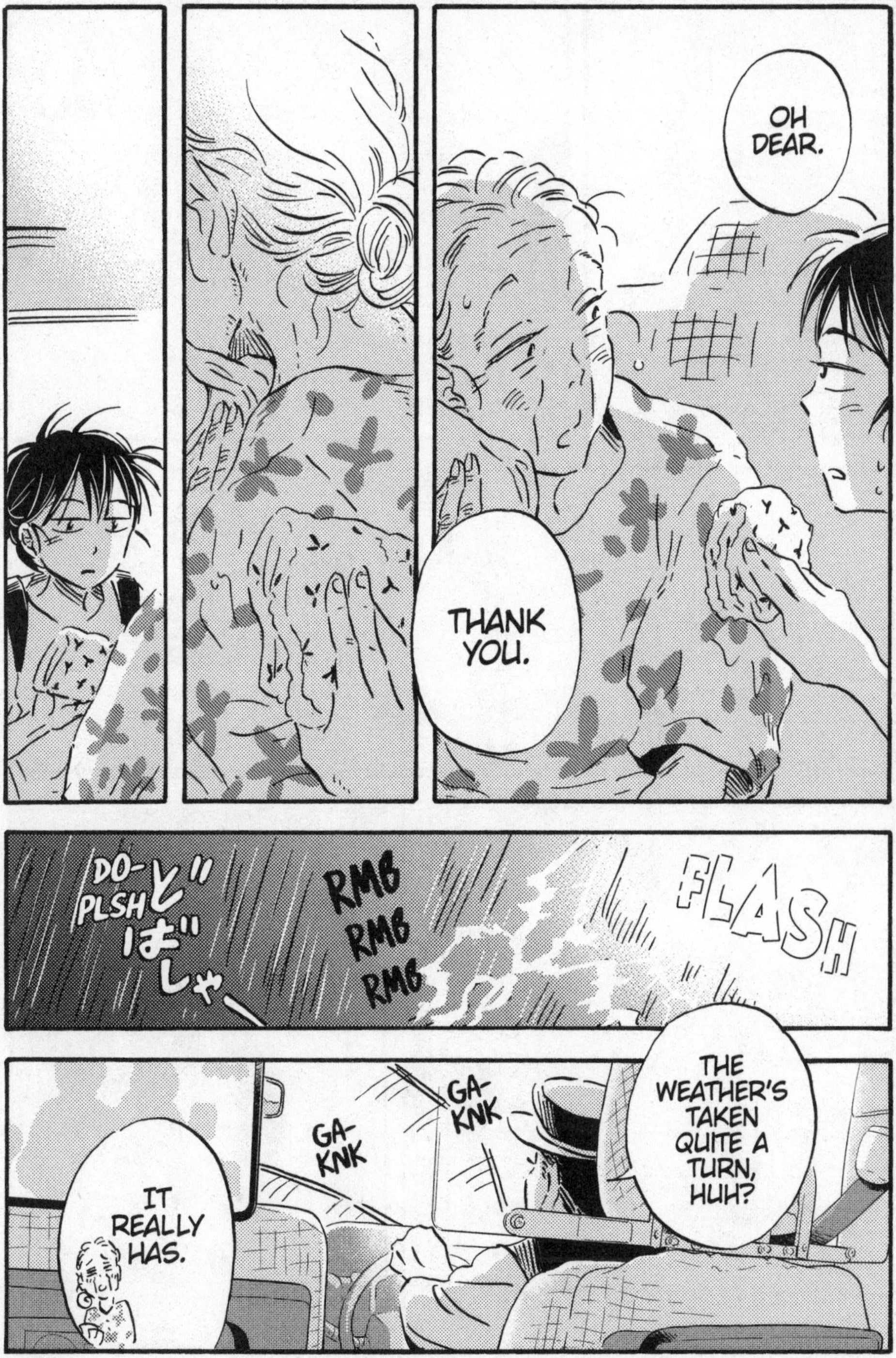
OH DEAR.
THANK YOU.
FLASH
RMB RMB RMB
DO-PLSH
どばしゃー
THE WEATHER'S TAKEN QUITE A TURN, HUH?
GA-KNK
GA-KNK
IT REALLY HAS.

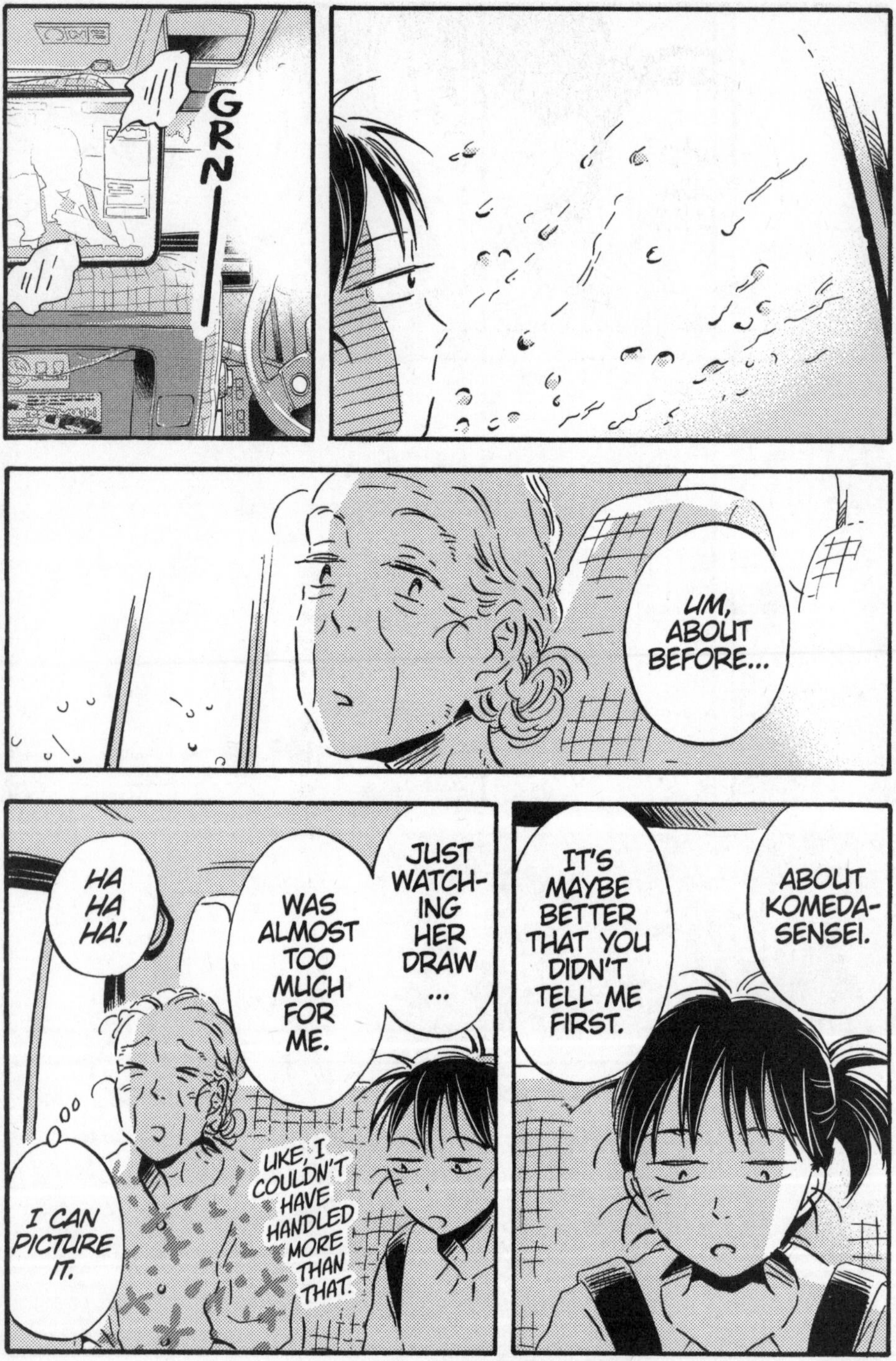
GRN
UM, ABOUT BEFORE...
ABOUT KOMEDA-SENSEI.
IT'S MAYBE BETTER THAT YOU DIDN'T TELL ME FIRST.
JUST WATCHING-ING HER DRAW...
WAS ALMOST TOO MUCH FOR ME.
LIKE, I COULDN'T HAVE HANDLED MORE THAN THAT.
HA HA HA!
I CAN PICTURE IT.

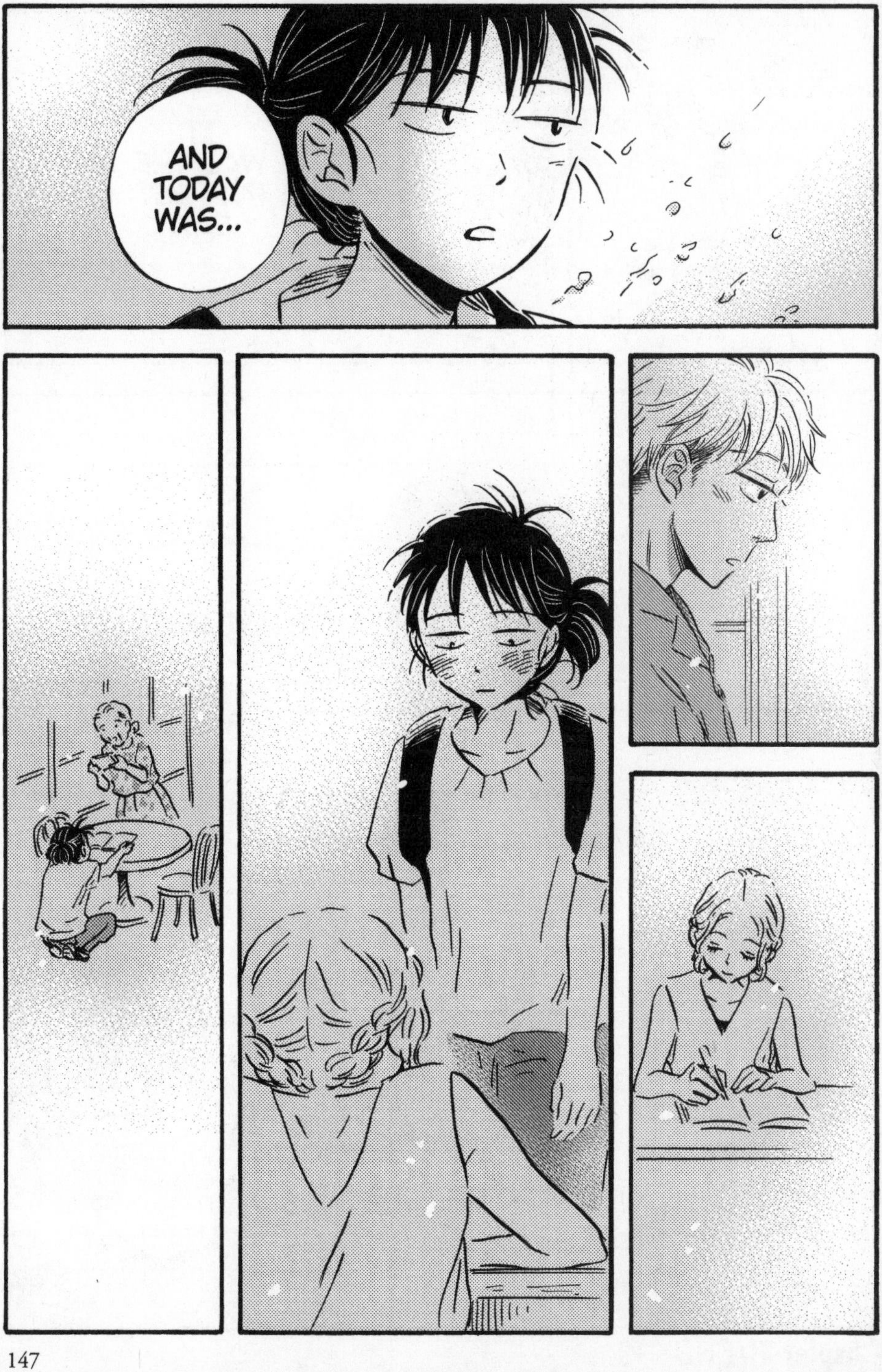
AND TODAY WAS...

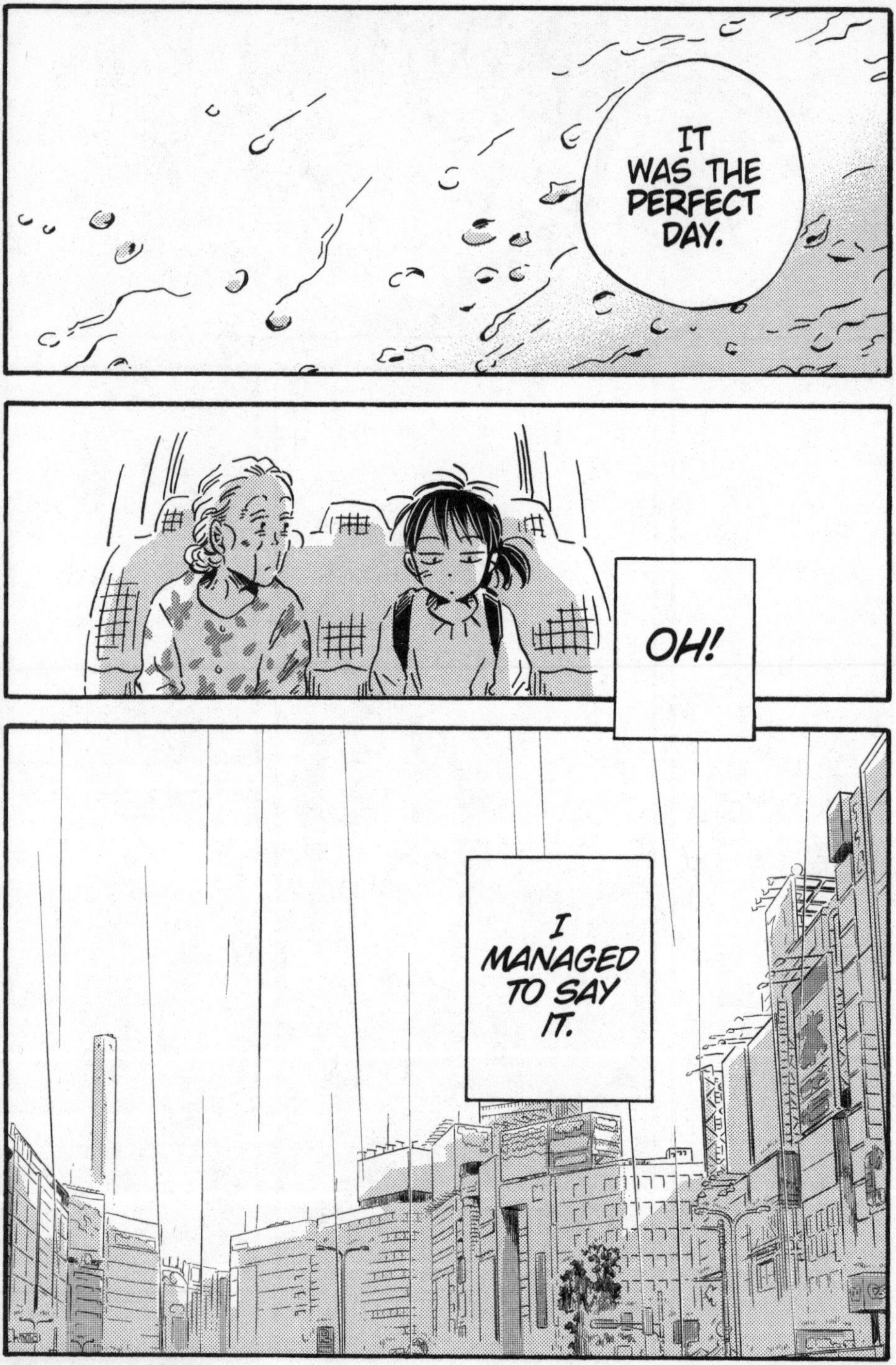
IT WAS THE PERFECT DAY.
OH!
I MANAGED TO SAY IT.

Chapter 51/END

metamorphosis

## Final Chapter

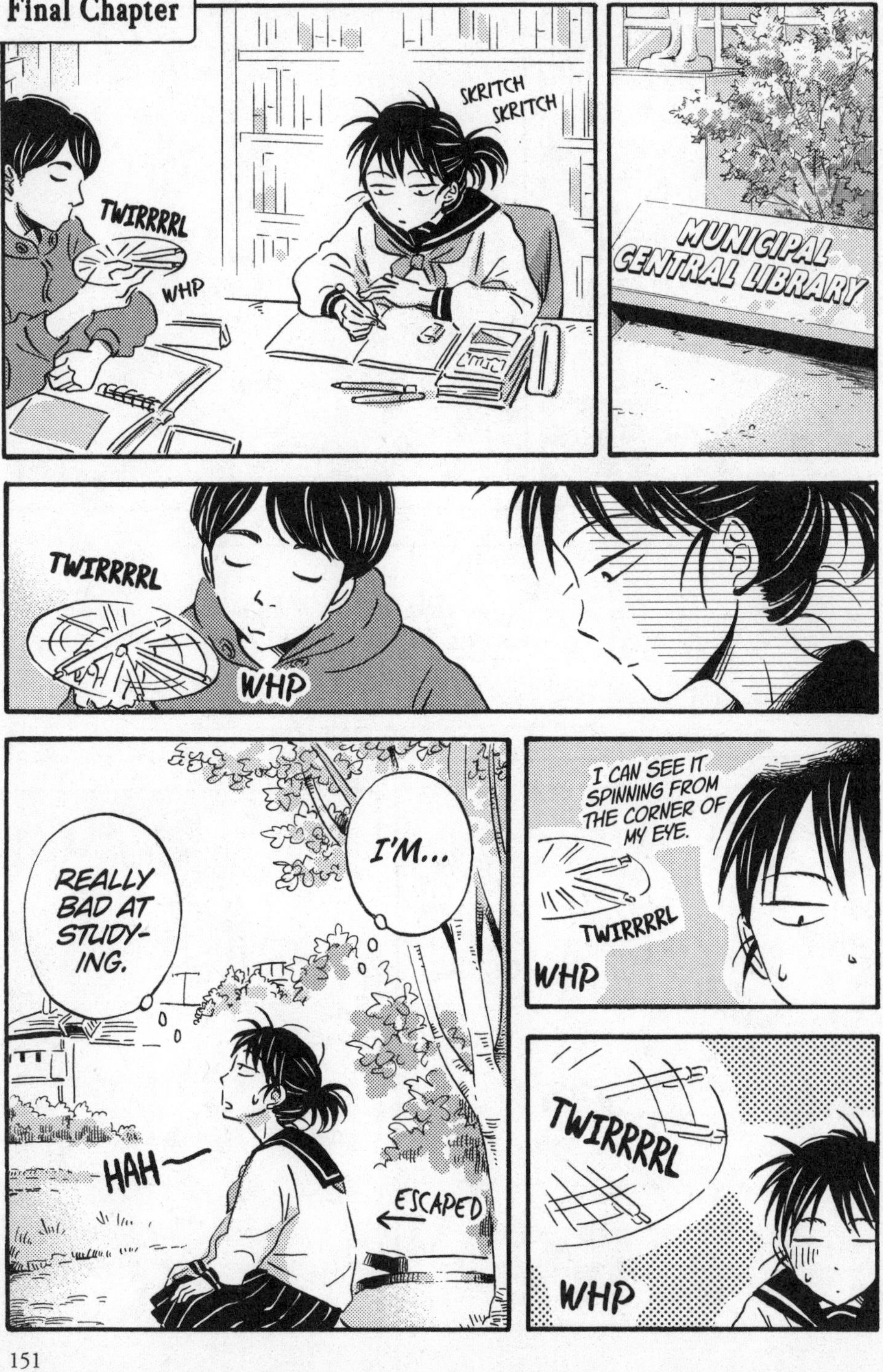
MUNICIPAL CENTRAL LIBRARY
SKRITCH SKRITCH
TWIRRRRL
WHP
TWIRRRRL
WHP
I CAN SEE IT SPINNING FROM THE CORNER OF MY EYE.
TWIRRRRL
WHP
TWIRRRRL
WHP
I'M...
REALLY BAD AT STUDY-ING.
HAH~
ESCAPED

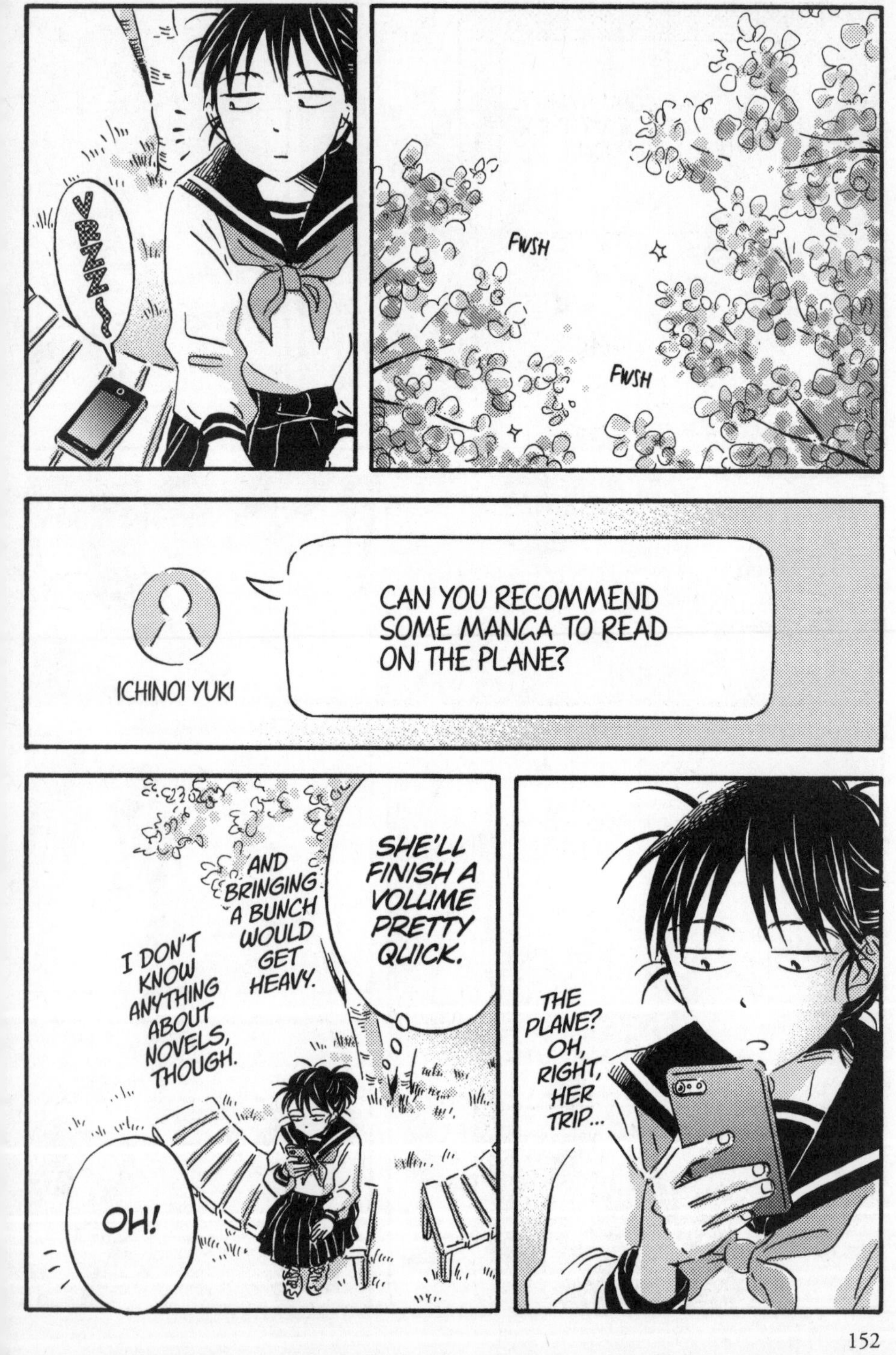
FWSH
FWSH
VRZZ~
ICHINOI YUKI
CAN YOU RECOMMEND SOME MANGA TO READ ON THE PLANE?
THE PLANE? OH, RIGHT, HER TRIP...
SHE'LL FINISH A VOLUME PRETTY QUICK.
AND BRINGING A BUNCH WOULD GET HEAVY.
I DON'T KNOW ANYTHING ABOUT NOVELS, THOUGH.
OH!

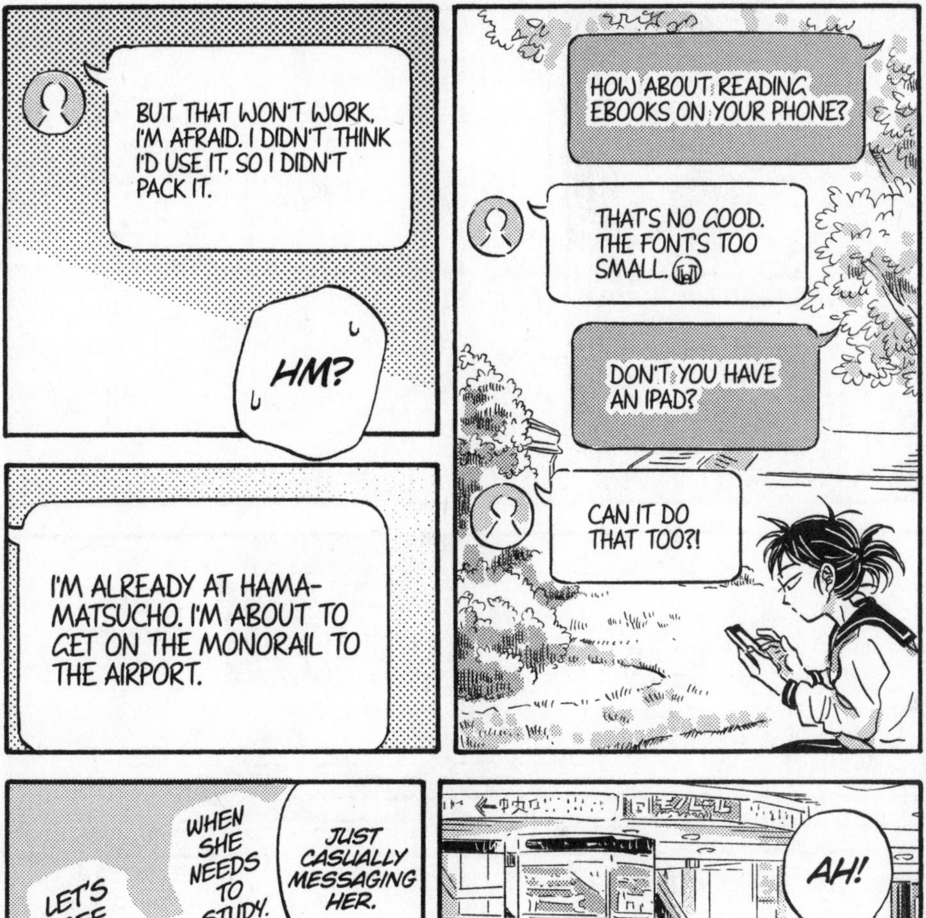
HOW ABOUT READING EBOOKS ON YOUR PHONE?
THAT'S NO GOOD. THE FONT'S TOO SMALL.
DON'T YOU HAVE AN IPAD?
CAN IT DO THAT TOO?!
BUT THAT WON'T WORK, I'M AFRAID. I DIDN'T THINK I'D USE IT, SO I DIDN'T PACK IT.
HM?
I'M ALREADY AT HAMA-MATSUCHO. I'M ABOUT TO GET ON THE MONORAIL TO THE AIRPORT.
AH!
I DID IT AGAIN.
JUST CASUALLY MESSAGING HER.
WHEN SHE NEEDS TO STUDY.
LET'S SEE, HMM.
Y-O-U-A-R-E-P-R-O-B-A-B-L-Y-S-T-U-D-Y...
URARA LINE AUDIO
AH!

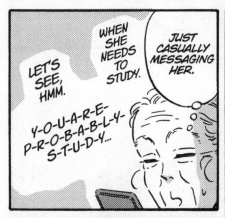

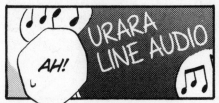

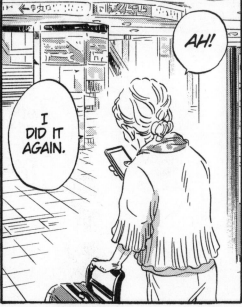

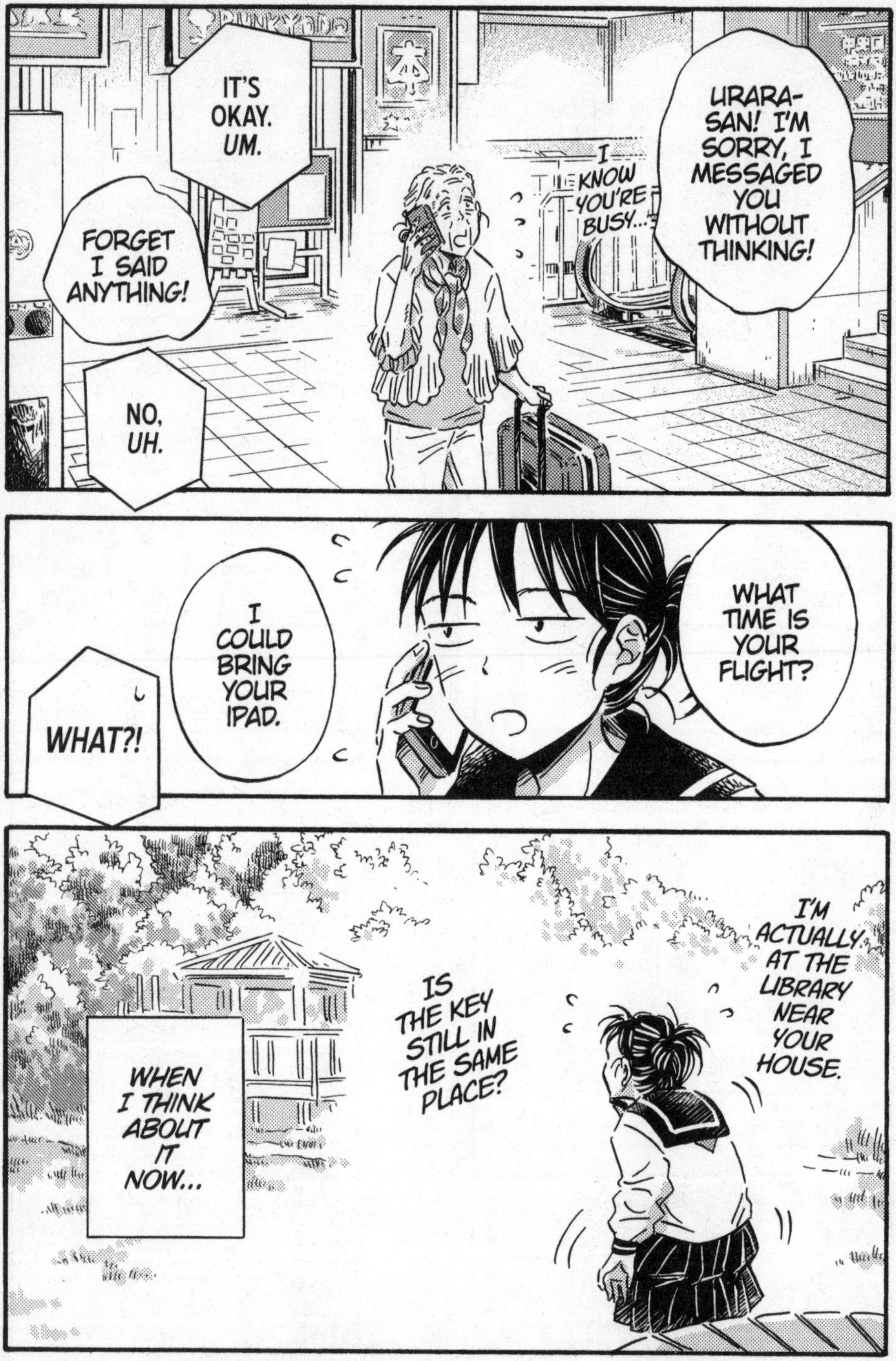
URARA-SAN! I'M SORRY, I MESSAGED YOU WITHOUT THINKING!
I KNOW YOU'RE BUSY...
IT'S OKAY. UM.
FORGET I SAID ANYTHING!
NO, UH.
WHAT TIME IS YOUR FLIGHT?
I COULD BRING YOUR IPAD.
WHAT?!
I'M ACTUALLY AT THE LIBRARY NEAR YOUR HOUSE.
IS THE KEY STILL IN THE SAME PLACE?
WHEN I THINK ABOUT IT NOW...

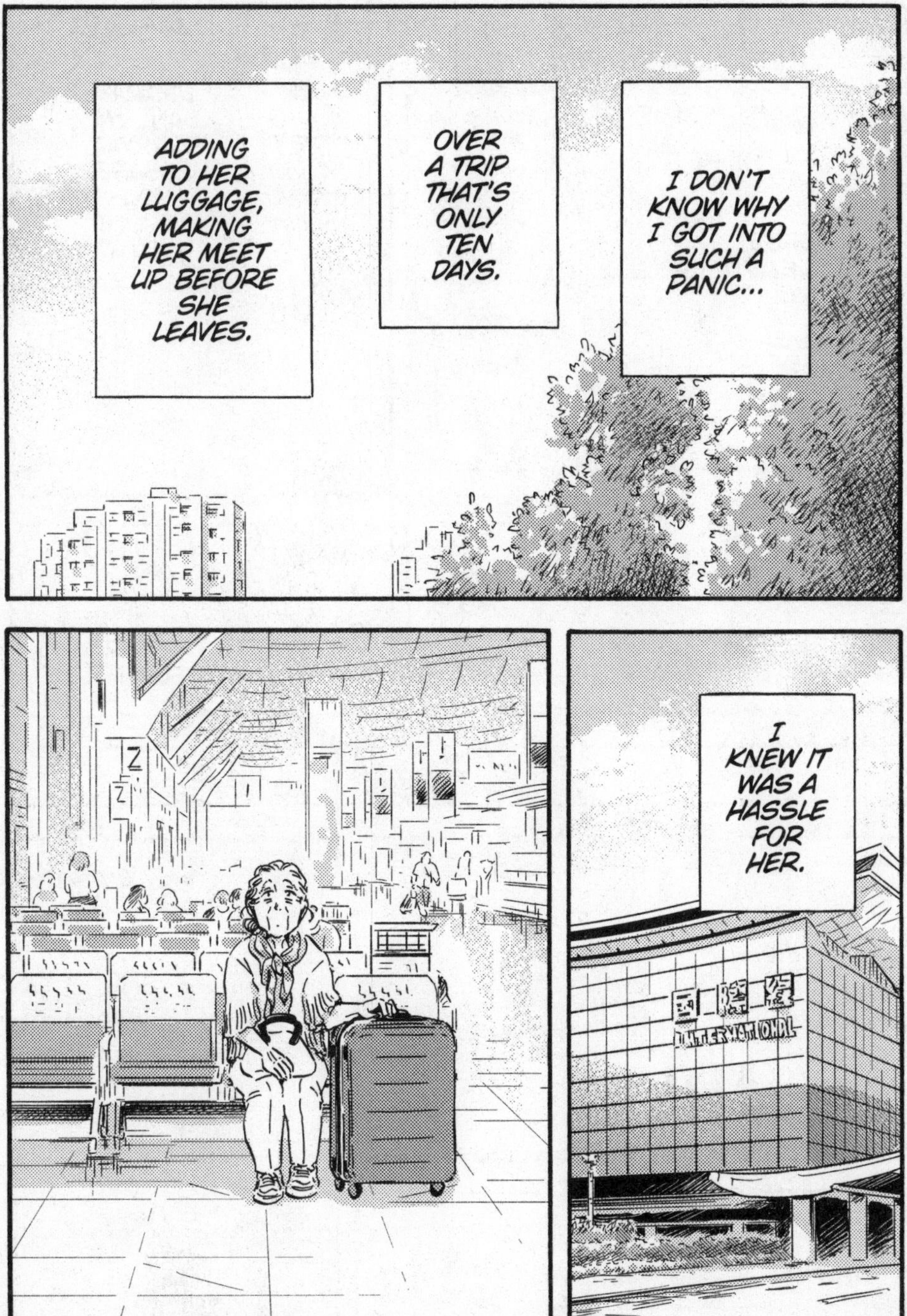
I DON'T KNOW WHY I GOT INTO SUCH A PANIC...
OVER A TRIP THAT'S ONLY TEN DAYS.
ADDING TO HER LUGGAGE, MAKING HER MEET UP BEFORE SHE LEAVES.
I KNEW IT WAS A HASSLE FOR HER.
INTERNATIONAL

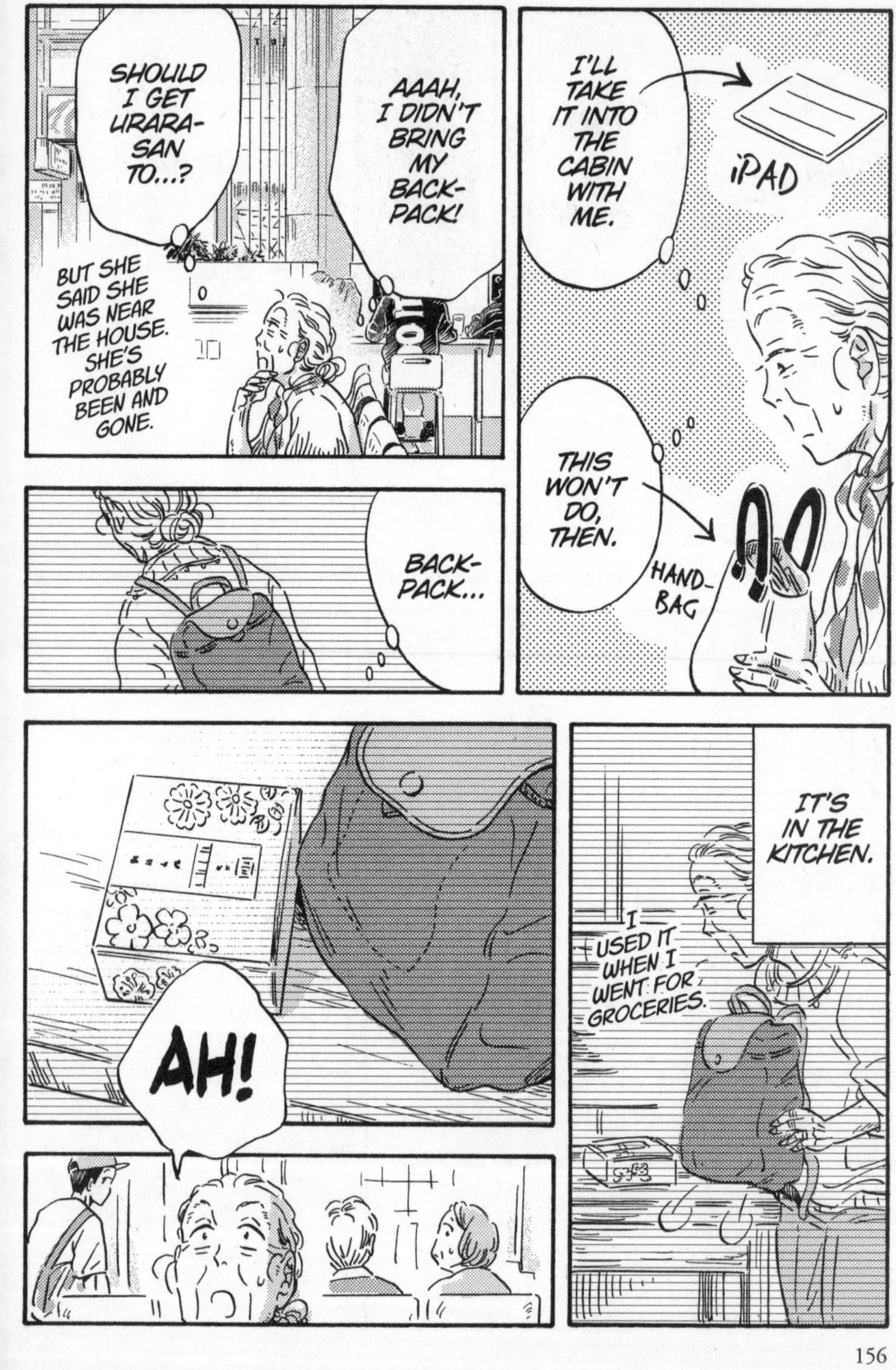
I'LL TAKE IT INTO THE CABIN WITH ME.
iPAD
THIS WON'T DO, THEN.
HANDBAG
AAAH, I DIDN'T BRING MY BACKPACK!
SHOULD I GET URARA-SAN TO...?
BUT SHE SAID SHE WAS NEAR THE HOUSE. SHE'S PROBABLY BEEN AND GONE.
BACKPACK...
IT'S IN THE KITCHEN.
I USED IT WHEN I WENT FOR GROCERIES.
AH!

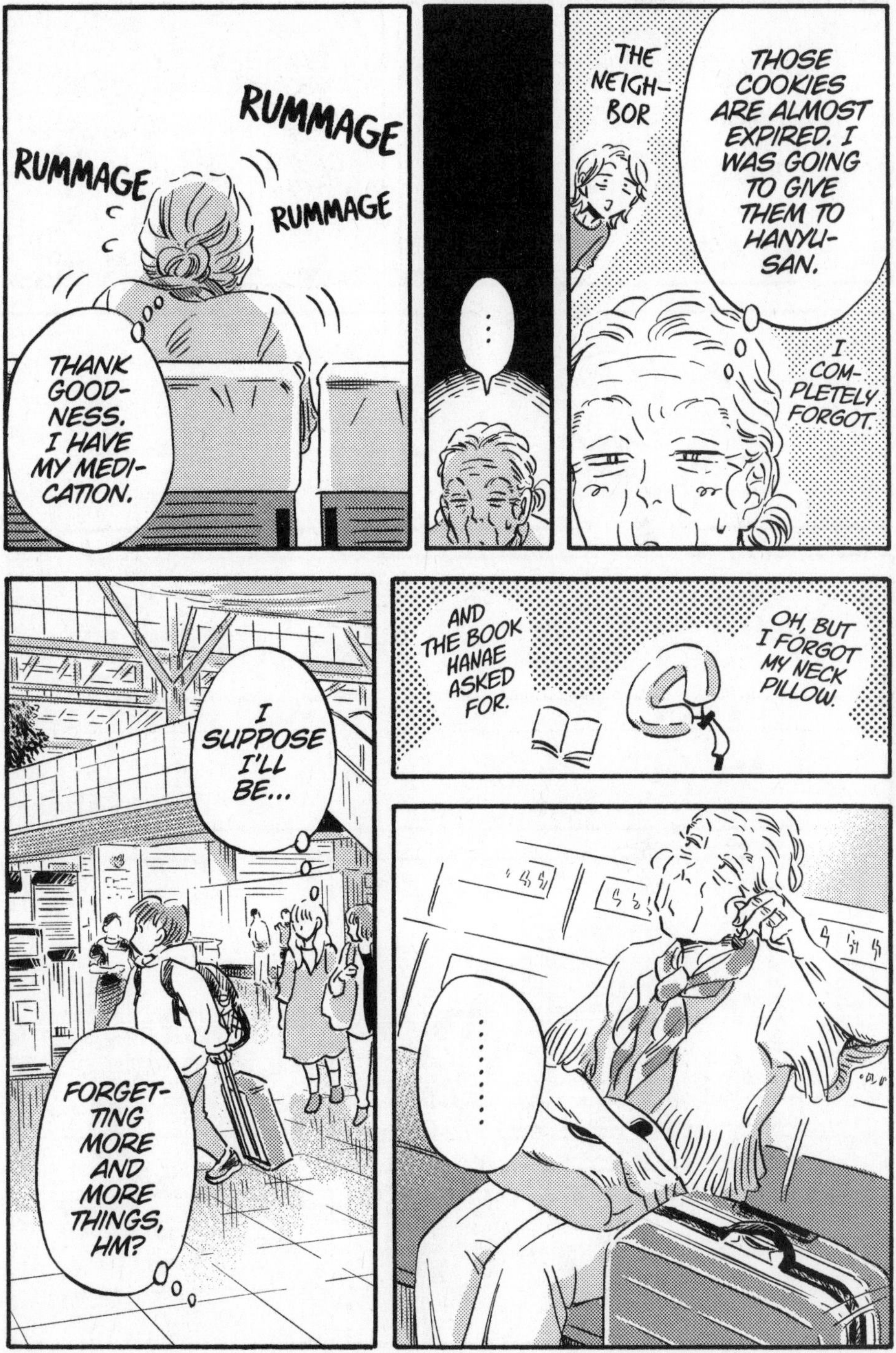
THOSE COOKIES ARE ALMOST EXPIRED. I WAS GOING TO GIVE THEM TO HANYU-SAN.
THE NEIGHBOR
I COMPLETELY FORGOT.
...
RUMMAGE
RUMMAGE
RUMMAGE
THANK GOODNESS. I HAVE MY MEDICATION.
OH, BUT I FORGOT MY NECK PILLOW.
AND THE BOOK HANAE ASKED FOR.
......
I SUPPOSE I'LL BE...
FORGETTING MORE AND MORE THINGS, HM?

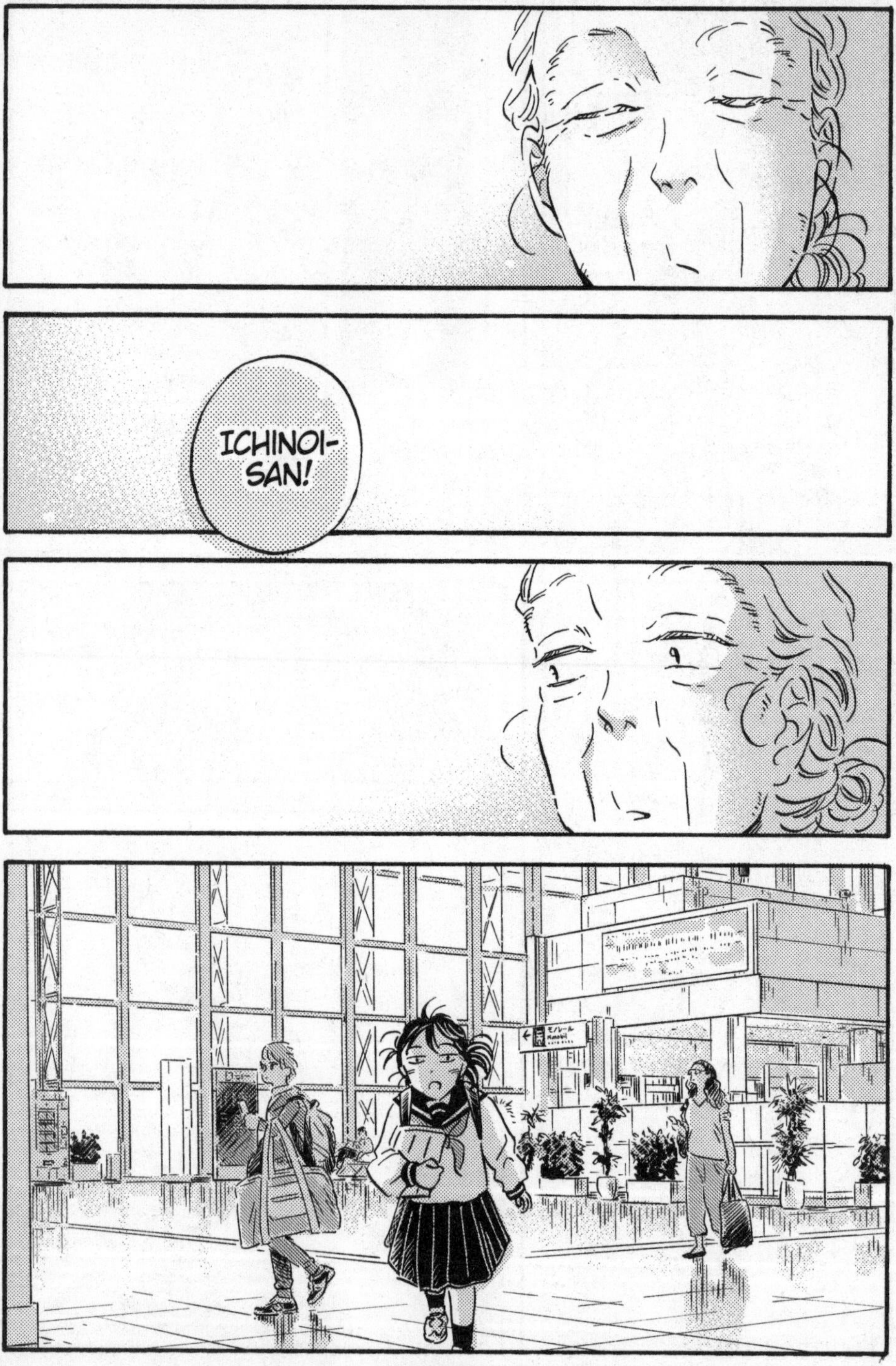
ICHINOI-SAN!

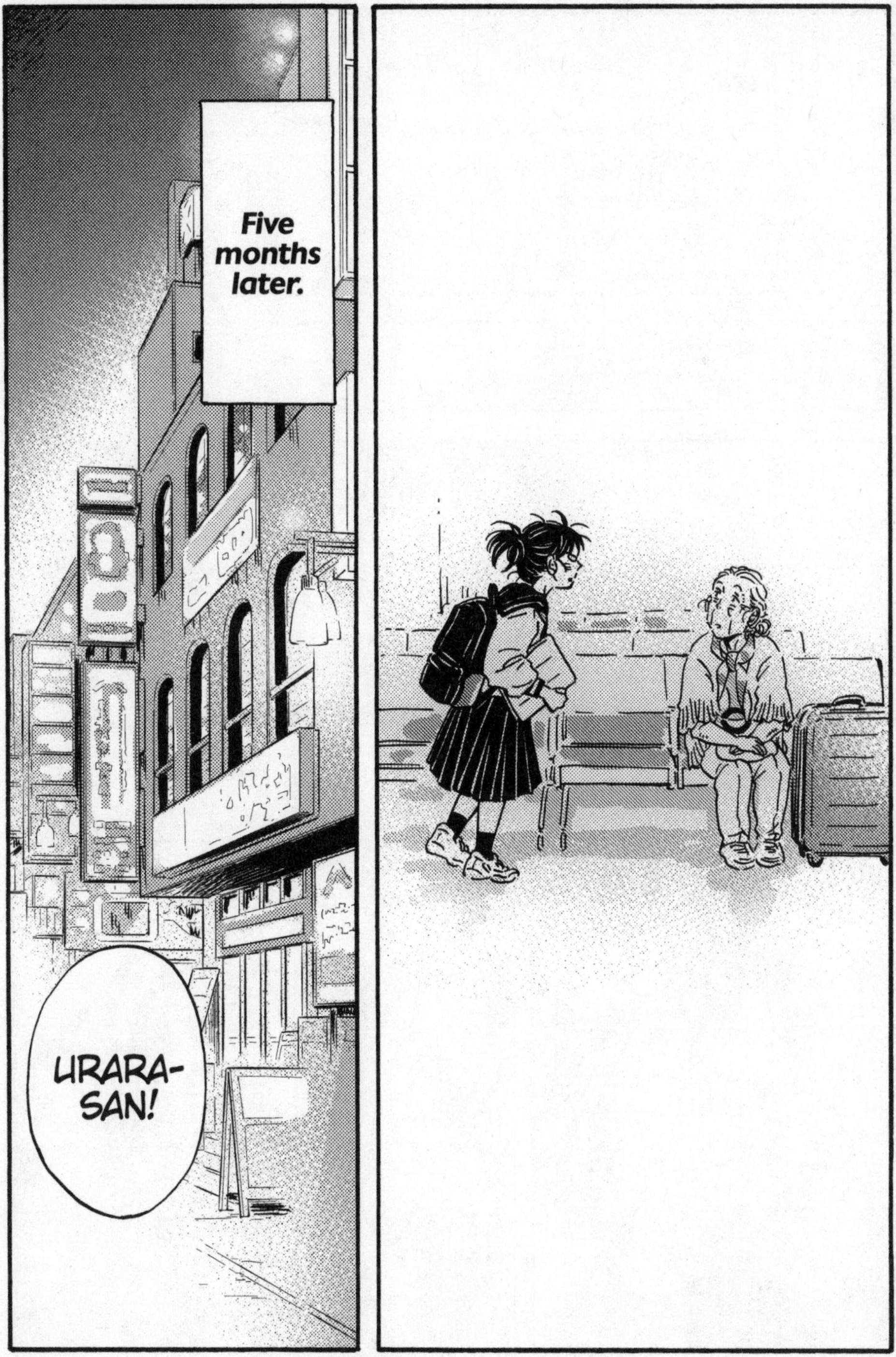
Five months later.
URARA-SAN!

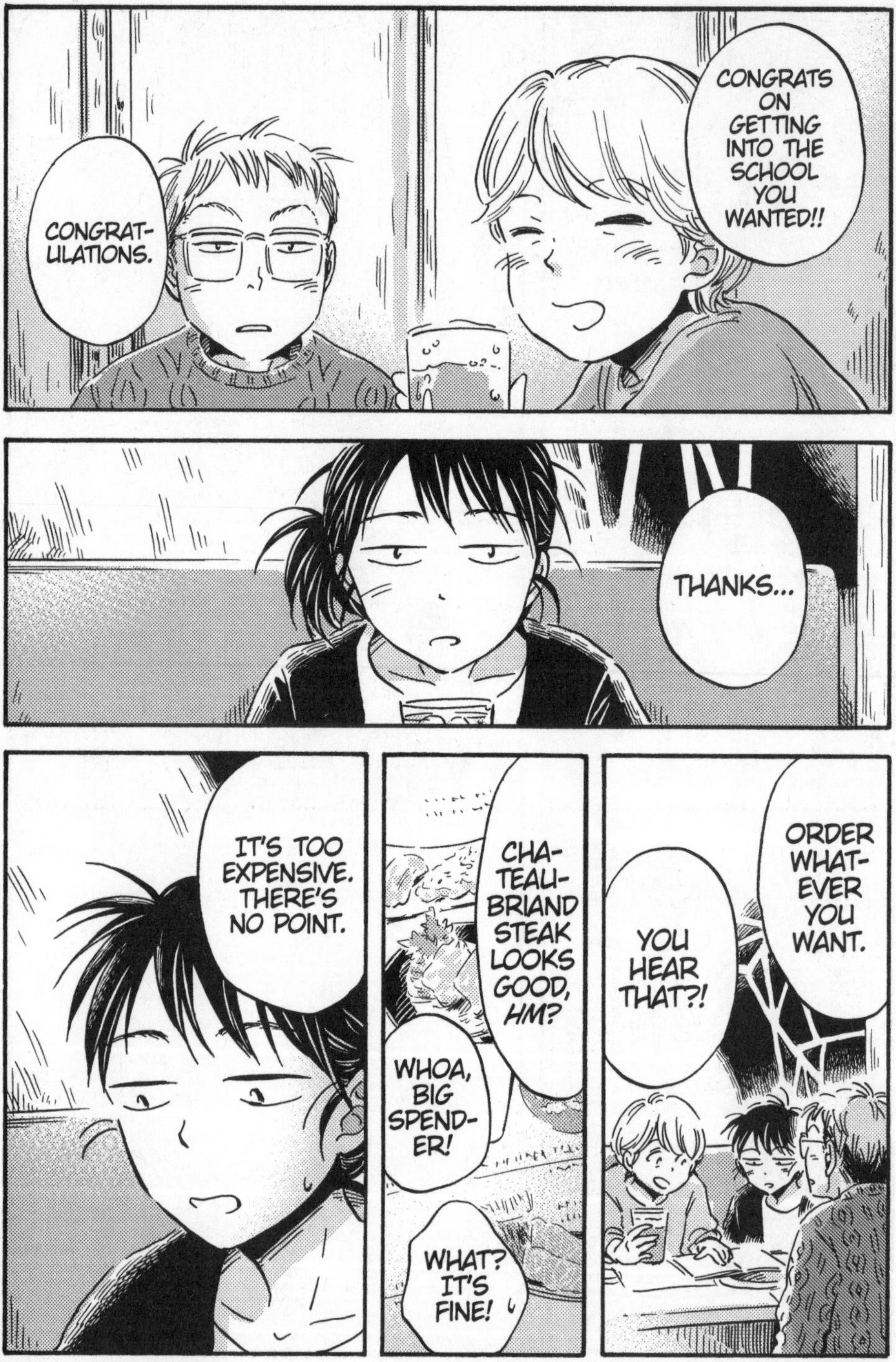
CONGRATS ON GETTING INTO THE SCHOOL YOU WANTED!!
CONGRATULATIONS.
THANKS...
ORDER WHATEVER YOU WANT.
YOU HEAR THAT?!
CHATEAUBRIAND STEAK LOOKS GOOD, HM?
WHOA, BIG SPENDER!
WHAT? IT'S FINE!
IT'S TOO EXPENSIVE. THERE'S NO POINT.

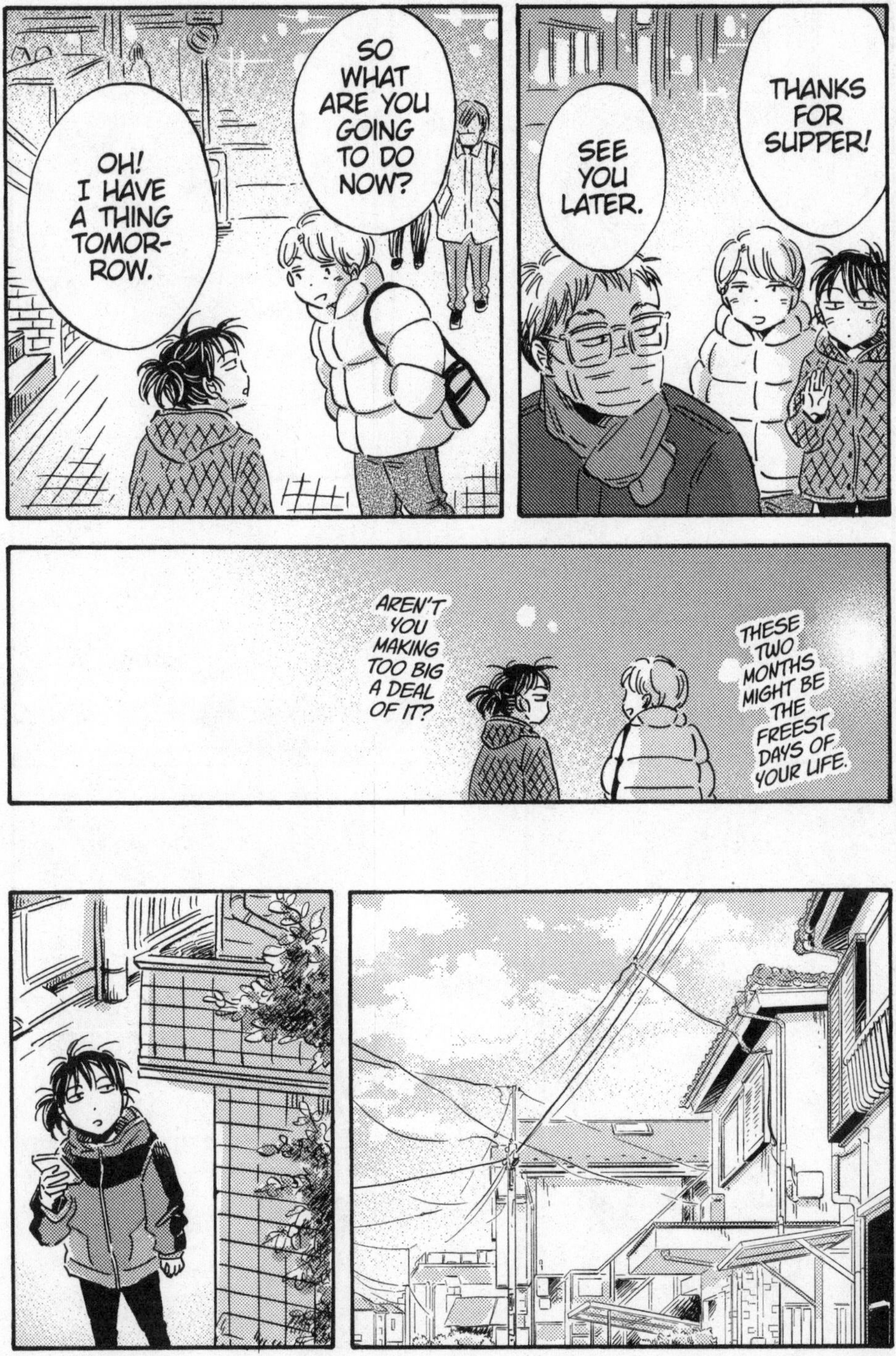
THANKS FOR SUPPER!
SEE YOU LATER.
SO WHAT ARE YOU GOING TO DO NOW?
OH! I HAVE A THING TOMORROW.
THESE TWO MONTHS MIGHT BE THE FREEST DAYS OF YOUR LIFE.
AREN'T YOU MAKING TOO BIG A DEAL OF IT?

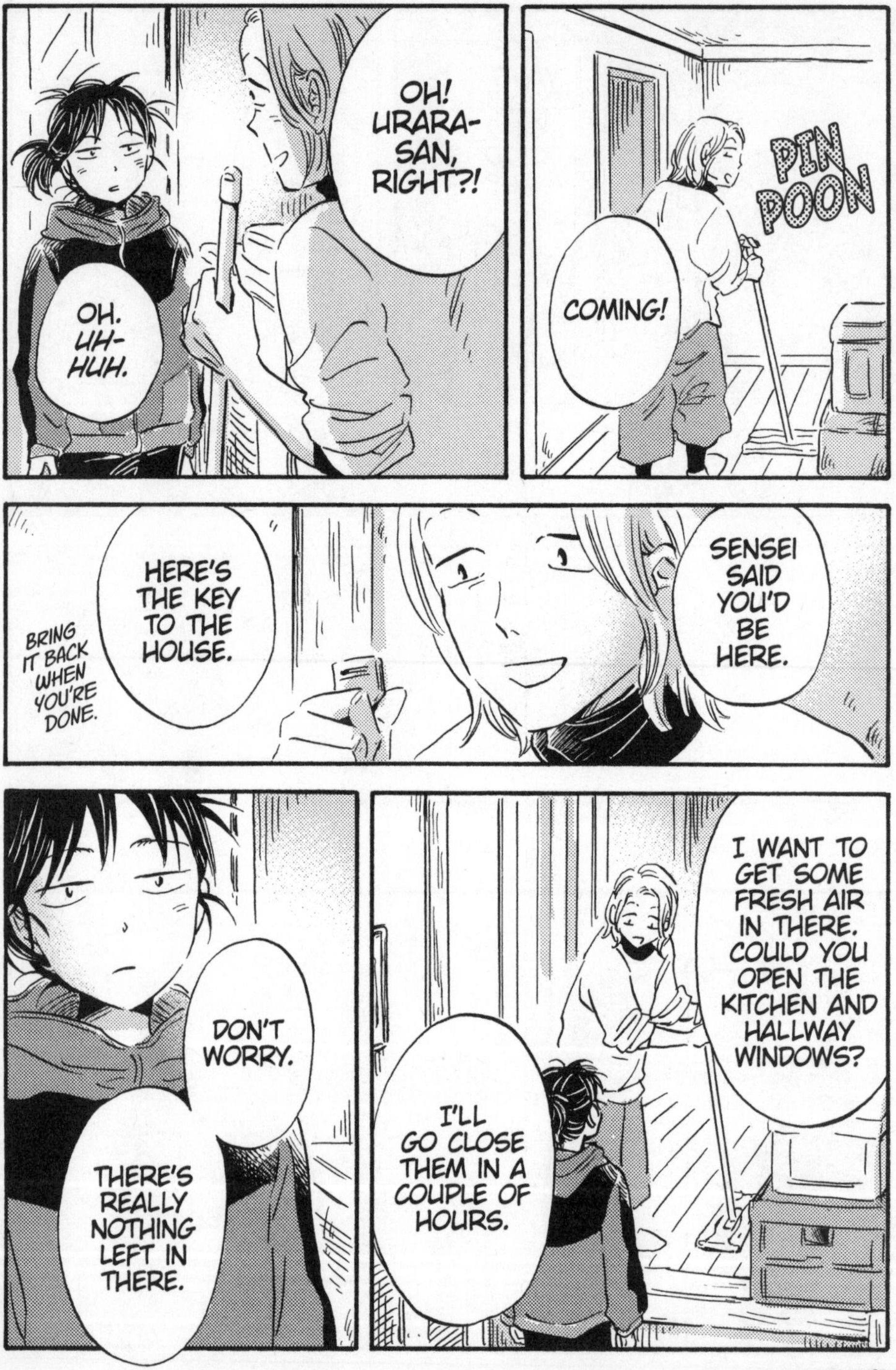
PIN POON
COMING!
OH! URARA-SAN, RIGHT?!
OH. UH-HUH.
SENSEI SAID YOU'D BE HERE.
HERE'S THE KEY TO THE HOUSE.
BRING IT BACK WHEN YOU'RE DONE.
I WANT TO GET SOME FRESH AIR IN THERE. COULD YOU OPEN THE KITCHEN AND HALLWAY WINDOWS?
I'LL GO CLOSE THEM IN A COUPLE OF HOURS.
DON'T WORRY.
THERE'S REALLY NOTHING LEFT IN THERE.

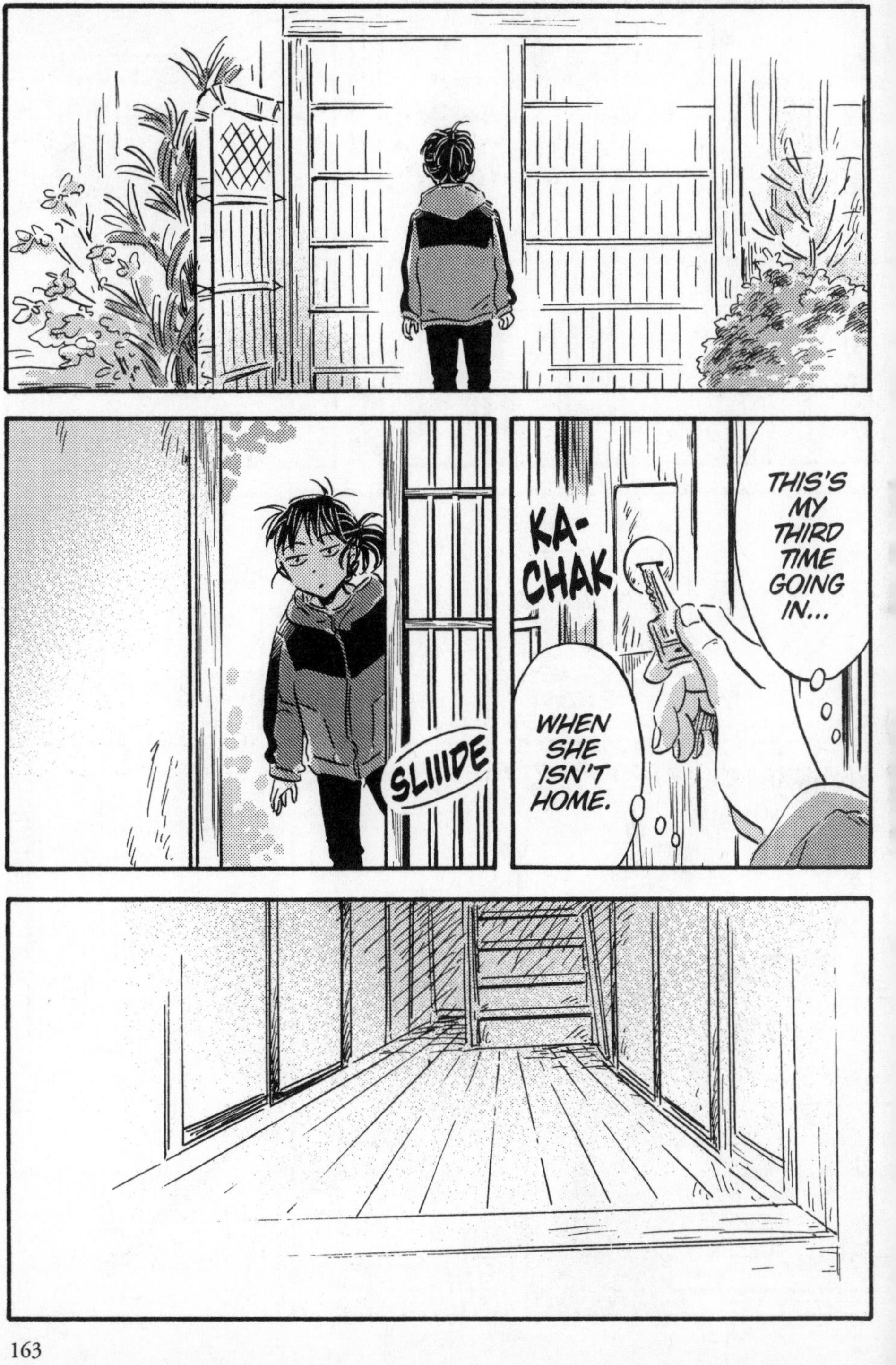
THIS'S MY THIRD TIME GOING IN...
KA-CHAK
WHEN SHE ISN'T HOME.
SLIIIDE

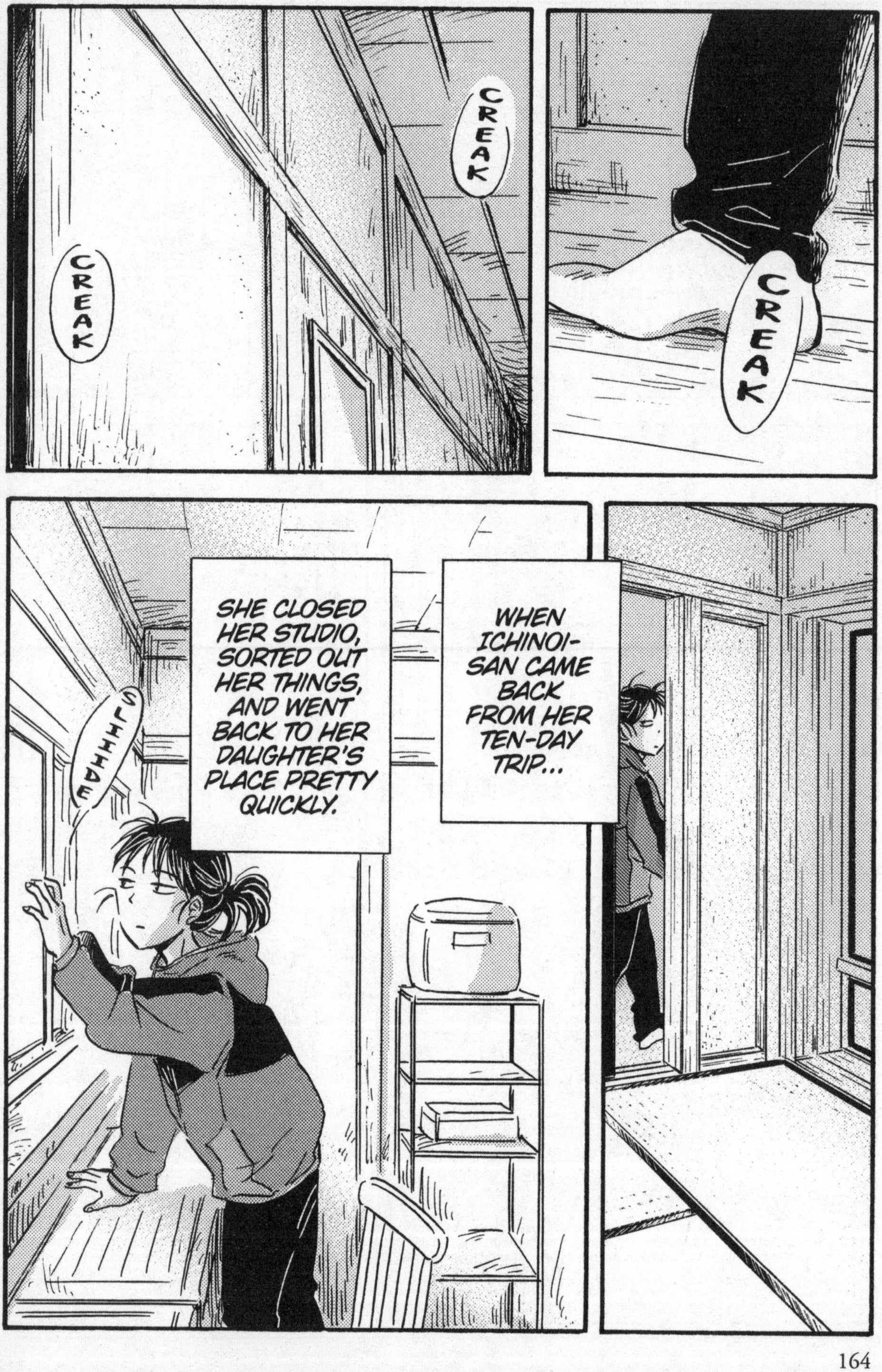
CREAK
CREAK
CREAK
WHEN ICHINOI-SAN CAME BACK FROM HER TEN-DAY TRIP...
SHE CLOSED HER STUDIO, SORTED OUT HER THINGS, AND WENT BACK TO HER DAUGHTER'S PLACE PRETTY QUICKLY.
SLIIIDE

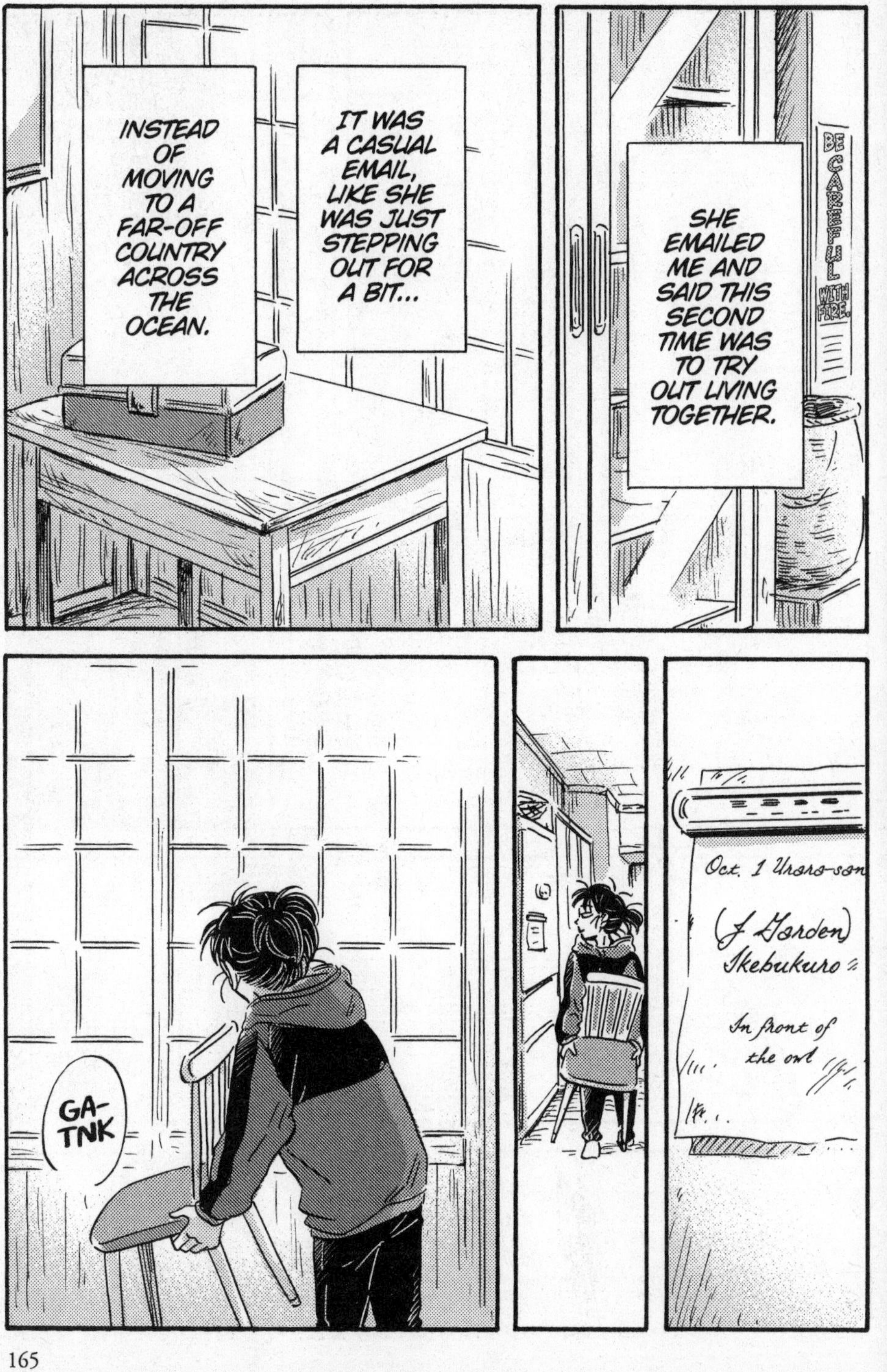
SHE EMAILED ME AND SAID THIS SECOND TIME WAS TO TRY OUT LIVING TOGETHER.
BE CAREFUL WITH FIRE.
IT WAS A CASUAL EMAIL, LIKE SHE WAS JUST STEPPING OUT FOR A BIT...
INSTEAD OF MOVING TO A FAR-OFF COUNTRY ACROSS THE OCEAN.
Oct. 1 Urara-san
(J Garden) Ikebukuro
In front of the owl
GA-TNK

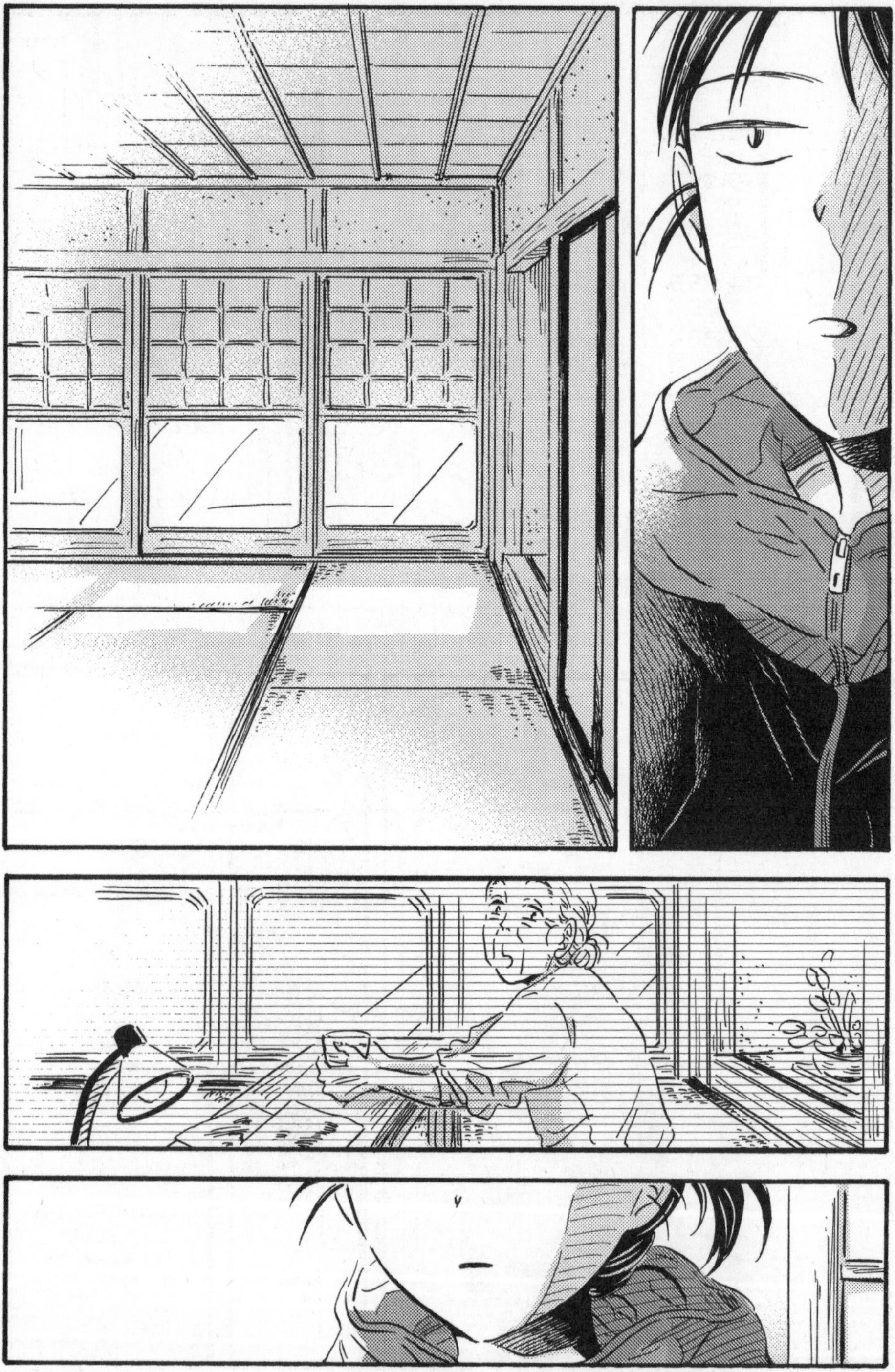

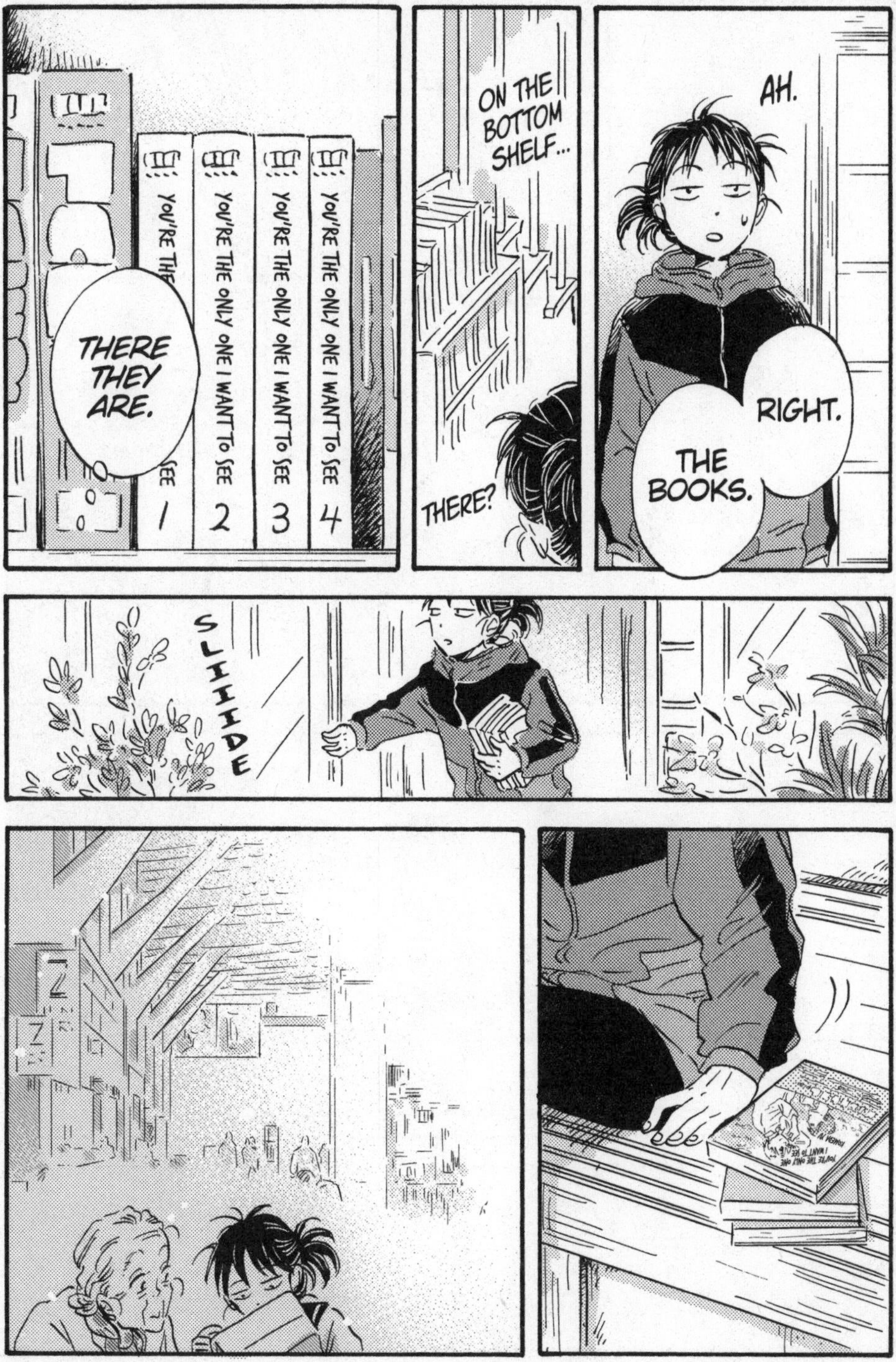
AH.
RIGHT.
THE BOOKS.
ON THE BOTTOM SHELF...
THERE?
THERE THEY ARE.
YOU'RE THE ONLY ONE I WANT TO SEE 2
YOU'RE THE ONLY ONE I WANT TO SEE 3
YOU'RE THE ONLY ONE I WANT TO SEE 4
SLIIIIDE

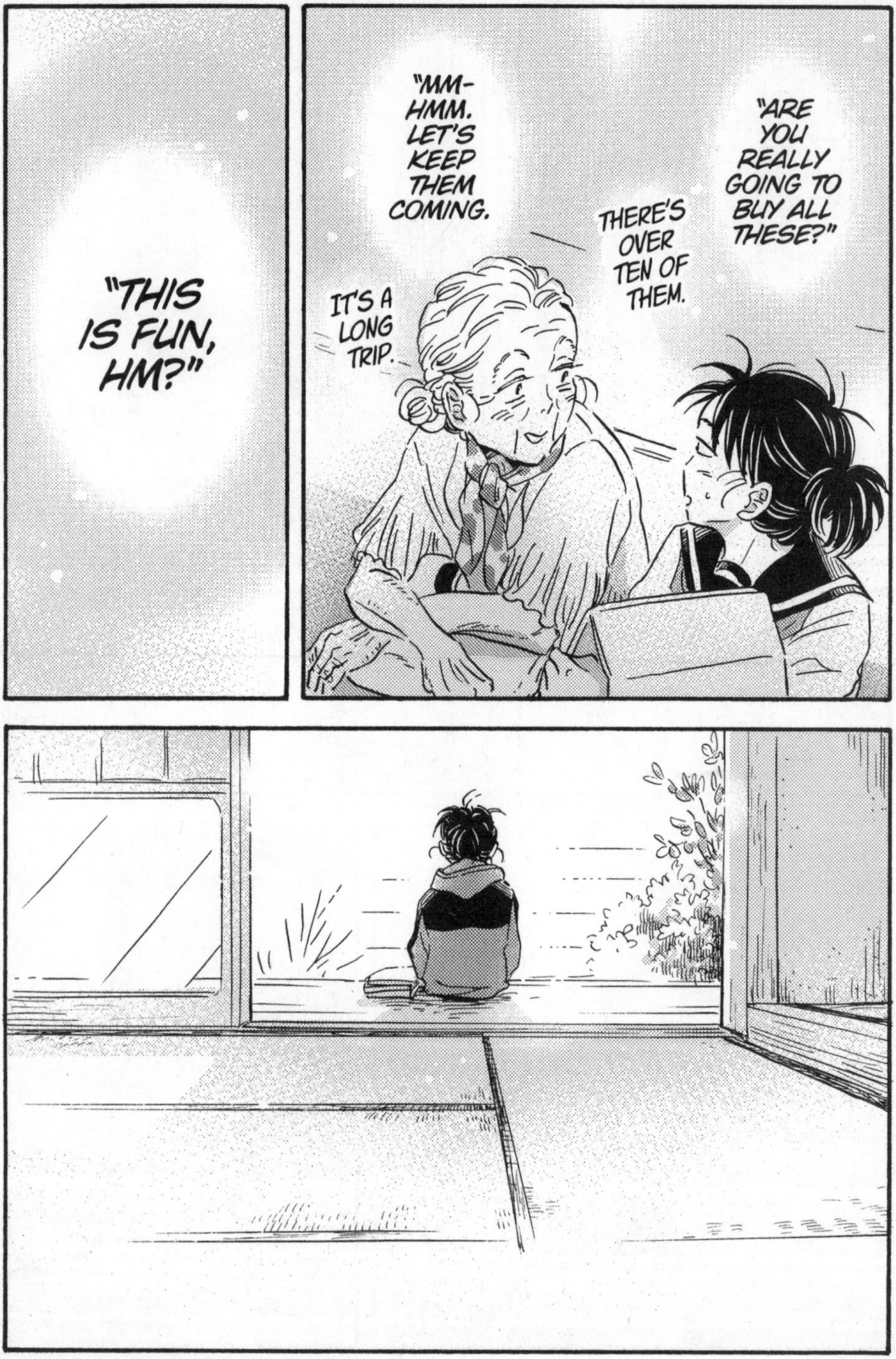
"ARE YOU REALLY GOING TO BUY ALL THESE?"
THERE'S OVER TEN OF THEM.
"MM-HMM. LET'S KEEP THEM COMING.
IT'S A LONG TRIP.
"THIS IS FUN, HM?"

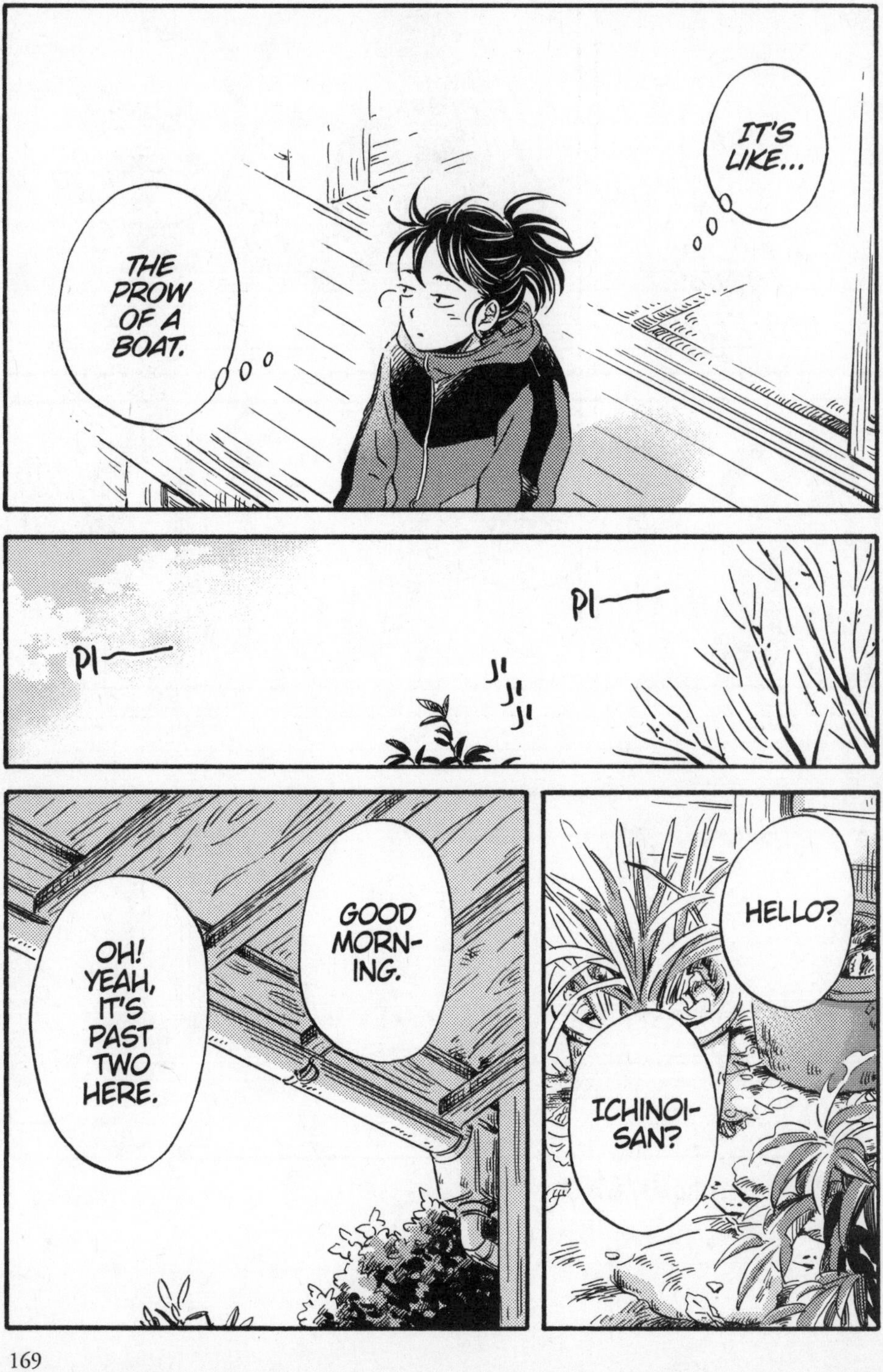
IT'S LIKE...
THE PROW OF A BOAT.
PI—
JI
JI
JI
PI—
HELLO?
ICHINOI-SAN?
GOOD MORN-ING.
OH! YEAH, IT'S PAST TWO HERE.

I FOUND THE BOOKS.
SH-TMP
OKAY.
I'LL SEND THEM TODAY.

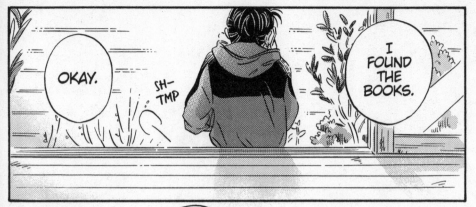

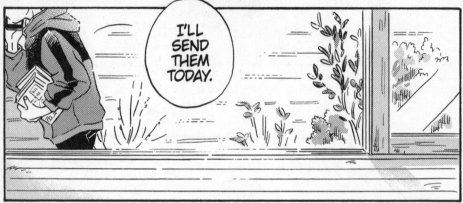

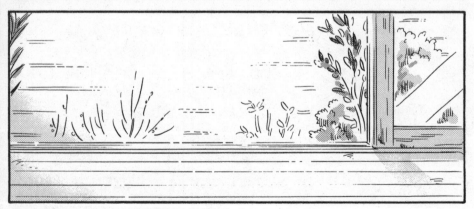

BL Metamorphosis/END

He Came from Far Away

FLASH

AAH, WORK WAS EXHAUST-ING.

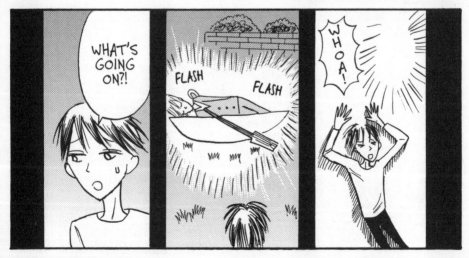

WHAT'S GOING ON?!

FLASH FLASH

WHOA!

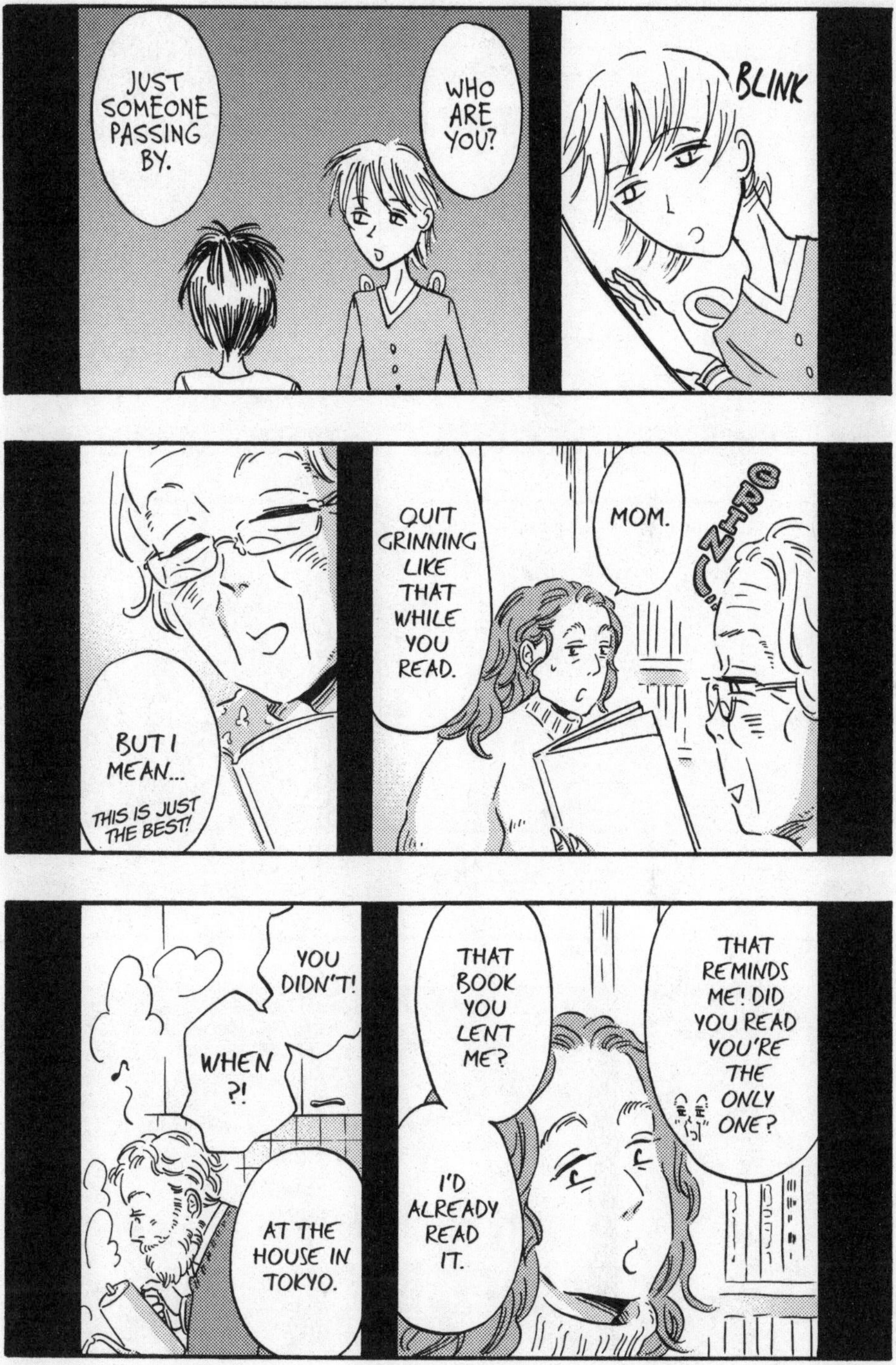

BLINK
WHO ARE YOU?
JUST SOMEONE PASSING BY.
ZING
MOM.
QUIT GRINNING LIKE THAT WHILE YOU READ.
BUT I MEAN... THIS IS JUST THE BEST!
THAT REMINDS ME! DID YOU READ YOU'RE THE ONLY ONE?
THAT BOOK YOU LENT ME?
I'D ALREADY READ IT.
YOU DIDN'T!
WHEN ?!
AT THE HOUSE IN TOKYO.

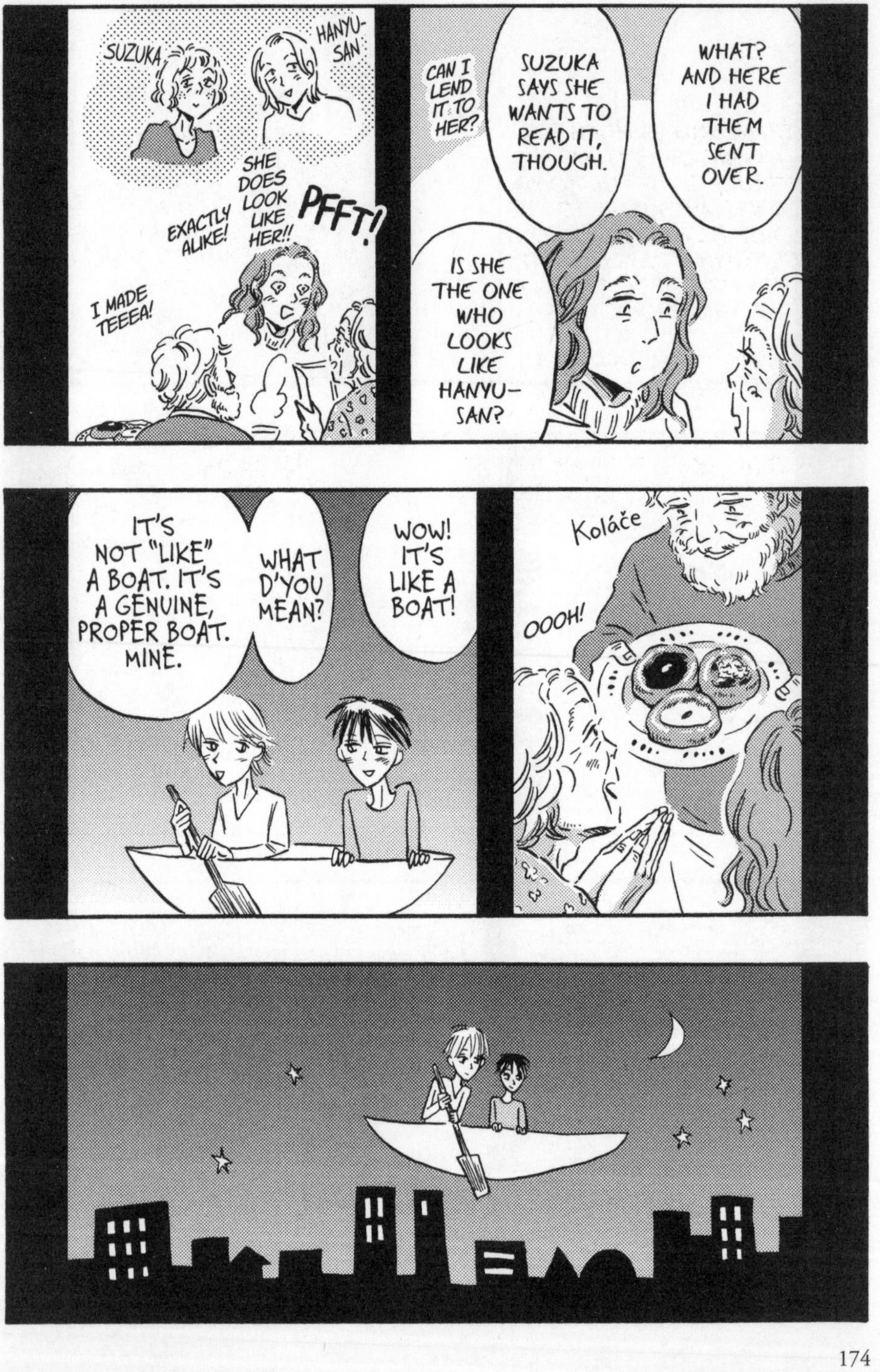
WHAT? AND HERE I HAD THEM SENT OVER.
SUZUKA SAYS SHE WANTS TO READ IT, THOUGH.
CAN I LEND IT TO HER?
IS SHE THE ONE WHO LOOKS LIKE HANYU-SAN?
HANYU-SAN
SUZUKA
PFFT!
SHE DOES LOOK LIKE HER!!
EXACTLY ALIKE!
I MADE TEEEA!
Koláče
OOOH!
WOW! IT'S LIKE A BOAT!
WHAT D'YOU MEAN?
IT'S NOT "LIKE" A BOAT. IT'S A GENUINE, PROPER BOAT. MINE.

THANK YOU SO MUCH FOR PICKING UP VOLUME 5! I'M TRULY GRATEFUL TO YOU FOR READING RIGHT TO THE END OF BL METAMORPHOSIS. IT'S THANKS TO ALL OF YOU THAT I WAS ABLE TO DRAW IT THIS WHOLE TIME.

EVERY TIME I READ THE QUESTIONNAIRE POSTCARDS OR THE THOUGHTS AND OPINIONS I'VE RECEIVED, I KEENLY FEEL THAT A WORK ISN'T ONLY CREATED BY THE ARTIST. THE READERS ARE PART OF IT, TOO.

COLORING THE PICTURES; ADDING THINGS...
I READ MY FIRST MANGA! NINE YEARS OLD.
THMP
YUKI-SAN'S REALLY LIKE THIS THEN.
EH HEH HEH.
DISCOVERING THINGS LIKE, "OH, I HAD NO IDEA!" POSTCARDS ABOUT URARA-SAN FROM MANGA ARTISTS I LOVE.
MY EDITOR COLLECTS THE QUESTIONNAIRE POSTCARDS AND SENDS ME IMAGES OF THEM, BUT I GET TOO EXCITED AND CAN'T READ THEM ALL AT ONCE. I ALWAYS TAKE A LOT OF BREAKS WHILE READING.

AND I WANT TO TAKE THIS OPPORTUNITY TO SAY THANK YOU TO MY LITTLE SISTER, WHO IS MY FIRST READER AND REALLY THE SECOND CREATOR OF THIS MANGA.

OH! BUT AT A TIME LIKE THIS, OUR GRANDMA WOULD...
MY YOUNGER SISTER THOUGHT UP SCENES AND DIALOGUE FOR ME TOO MANY TIMES TO COUNT.
OHOO!
NOW LOOK, YOU! THAT SORT OF THING'S JUST THIS AND THAT!
IMMEDIATE IMPERSONATION

I'M LOOKING FORWARD TO THE DAY WHEN I SEE YOU ALL AGAIN.

THANK YOU!

KAORI TSURUTANI DEC. 7, 2020

COVER DESIGN
Kohei Nawata Design Office

STAFF
Mayumi Tsuge
Akari Mikumo
Yamada
Niniko Yusa

EDITOR
Masayasu Noguchi

SPECIAL THANKS
Comitia executive committee
Junkudo Ikebukuro branch
Books Ruhe
Konno Shoten
Shogaku Asagaya branch

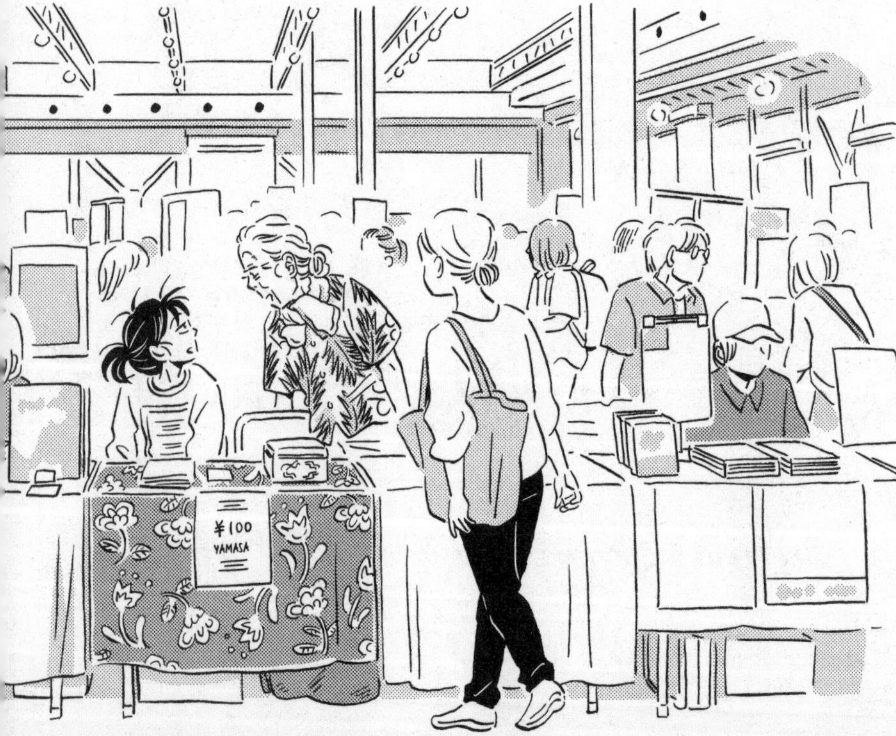
¥100
YAMASA

# SEVEN SEAS ENTERTAINMENT PRESENTS

## BL metamorphosis

story and art by KAORI TSURUTANI     VOL. 5

TRANSLATION
**Jocelyne Allen**

ADAPTATION
**Ysabet Reinhardt MacFarlane**

LETTERING
**Ray Steeves**

COVER DESIGN
**Nicky Lim**

LOGO DESIGN
**Ki-oon**

PROOFREADER
**Dawn Davis**
**Danielle King**

EDITOR
**Jenn Grunigen**

PREPRESS TECHNICIAN
**Rhiannon Rasmussen-Silverstein**

PRODUCTION MANAGER
**Lissa Pattillo**

MANAGING EDITOR
**Julie Davis**

ASSOCIATE PUBLISHER
**Adam Arnold**

PUBLISHER
**Jason DeAngelis**

METAMORPHOSE NO ENGAWA Vol. 5
© Kaori Tsurutani 2021
First published in Japan in 2021 by KADOKAWA CORPORATION, Tokyo.
English translation rights reserved by Seven Seas Entertainment
under the license from KADOKAWA CORPORATION, Tokyo.

Seven Seas press and purchase enquiries can be sent to Marketing Manager
Lianne Sentar at press@gomanga.com. Information regarding the distribution
and purchase of digital editions is available from Digital Manager CK Russell
at digital@gomanga.com.

Seven Seas and the Seven Seas logo are trademarks of
Seven Seas Entertainment. All rights reserved.

ISBN: 978-1-64827-304-9

Printed in Canada

First Printing: September 2021

10 9 8 7 6 5 4 3 2 1

**FOLLOW US ONLINE:** *www.sevenseasentertainment.com*

# READING DIRECTIONS

This book reads from *right to left*, Japanese style.
If this is your first time reading manga, you start
reading from the top right panel on each page and
take it from there. If you get lost, just follow the
numbered diagram here. It may seem backwards at
first, but you'll get the hang of it! Have fun!!

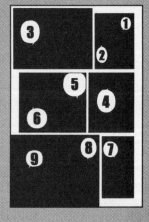